D1327413

Myth from the Ice Age to Mickey Mouse

Myth from the Ice Age to Mickey Mouse

◆

Robert W. Brockway

STATE UNIVERSITY OF NEW YORK PRESS

Published by
State University of New York Press, Albany

For information, address State University of New York Press,
State University Plaza, Albany, N.Y., 12246

Production by Marilyn P. Semerad
Marketing by Dana E. Yanulavich

Library of Congress Cataloging-in-Publication Data

Brockway, Robert, 1923-
    Myth from the Ice Age to Mickey Mouse / Robert W. Brockway.
        p.   cm.
    Includes bibliographical references and index.
    ISBN 0-7914-1713-1 (alk. paper). – ISBN 0-7914-1714-X (pbk. :
alk. paper)
    1. Myth. 2. Intellectual life. 3. Popular culture.
4. Civilization, Modern. I. Title.
BL304.B75 1993
291.1'3—dc20   93-2690
                                                                          CIP

10 9 8 7 6 5 4 3 2 1

To My Wife Katie
Who is Also My Best Friend

CONTENTS

PREFACE

Many THANKS ARE OWED to friends and colleagues. Dr. Robert E. Florida, Professor Susan Medd, and Mr. David Pulak critically read and commented upon earlier versions of this book. I would also like to thank Dr. Peter Hordern, friend, colleague, and dean, for encouragement, advice, and financial assistance. Dr. Edward Milton, chairman of the Department of Religion, Brandon University has given me encouragement and continued, post-retirement teaching opportunities. The Research Council of the university awarded me several research grants over the years. Very warm thanks are due the library staff of Brandon University and especially Ms. Alice Brancewicz for interlibrary loan assistance, and the procuring of books and articles difficult to locate.

During the summer of 1973 I was awarded a research grant by the British Council which enabled me to do research at the British Museum and the Bodleian, Oxford. The British Council also arranged interviews with Glyn Daniel, Sir Mortimer Wheeler, Jacquetta Hawkes, folklorist Christina Hole, and novelist Joseph Priestley. Many other distinguished scholars whom I have met gave me insights and ideas. They include the following: Dr. and Mrs. Emmanuel Anati of the International Association for the Study of Prehistoric and Ethnic Religion, Italy, Dr. Franz Jung and Ms. Aniela Jaffé of Zürich, Switzerland; Dr. Kenneth Emory of Bernice Pauahi Bishop Museum, Honolulu; and Dr. John Charlot of the University of Hawaii. My thanks as well to the librarian of Disney Archives, Burbank, California.

I have appreciated the encouragement, suggestions, advice, and help which I have received from distinguished correspondents who are now deceased. They include the late Joseph Campbell and Mircea Eliade, historians of religion, and Raymond Dart, the discoverer of *Australopithecus africanus*.

May I take this opportunity, as well, to compliment the editors and staff of the State University of New York Press, Albany, and to thank them for their encouragement, advice, and assistance? I am particularly grateful to Director William Eastman, acquisition editor Carola Sautter, and production editor Marilyn Semerad.

Finally, my wife Katie has given me encouragement, support, gifts of typewriters, computers, and printer, much help with equipment, and for more than I can possibly say. Thanks, too, to our two dogs, Sandy and Little Guy, who barked a lot.

1

ALL MYTHS ARE STORIES

ONE SUMMER DAY IN 1960, when my wife and I were living in Coventry, England, I strolled into the tiny public library next to the ruins of the old cathedral and browsed. By chance I came across Mircea Eliade's *Myths, Dreams, and Mysteries*. I devoured it at one reading. It was one of the most exciting books I had ever read. It roused my interest in prehistory and myth.

In Britain prehistory is very real, a living substratum of contemporary society, like the unconscious in the mind of an individual. Vestiges of the prehistoric are all around. The Rollright Stones in the Cotswold are an hour's drive from Coventry. The hills around the Severn are also near. There one can see neolithic long barrows such as Hetty Pegler's Tump. Stonehenge in Wiltshire is not far away.

In England, as in other Old World countries, prehistory lives in ancient rites and customs which are still performed at certain times during the year even though the participants are frequently unaware of the antiquity of the ceremonies. There are well-dressers in Derby and furry dancers in Cornwall; in some villages young men don antlers and chase young women through the streets. Elsewhere, in the same season, small boys roll cheeses down hills to commemorate the revival of the sun. The ancient Celtic rite of Samhain survives in Halloween which came to us from Celtic lands. All of these rituals survive from pagan Britain, as does folklore about elves, fairies, and pixies. Old stories are still recited in the countryside and there are witches. I have met a few. There is a wealth of living lore in all old world countries, a vital inheritance which still flourishes under the veneer of modern civilization.

Archaic myth lives in the Old World. It is a heritage from the past shared by all. People of the New World are less fortunate, especially in those countries where native cultures have been displaced or destroyed.

The European conquerors were all too successful in some countries. They annihilated the native cultures. This, however, did not happen in most of Latin America, Africa, Eurasia, nor Oceania, where synthesis occurred instead. These lands are actually Old World even though some of them may be geographically located in the western hemisphere. Mexico is a prime example.

The New World is where traditional cultures have been displaced or marginalized by European colonists to the impoverishment of both conquered and conquerors. Native cultures were aborted, and the migrants lost their roots. White Canadians, Americans, Australians, New Zealanders, and other overseas people of European stock live in cut-flower civilizations.

Myth is part of the traditional heritage of the Old World. It has been aborted or lost in the new. Archaic myths are traditional stories which are usually about gods and heroes. Strictly speaking, myths are folk-tales which are part of an oral heritage. True mythic traditions now survive in only a few isolated parts of the world such as the rain forests of Brazil and the highlands of New Guinea. However, since the beginning of the nineteenth century, the definition of myth has been broadened to include sacred history (Heilgeschichte), literary epics, and popular genre literature such as westerns, gothics, science fiction, fantasy tales, and romances. What is more, mythic implications are sometimes discerned in modern scientific theories, philosophical systems, theories of history and political ideologies.

While these modern theories and ideologies are not myths, strictly speaking, they have mythic overtones and implications. They stand where myths once stood. The chief differences between archaic myths and modern theories are linguistic, as Ernst Cassirer showed in Language and Myth. Traditional myths are metaphors; they are usually presented in mythopoetic language, partly because rhythm and the repetition of images like "wine dark sea" are useful mnemonic devices. At the same time, many myths, such as the creation stories in Genesis, are archaic scientific theories based on the best information available at the time. Indeed, Mircea Eliade argued that all myths are myths of origin. They tell how the cosmos began, why humanity is sexed, and how nations, classes, families, and occupations came to be. In that way they are archaic scientific theories.

According to Eliade, myth is the content of religion. He writes:

Speaking for myself, the definition that seems least inadequate because most embracing is this: Myth narrates a sacred history; it relates an event that took place in primordial Time, the fabled time of the "beginnings." In other words, myth tells how, through the deeds of Supernatural Beings, a reality came into existence, be it the whole of reality, the Cosmos, or only a fragment of reality—an island, a species of plant, a particular kind of human behavior, an institution. Myth, then, is always an account of a "creation"; it relates how something was produced, began to *be*. Myth tells only of that which really happened, which manifested itself completely. The actors in myths are Supernatural Beings. They are known primarily by what they did in the transcendent times of the "beginnings." Hence, myths disclose their creative activity, and reveal their sacredness (or simply the "supernaturalness") of their works; in short, myths describe the sudden and sometimes dramatic breakthroughs of the sacred (or the "supernatural") into the World. It is this sudden breakthrough of the sacred that really *establishes* the World and makes it what it is today. Furthermore, it is a result of the intervention of Supernatural Beings that man himself is what he is today, a mortal, sexed, and cultural being.[1]

Eliade defines myth as *sacred history, hierophany,* the disclosure of the sacred. Anything can be sacred, a rock, a tree, an animal, a man, or a story. From Eliade's point of view, myths are necessarily sacred. They are metaphorical and symbolic. What Eliade calls *hierophanies* were revealed *in illo tempo,* "in that time" or "one upon a time" but are realized in the present through ritual reenactment. In that way, for example, the death and resurrection of Christ are made real in the present through the sacrifice of the mass. It is a dramatic reenactment of the holy event which is not a historical event set in the past, from the Catholic Christian viewpoint, but a real event in any time or place.

How did myths originate? This question will be addressed in detail in the following chapter. Suffice it to say here that myths originated in what Joseph Campbell calls "mythogenetic zones" which are defined by cultural horizons. The mythogenetic zone is an area in which the people have roughly the same recurrent experiences and share the same cultural values.[2] Myths, according to Campbell, rise from collective experience. This idea is akin to Jung's concept of archetypes which arise from recurrent, common experiences such as the rising and setting of the sun, the phases of the moon, man's experience with woman,

woman's with man, birth, childhood, youth, maturity, old age, and death, the chase, food gathering, and courtship.[3] Campbell held that all particular mythogenetic zones gave way to a single global mythogenetic zone beginning with the age of discovery around 1500. The modern zone is the creative imagination of the individual. I do not entirely agree but think that there are still collective mythogenetic zones today though not necessarily in the geographical sense.

There have been a series of mythic transformations throughout historical times which presumably began during the prehistoric era. By this I mean displacements from myth to other aspects of culture. Here I adapt an idea advanced by Northrop Frye, the Canadian literary critic. He suggests that all forms of Western literature are displaced from myth.. Myths are stories about gods; epics are stories about heroes; and romances are about heroic figures who are somewhat larger than life; those that Frye calls high mimesis or imitation are somewhat more powerful than we are but not overwhelmingly so. In lower mimesis we encounter characters who are like ourselves, in irony, hapless victims who are beneath us.[4] In a sense, this idea can be applied to other areas of culture with regard to myth. There are degrees of displacement from myth with modern scientific theory at the opposite extreme from myth yet bearing the mythic watermark.

Writing was first invented in Sumeria in lower Mesopotamia around 3000 B.C.E. Our earliest-known myths are therefore Sumerian. However, these are literary compositions based on myths rather than the actual myths themselves. They were written by scribes who probably modified them in the process of recording them. They are compositions. We have no original Mesopotamian myths. The same is true of Egyptian, Greek, Canaanite, and Hebrew myths. We have literary compositions which are based on myths but no archaic myths in original form.[5]

Myth-making primarily occurs in literature because all myths are stories. However, there are also mythic themes in art and music, scientific theories, and historiography. Myth also flourishes in the popular arts where it is purest. In part, myth legitimates religious and social values. According to Peter Berger in *The Sacred Canopy*:

> Both religious acts and religious legitimations, ritual and mythology, *dromena* and *legoumena*, together serve to "recall traditional meanings embodied in culture" and its many institutions.[6]

In archaic or modern native cultures (what we used to call "primitive"), science and myth are inextricably related. In *The Savage Mind*, the structural anthropologist Claude Lévi-Strauss shows that much primitive lore is made up of botanical classifications, meteorological and astronomical observations, the knowledge of animal behavior, medical knowledge and much else which we moderns classify as scientific information.[7] In this way, myth is science in archaic or "primitive" cultures. However, the methodological techniques of data-gathering are very different. The essence of modern science is the scientific method which involves testing and other verification techniques. Primitive science is usually anecdotal, improvised, and based on tradition. For these reasons alone, folklore and scientific data are very different. This is certainly true where specialized scientific experimentation is concerned in the hard sciences such as physics.

There are many soft areas in modern science, however, and these are comparable to the way that archaic peoples gathered information and interpreted phenomena. Modern science is secular and non-metaphysical. However, certain parallels that can be made between archaic myth and modern scientific theory which show the historical continuity between them and in which the unintended mythic watermark is detectable in the scientific hypothesis.

Examples of the former include the speculations of certain nineteenth-century scientists who insisted that there was absolute scientific authority for their philosophical opinions. For instance, Charles Darwin's *The Descent of Man* is an exercise in speculation based on very fragile evidence. It is particularly true of nineteenth-century physicists such as Emil Heinrich DuBois-Reymond who asserted that there was scientific proof for mechanistic-materialism. Today mechanistic-materialism is regarded as a philosophical idea. It also could be called a myth. Biological evolution is not a myth. The supportive data is overwhelming. However, some of Darwin's ideas were highly speculative and gave rise to movements such as Social Darwinism which Darwin himself deplored. Social Darwinism is an ideology and, as such, a modern myth.

Today, there is much debate concerning objectivity. Is it possible? Some scholars of the deconstructionist school hold that we live in a postmodern era in which much that was held with great confidence during the eighteenth and nineteenth centuries is highly dubious. Another way of saying this is to acknowledge that there is a great deal of myth-making among academics and scientists.

The physicist Fritjov Capra argues in *The Tao of Physics* that there are parallels between mysticism and science, both in methodology and theories. He asserts that the mystic as well as the scientist uses rational/empirical methods and that both mystical meditation and scientific experimentation are highly disciplined, rigorous pursuits. He suggests that most scientific theories had their genesis in random ideas which have occurred spontaneously to the scientist and are like what artists, composers, novelists, and myth-makers do. His argument is that the contrast between science and the humanities has been exaggerated.

There are certain grey areas where mythic and scientific thinking coincide. However, mythic thinking is spontaneous, imaginative, and creative; scientific thinking is systematic, rigorous, and logical. What is variously called psychodynamic or depth psychology is a good example of a soft science which has a strong mythic component. Psychodynamic psychology is founded on the concept of the unconscious. This idea emerged from the German romantic tradition and other nineteenth-century intellectual movements. It was originally a mystical notion, the idea that God lurks in the depths of soul.

Both Sigmund Freud and C. G. Jung based their respective psychological systems on biology. Freud argued that his therapeutic technique of psychoanalysis was a makeshift one which would have to do until science proved the physiological basis of all mental problems. At that time chemotherapy would replace psychotherapy. Jung did not agree. While his analytic psychology was also based on biology, he insisted that there is an irreducible psychic factor as well.

Today, Freud's prediction has been proven. Psychotherapy has given way to chemotherapy and hormone treatment. Psychoanalysis and its supporting theories now seem to be ideological, and therefore very much like myths although there is no supernatural or metaphysical component. Jung's analytic psychology is frankly mythical. Jung used myths as psychotherapeutic tools. In recent years there have been colloquiums between psychoanalysts and Buddhists such as the Zen master Daisetzu Suzuki. The latter held that psychoanalysis and Zen are very much alike. The psychoanalyst Erich Fromm agreed. Both psychoanalysis and Zen are based on the concept of the unconscious although they use very different terminologies. Both are rigorous forms of meditation.[8]

Jung found many parallels between his analytic psychology and Gnostic Christianity, Hinduism, and native religions such as that of the Elgoni in East Africa among whom he lived for several months during the 1920s. Jung and his followers have an affirmative and appreciative approach to religion and see no conflict between religion and science.

Today many scholars and scientists maintain that science and myth are akin to one another, and that both are valid. They are not mutually exclusive. Those who have this outlook are often called holistic thinkers. Holists prefer synthesis to analysis. They are also generalists rather than specialists.

In recent years, holistic thinkers such as Sam Keene and José Argüelles have argued that we of the West have neglected right hemispheric, synthetic, and spontaneous thinking, that we have over-emphasized the left hemispheric, analytical approach. We need to correct the imbalance. We need to value music and the arts more highly than we do, and also acknowledge the importance of meditation and the cultivation of psychic experiences. Those who think in these terms interpret mythic thinking as psychism and hold that it is entirely consistent with modern thought.

Holistic thinkers argue that modern people are not qualitatively different from archaic people. Our thinking has not been purged of illusion and myth-making by modern science and philosophy. They deny that pure reason is either possible or desirable. They also question the idea of progress.

Whether or not there are modern myths is an open question. If we insist on precise definitions of myth as set forth in most dictionaries, myth-making ceased with the rise of modern secular culture. Modern people seldom dream of gods, demons, and other supernatural beings. When they do they are usually candidates for the mental hospital. If we do not insist on metaphysics in myth-making, however, there are many ways in which it flourishes today.

Modern people are no less prone to create myths than our archaic ancestors. Perhaps we should speak of *Homo Mythologicus* in the way that we speak of *Homo Religiosus* or *Homo Ludens* meaning "religious man" and "playful man," implying that these traits are natural to us as human beings. It is our nature to weave myths and to think in mythic terms. Mythic thinking is imaginative and also imaginal, which refers to image-making. We tell stories; we cannot avoid it. Much of our storytelling is unintentional; some of it is deliberate and contrived. It is a way of thinking which is at the opposite pole from critical thinking. The analytic thinker takes things apart to see how they are put together. The mythic thinker puts the parts together. He or she is a holistic thinker. Mythic thinking is connected, structured, and linear. Stories always have a beginning, middle, and end.

Mythic thinking narrates, integrates, and makes whole; it does not fracture experience into fragments. It is not expressionistic. In that way, mythic thinking contravenes some of the dominant modes of the late twentieth century. It is at opposite poles from rock music, special effects in films, or the "Sesame Street" effect of rapid-fire impressions, quick takes, and momentary gestures. Instead, mythic thinking is metaphorical, sequential, and demands sustained attention span. It is by no means the approach everyone prefers. In his *Poetics*, Aristotle defined *mythos* as "plot," what the story or drama is about. Not all contemporary *New Yorker* stories, for example, have plots, but consist of quick impressions in series. Sensationalism is a characteristic of twentieth-century culture which permeates modern music and modern art, and which many people find congenial. Those people are often bored with prolonged, connected narrative, and therefore with myth.

Myth is personal and individual as well as ethnic and national. I have the diaries which I kept when I was a teenager in Hawaii. One of them records my personal experience of the Pearl Harbor raid of December 7, 1941. I was present at an historical event which was also a deeply significant event in my personal history. In retrospect, I have subtly transformed my war story into a myth which I call "Loss of Innocence" or "Expulsion from Paradise," titles which apply to Hawaii itself. My diary entry is a chronicle without commentary. However, I have molded and remolded my version of Pearl Harbor in the course of retelling the story. Jung stressed the importance of the personal myth in the prologue to his *Memories, Dreams, Reflections*. He writes:

> My life is a story of the self-realization of the unconscious. Everything in the unconscious seeks outward manifestation, and the personality too desires to evolve out of its unconscious conditions and to experience itself as a whole. I cannot employ the language of science to trace this process of growth in myself, for I cannot experience myself as a scientific problem.
>
> What we are to our inward vision, and what man appears to be *sub specie aeternitatis*, can only be expressed by way of myth. Myth is more individual and expresses life more precisely than does science. Science works with concepts of averages which are far too general to do justice to the subjective variety of an individual life.
>
> Thus it is that I have now undertaken, in my eighty-third year, to tell my personal myth. I can only make direct statements, only "tell stories." Whether or not the stories are "true" is not the problem. The only question is whether what I tell is *my* fable, *my* truth.[9]

An entire book could be written on the definition of myth—should be written in fact. It is a vast topic, and a thorny one. The basic problem is that there are so many definitions of myth, a problem with all abstract terms, "religion," for example, as Wilfred Cantwell Smith shows in *The Meaning and End of Religion*.[10]

As with "religion," the problem is the proliferation of meanings. Every theorist has a private definition of myth, and most theorists work at cross-purposes with one another. There is little consensus. The field is a chaos. Consequently, dictionary definitions and encyclopedia articles express particular interpretations rather than ones generally held. The religion professor Ivan Strenski stresses this point in *Four Theories of Myth in Twentieth Century History*. According to Strenski:

> Myth is everything and nothing at the same time. It is *the* true story or a false one, revelation or deception, sacred or vulgar, real or fictional, symbol or tool, archetype or stereotype. It is either strongly structured and logical or emotional and pre-logical, traditional or primitive or part of contemporary ideology. Myth is about the gods, but often also the ancestors and sometimes certain men. . . . It is charter, recurring theme, character type, received idea, half-truth, tale or just plain lie.[11]

To illustrate, Strenski cites the definition of "Myth" in the *American Heritage Dictionary*:

> MYTH is a traditional story originating in a preliterate society, dealing with supernatural beings. . . . Any real or fictional story, recurring theme, or character type that appeals to the consciousness of a people by embodying its cultural ideals or by giving expression to deep, commonly felt emotions . . . one of the fictions or half-truths forming part of the ideology: *the myth of Anglo-Saxon superiority*," or "any fictitious or imaginary story, explanation, person, or thing: *German artillery superiority on the Western Front was a myth* (Leon Wolff). It is also a "notion based more on tradition or convenience than of fact: a received idea: *Without such uncertainty we are left with a set of dogmas and myths.* (I. L. Horowitz)[12]

According to the German philosopher Ernst Cassirer, most of the confusion concerning myth is caused by philosophers and can be traced to the pre-Socratics. As Cassirer says, the sophists regarded myths as scientific and ethical truths expressed in metaphorical language. Plato defined myth as "conceptual language in which alone the world of becoming can be expressed." It is a way of knowing the world just as mathematics and logic are ways of interpreting reality.[13] Plato contrasted *múθos* with *λóros*. Both mean "word," he said, but *múθos* is presented with authority whereas *λóros* is open to dialogue.

The New Latin spelling *mythus* is the immediate source of the term "myth" in all modern languages including English. The French adapted their word *mythe* from it and some English-speaking writers appear to have used that spelling as well. For instance, in the *English Oxford Dictionary*, the classics writer T. Keightley wrote in 1846: "From the Greek *múθos* I have made *mythe* in which no one has followed, the form adopted generally being *myth*."

To me the common denominator in all definitions of myth, ancient and modern, is the word "story." A myth is not necessarily a story about gods and supernatural beings, nor necessarily a traditional tale. It is, however, a story. The narrative might be fictional, historical, or cosmological in form. It might be either prose or poetry. Yet not all stories are myths, and this is the chief problem in the definition. Essentially, a myth is an important story which interprets reality. It is also something presented and not a topic for rational analysis and discussion unlike (*logos*).

One feels that a myth should deal with vast events such as the creation of the cosmos or its destruction by flood and fire, or the Russian Revolution and the collapse of the Soviet Union seventy years later. Family and personal histories are grey areas unless they concern heroes, kings, and royal households. Myths are usually interpretative on a grand scale.

The confusions with the word myth rest, in part, with its modern usages, as in "the American dream," and, with philosophers, as Cassirer says. Twentieth century theorists in various relevant disciplines such as the history of religions, literature, anthropology, archeology, and popular culture have coined private definitions so that definitions have proliferated to the point of chaos. Their problem and ours is the isolation of the disciplines from one another where mythic studies are concerned. There is very little dialogue between workers in these various fields. As a result, we are bedeviled by problems in definition and meaning, some of which are contradictory.

Since archaic myths are only known to us in literary form, literary critics are best equipped to deal with them in my view. Classical scholars such as Robert Graves and G. S. Kirk tell us that we do not have a single Greek myth, by which they mean that all so-called Greek myths are authored works of literature. The same is true of other archaic cultures as well, such as Egypt and Mesopotamia. What we call "myth" is literature unless we refer to the traditional stories of native peoples. Even here, most are known because they have been written and, when written, they have been altered.

All myths are stories. The word "story" is derived from the Latin *historia* which is the root of both "narrative" and our word "history." The Latin lumping of fictional and non-fictional narrative is common to all or most languages. In all languages, the same root words originally meant both "story" in the fictional sense and "history," the narrative of events which actually happened. Distinctions between fiction and non-fiction were made later. The Greeks were the first to make them. Their word *múθos (múthos)* originally meant "utterance," something said. Later it was defined as "folk-tale" or "traditional story." In usage, the Greeks also distinguished between divine myths, stories about supernatural beings, and stories about heroes. By definition, a hero was the child of a god, usually the father, and a mortal, usually the mother. This meant that heroes had some supernatural powers but were mortal.

In practice, the Greeks also tended to use myths for stories which dealt with grand subjects such as gods and heroes who act in magic landscapes in which natural laws are suspended. Folk-tales were homely stories about ordinary people such as goose girls and shepherds. There was sometimes a supernatural or magical component, encounters with elemental spirits and spirits of the dead, for instance, but the scope of the stories was limited. Myths often deal with tragic themes such as the fall of kings like Oedipus Rex or heroic descents into the infernal regions, as in the story of Orpheus and Eurydice. These stories were symbolic and were meant to convey more than they said explicitly and on the surface.

By medieval times, the distinctions among sacred history, secular history, hero tale, and folk story had become quite sharp and clear. Our familiar fairy tales such as *Jack and the Beanstalk* and *Hansel and Gretel* are mainly of medieval origin. They were not originally children's stories, but folk-tales told for the entertainment of adults. They are related to myths, however, in that they often have hidden meanings. Anna-Marie Von Franz and other Jungian psychologists hold that both myths and fairy tales disclose archetypes of the collective unconscious. The psychoanalyst Bruno Bettelheim, of the Freudian school, holds that fairy tales have hidden erotic components. The idea that the folk-tale has hidden meaning occurs among native peoples throughout the world. The Hawaiian word *kaona*, for example, refers to the hidden meaning in stories. We have little difficulty identifying an archaic myth as a story about gods, heroes, and other supernatural beings. Our problems are chiefly with modern myths. As Strenski complains, the meaning of myth has been so broadened during the twentieth century that it means everything and therefore nothing at all. Dictionary definitions usually refer first to archaic myths or traditional stories with a supernatural component. The third or fourth definition listed is broader. Possibly such inclusive definitions should not have been made. In language, however, usage dictates meaning rather than purity of definition.

Strenski's objections are not altogether valid. Even though we cannot be precise in our definitions, most of us sense that a myth is a "big story" just as the Elgoni of East Africa, whom Jung lived among, distinguished between "big" and "little" dreams. By the former they meant dreams in which the dreamer encounters ancestors or gods, or else finds himself or herself in a labyrinth, the heavens, or the depths of the sea, and encounters beings of extraordinary power or awesome mystery. These dreams are very different from the usual day residue dreams about ordinary, everyday events.

The problem with myth in twentieth-century contexts is the usual absence of the supernatural component. Modern people seldom dream of gods, demons, and other metaphysical beings. When they do, the dreamer is usually a person with a medieval or seventeenth-century mind even though he or she lives in a modern metropolis. Such dreams usually have a traditional religious context.

Some dreams and stories are easy to identify as mythic motifs. These are the stories which are directly based on traditional religious beliefs. Religious myths are archaic stories which persist in the modern day in the context of traditional religions. In the West, such stories usually derive from the Bible and, to a lesser extent, Greek, Celtic, and Germanic mythology. They were dominant in our literary and aesthetic traditions until the late seventeenth century, the beginning of the Enlightenment. They are much less so today and are chiefly encountered where modern ideas have not intruded, as in traditional Jewish ghettos, or where they have been rejected, as among the Christian and Moslem fundamentalists.

Non-religious myths are much more difficult to classify and, indeed, whether or not they should be classed as myths at all is an open question. Even so, scholars who have studied the persistence of myth in the modern world usually insist that they are ultimately derived from traditional religious roots. These roots are very apparent in the Far East, India, and the Islamic world. Confucianism, Taoism, Hinduism, and Buddhism are very apparent in village life which is predominantly traditional, especially in India. Educated urban minorities, on the other hand, are usually Westernized, and Westernization and modernism are equivocated. In countries, such as Iran, where Westernization has been violently rejected, there has been a return to traditional values and ideas which, to us, at least, seem medieval.

Eliade, Reinhold Niehbuhr, and other scholars in the field of religion identified Marxism, for example, as a secular version of the Judeo-Christian Messianic myth. This does not mean that Marx consciously derived his economic, political, and social theories from Christianity. We know that he was an atheist and that dialectical materialism was adapted from Hegel. However, it is argued that certain Biblical ideas such as the messianic hope, the chosen people, and the coming day of judgment are so deeply ingrained in the culture that they permeate all aspects of it. They have a way of surfacing in disguise but do so unconsciously. Marxists certainly do not consciously derive their ideas from the Bible. It is rather that the Bible has had such impact on Western thought that *all* philosophical, political, social, literary, and social ideas are affected even when the supernatural element is vigorously rejected. The Marxists have adapted and transformed Biblical ideas unwittingly.

Exactly the same arguments apply to other political and economic theories. Many American intellectual historians, such as Vernon Parrington, derive American democracy from the Puritan wilderness Zion. Scratch the surface of the American dream and you find the Biblical Messianic ideal once more. The same is true of National Socialism, which scholars such as Georg Mosse derive from the Volkishness of German romanticism with its roots in Teutonic paganism.

The argument is that myths are masks of God, to use the title of Campbell's multi-volume master work. Certain mythic themes which occur in the Bible, the Greek classics, and, to a lesser degree, Celtic and Germanic lore, recur as themes into the present. They are usually undercurrents, however, and are only detected by critics. They include motifs such as creation, the heroic quest, the earth mother, death and rebirth, *descensus ad inferos, ascensus ad paradiso,* the sacred marriage, and others. They constantly recur in our literature and art, where we might expect them to. However, they also crop up in unexpected places such as in our political theories, in interpretations of history, and even in some of our scientific theories. We see them in the movies, read them in the funny papers, and encounter them when we go to Disneyland. They are particularly apparent in the popular culture, more so than in the so-called high culture in which one chiefly encounters the mind of the artist, composer, or author.

Thus, even today, we continue to be myth-making animals even though most of our myths do not have an explicit supernatural dimension. This is because of the skepticism which has prevailed among the educated classes since the eighteenth-century Enlightenment.

There are other forms of myth-making as well, perennial forms which fit neither the idea of the traditional tale nor the modern story based on the traditional tale. These are the theories that we compose partly out of empirical evidence and partly out of our imaginations. Many archeological theories, for example, are the subjective interpretations of highly prestigious scholars such as Marcus Childe or Abbé Breuil; the theories persist long after anomalies occur in them which finally result in their disintegration. The megalithic religion theory of Childe became an academic myth. It did not originate in the Bible or any other archaic work but in Childe's mind, and it was perpetuated until the mid-1960s because of his great prestige. The same is true of Breuil's theory of hunting magic where palaeolithic cave art is concerned, and, today, with Marija Gimbutas' theories of goddesses in Old Europe or James Mellaart's of neolithic Anatolian goddess cults. Today such theories are under attack and will probably collapse, but they were accepted as received standard opinion for a number of years. Theories such as these are very similar to the myths of archaic peoples and play very similar roles. The Ptolemaic model of the cosmos is an example. It persisted into the seventeenth century even though many anomalies had occurred long before. However, the theory had such prestige and authority that challengers were threatened with torture and death if they did not adhere to it.

There are two kinds of myth in antiquity and today's world. One is the traditional religious myth which flourishes in the context of the traditional religions. This is myth as we always have understood it. It is *hierophany* or the "sacred history." As such it is the content of all religion. To the unbeliever myths are fictions, illusions, or lies. To the believer myths are true. The religious myth may be either a divine myth about gods or a saga about heroes.

The other kind of myth could be called *the secular myth*. It is derived from religious myth, but the supernatural aspect is either missing altogether or has none of the qualities Rudolf Otto identifies as the numinous, or *mysterium tremendum et fascinans*. Most literary myths fall into this category from Sumerian tales of the third millennium B.C.E. to modern novels such as Melville's *Moby Dick* or Thomas Mann's *The Magic Mountain*. Mythic themes are also detectable in theories of history such as the frontier thesis of Frederick Jackson Turner. Most nations have national myths: the Portuguese as expressed in Camoens' *Os Lusiads*; for instance, the American as revealed in Jefferson's preamble to the American Declaration of Independence or Lincoln's Gettysburg Address. Such myths express the teleological aspirations of whole peoples and are based on archaic religious traditions. Those of the West emerge from the Bible and classics.

Finally, myth manifests itself in its purest forms in modern popular culture, no matter how bowdlerized, commercial, or tasteless. Indeed, as Jung insisted, it is much more apt to be found here than elsewhere. In the high culture one encounters the soul of the artist, writer, or composer, as mentioned, but in the popular culture, one encounters the anonymous and collective dreams of whole peoples. Children's literature, as a species of popular culture, is a particularly interesting source of continuing myth in the modern age. Frank Baum's *The Wizard of Oz*, the Dr. Seuss books, the Ninja Turtles, and, of course, Lewis Carroll's Alice stories are obvious examples.

A collective definition of myth composed of many theories might be framed by the following paraphrases:

> Myths are stories, usually, about gods and other supernatural beings (Frye). They are often stories of origins, how the world and everything in it came to be *in illo tempore* (Eliade). They are usually strongly structured and their meaning is only discerned by linguistic analysis (Lévi-Strauss). Sometimes they are public dreams which, like private dreams, emerge from the unconscious mind (Freud). Indeed, they often reveal the archetypes of the collective unconscious (Jung). They are symbolic and metaphorical (Cassirer). They orient people to the metaphysical dimension, explain the origins and nature of the cosmos, validate social values, and, on the psychological plane, address themselves to the innermost depths of the psyche (Campbell). Some of them are explanatory, being prescientific attempts to interpret the natural world (Frazer). As such, they are usually functional and are the science of primitive peoples (Malinowski). Often, they are enacted in rituals (Hooke). Religious myths are sacred histories (Eliade), and distinguished from the profane (Durkheim). But, being semiotic expressions (Saussure), they are a "disease of language" (Müller). They are both individual and social in scope, but they are first and foremost stories (Kirk).

As C. G. Jung showed in his *Memories Dreams Reflections*, each of us has a personal myth, our story about ourselves, that which we tell ourselves about our life history and our place in time and space. This story is subjective and, in part, stems from subconscious and unconscious depths of psyche. It is not necessarily accurate. It is not at all objective. Instead, it is as we perceive and interpret it.

By definition then, a myth is a story, a narration. But what is a story? According to E. M. Forster in *Aspects of the Novel*:

> Daily life is . . . full of time sense. We think one event occurs after another, the thought is often in our minds, and much of our talk and action proceeds on the assumption. Much of our talk and action, but not all; there seems to be something else in life besides time, something which may conveniently be called "value," something which is measured not by minutes or hours, but by intensity, so that when we look at our past it does not stretch back evenly but piles up into a few notable pinnacles, and when we look at the future it seems, sometimes a wall, sometimes a cloud, sometimes a sun but never a chronological chart.[14]

Story mirrors life and interprets it, but the mirror-image being is distorted, as in a fun house, and the interpretations are always subject to error and misunderstanding. We are like baby chimpanzees before a looking glass, seeing another chimpanzee before us but bewildered when we see only the image and find nothing behind the glass. Neither science nor philosophy are able to solve our perennial epistemological problems and give us the certainty that we seek, and so we tell stories. Each is an attempt to perceive and interpret objective reality.

Forster illustrates the concept of story as follows:

> "The king died and then the queen died" is a story. "The king died and then the queen died of grief" is a plot. The time-sequence is preserved but the sense of causality overshadows it. Or again, "The queen died, no one knew why, until it was discovered that it was through grief at the death of the king." This is a plot with a mystery in it, a form capable of development. It suspends the time-sequence, it moves as far away from the story as its limitations will allow.[15]

However, not every kind of story is a traditional myth, but only those which deal with significant themes, and especially those which are about gods, demons, and other supernatural beings. These are sacred histories. Consequently, traditional myths are comparatively easy to identify and define. Although the etymology of the Greek word *mythos* is simply "utterance" or "story," we have used the term in a special sense since the Greek Enlightenment of the sixth century B.C.E. and after. Until the eighteenth-century Enlightenment, myth necessarily had a metaphysical component.

The rise of skepticism concerning the deity and revelation during the Age of Reason led to a new definition of myth. Now it meant a fiction or deception. That was not an altogether new definition because Plato had used it in that sense and so had the early Christians. However, this definition became deeply ingrained during the eighteenth century and after, and, to most of us, "myth" is still a synonym for a fantasy or fiction.

2

HOW IT ALL BEGAN

THE DESCENT OF HUMANITY

BIOLOGICALLY SPEAKING, we are animals, placental mammals of the Animal Kingdom, Primates, an order which includes the apes, monkeys, lemurs and lorises. We are Hominoids, a superfamily which includes the apes; we are Hominidae, the family which includes the large bodied apes such as chimpanzees and gorillas. Our genus is Homo of which we *Homo sapiens sapiens* are the only surviving species. The term *Homo sapiens* means "wise man."

According to the fossil evidence, we originated in East Africa in the neighborhood of the Rift Valley from 5 to 8 million years ago. One of our ancestors was the 3,600,000 year old "Lucy" discovered by a team led by Donald Johanson. In three expeditions, the team discovered 6,000 specimens. These included remains from thirty-five to sixty-five hominid individuals. In 1975, Johanson and his colleagues found dozens of hominid bones in a hillside. They were identified as a group apparently killed in a flash flood. They included adults and four infants. Johanson and his colleagues called them "First Family."[1]

The discovery of Lucy was preceded by other East African discoveries of very early hominids, beginning with those of Louis and Mary Leakey in the Olduvai Gorge in Tanzania, and of Richard Leakey at Lake Turkana. These discoveries were preceded by the discovery of *Australopithecus africanus* in Southern Africa by Raymond Dart in 1924.

As a result of these finds, the descent of humanity has been firmly documented as of two million years ago. The 1,800,000 year old *Homo Habilis*, discovered by the Leakeys at Olduvai Gorge, was a tool-maker who was very human in appearance and of upright gait from the neck down. From the neck up, these early humans were rather ape-like. With brain cases of around 700 to 800 cubic centimeters, *Homo Habilis* was probably more intelligent than chimpanzees and gorillas, but very probably was not intelligent enough to carry on conversations and tell stories. All authorities, however, agree that *Homo Habilis* was in our line of descent.

Australopithecines, such as "Lucy," are much more controversial. Johanson and his colleagues maintain that her species, *Australopithecus afarensis* was ancestral to ours. Richard Leakey disagrees. Either way, it is highly probable that our earliest ancestors of four or five million years ago were only slightly beyond the chimpanzees and gorillas in intelligence and communication abilities. It is doubtful that they had language enough to compose stories.

Most authorities hold that human evolution is a continuum in which *Homo Habilis*, *Homo erectus*, and other later types were stages of development rather than distinct species. The earliest examples of *Homo erectus* appeared around 2,000,000 years ago, or Neanderthalers (now classed as a race) around 150,000 years ago. The earliest appearance of *Homo sapiens* is very much in dispute, and appears to have been much older than originally thought. Modern humans are called *Homo sapiens sapiens*.

Today there are two lines of inquiry, each based on entirely different evidence and methodology. These are the fossil studies of the paleoanthropologists and the genetic studies, a comparatively new approach, pioneered by the late Allan C. Wilson and other molecular biologists.

Two entirely different pictures of human evolution have emerged. One is nicknamed the "Noah's Ark" school and the other, based on fossil evidence, the "Candelabra" school. The first school is made up of molecular biologists. It was founded by Allan C. Wilson, Vincent Sarich, and others during the 1960s. Their research is based on a "molecular clock" by which the blood protein distance between humans and chimpanzees is calibrated.

According to the molecular biologists, genetic studies indicate that modern humane evolved from archaic forebears around 200,000 years ago.

The molecular approach is free from several . . . limitations of paleontology. It does not require well-dated fossils or tools from each part of the family tree it hopes to describe. It is not vitiated by doubts about whether tools found near fossil remains were in fact made and used by the population those remains represent. Finally, it concerns itself with a set of characteristics which is complete and objective.[2]

These evidences include the genome or full set of genes which hold all of the inherited biological information of an individual. "Genomes are objective sources of data because they present evidence that has not been defined, at the outset, by any particular evolutionary model." Genes are not subject to theoretical prejudices. Fossil evidences, on the other hand, are. They are spotty, and they cannot be evaluated objectively. This is the substance of a very technical argument, the details of which we will not enter into here.[3]

According to the molecular biologists, all *Homo sapiens* are descendants of a woman who lived in Africa around 200,000 years ago. She is nicknamed "Eve." Wilson, Thomas Kocher, and other molecular biologists discovered that the split between the common ancestor of the apes and human beings occurred around 5,000,000 years ago.

The "Candelabra" theory is based on fossil evidence, and is held by paleoanthropologists. The exponents of this view fault the molecular biologists for ignoring the massive fossil evidence and have less confidence than they do in the objectivity and accuracy of genetic research.

They are not convinced that modern humanity is descended from a single group of hunter-gatherers who completely replaced all others worldwide around 200,000 years ago:

> We are troubled by the allegations that beginning about 200,000 years ago one group of hunter-gatherers totally replaced all others worldwide. Although it is not uncommon for one animal species to replace another locally in a fairly short time, the claim that a replacement could occur rapidly in every climate and environment is unprecedented.[4]

The adherents of the "Candelabra" theory agree that the earliest hominids probably evolved in Africa, as the fossil evidence indicates. They agree that it could have been around 5,000,000 years ago. They agree that *Australopithecus* and *Homo Habilis* only appeared on that continent since there is no fossil evidence for them elsewhere. They also agree that *Homo erectus* evolved in Africa. During the early Pleistocene, *Homo erectus* bands migrated to Eurasia from Africa and, in the course of time, evolved into modern humans in Africa, North China, southern

Asia, western Asia, and Europe. Modern humans evolved in a number of separate places in the Old World from fifty to a hundred thousand years ago, possibly earlier.[5]

Northern Eurasia, under a vast ice pack until around 10,000 C.E., was a forbidding place. However, the woolly mammoths, woolly rhinoceri, saber tooth tigers, reindeer, and other animals adapted to the cold northland and, in their wake, came the Neanderthalers, whose appearance would not arouse interest in a New York subway because they looked so much like modern humans. They emerged around 150,000 years ago in Eurasia. The earliest traces of *Homo sapiens sapiens*, or modern humans, in Europe have been dated 43,000 years ago in the Balkans. *Homo sapiens sapiens* and Neanderthalers co-existed in France until around 33,000 years ago. Since then there only have been us. No Neanderthal fossils more recent than 33,000 years ago have as yet been found.

Culturally speaking, anthropologists class the early forms of humanity as lower palaeolithic. This era was from around 5,000,000 to 150,000 years ago. The middle palaeolithic extends from around 150,000 to 40,000 years ago. The upper palaeolithic was from 40,000 years ago to the end of the Ice Age, around 12,000 years ago. *Homo sapiens* is a category which includes archaic types such as the Neanderthalers. *Homo sapiens sapiens* refers specifically to modern human beings. Culturally speaking, the earliest modern human beings were upper palaeolithic.

Myth-making originated with story-telling. That of course depends both on the ability to speak and having brains enough to have something to say. Some stories were undoubtedly heroic adventures. Others may have been inspired by visions, dreams, and hallucinations. The second type may have given rise to religious myths.

As John McCrone says in *The Ape that Spoke*, there are a few very fragile clues which help us guess at what stage human beings began to talk. These have to do with the structure of the palate and the position of the larynx. In the new-born child, the larynx is high in the throat but, after six months, it drops lower and this makes speech possible. Apes do not have a curved palate and neither do the fossil skulls of Australopithecines or *Homo Habilis*. *Homo erectus* fossils dated 1,500,000 years ago do but the arch is slight. It is not pronounced until the earliest Neanderthalers of around 100,000 years ago. Louis Leakey guessed that *Homo erectus* may have spoken a few words and used a great many gestures. Others guess that Neanderthalers also spoke haltingly, with limited vocabulary and very rudimentary structure.[6]

North American native people tell stories using gestures and something of the sort may have occurred before oral speech. Australo-pithecines were only a little more intelligent than chimpanzees; *Homo Habilis* were more intelligent than chimps, but only a little more. *Homo erectus* was much more intelligent than *Homo Habilis*, but since these early ancestors of ours made the same kind of tools for a million years they were not geniuses. However, they did tend fire. That is a very complex process and, for that reason, *Homo erectus* intelligence is regarded with some respect by Alexander Marshack. These are clues to lower palaeolithic intelligence, and some archaeologists, such as Raymond Dart, who discovered *Australopithecus Africanus*, have guessed that the latter had religious rituals of some kind, perhaps the veneration of the skulls of animals. Dart held that such hominids may have had myths as well.[7] It is highly improbably that Australopithecines could talk let alone tell stories.

In his *Prehistoric Religion*, E. O. James speculated on the possibility of there being a *Homo erectus* cult of skulls based on evidences from Beijing, China. At the Choukoutian site near Beijing, the half million year old site yielded evidences of skull mutilation in much the same way as the Karens of Borneo. The skulls were artificially widened at the base, possibly to draw out and consume brains. James thought that it might have been to consume "soul substance."[8] If so, it would repre-sent a very long leap in the capacity of *Homo erectus* to think in abstract terms. The "soul" is the beginning point of supernatural beliefs in spir-its, demons, and gods. Supernaturalist thinking may have begun with *Homo erectus*. The fact that *Homo erectus* tended fire also suggests con-siderable intellect which leads Marshack to suggest that *Homo erectus* could not only speak but compose and tell stories.

Raymond Dart claimed to have found evidences of fire in an Aus-tralopithecine site at Swartkrans, and labelled the fossil "Australop-ithecus Prometheus."[9] However C. K. Brain, who also investigated the site, discovered strong evidence of the fire being on a level dated much later than the level of the Australopithecine remains. With that, Dart's theory of an Osteodontokeratic (bone and teeth) culture of fire-tend-ing, myth-and-ritual making Australopithecines collapsed.

Most authorities now consider the Australopithecines to have been only a little more intelligent than the chimpanzees and gorillas if at all. Both primates communicate by gestures, art, and have been taught to verbalize a few words such as "cup" by University of California experimenters. But it is very improbable that chimps and gorillas com-pose stories unless that term is understood on a very rudimentary basis.

Australopithecus probably did not invent stories. *Homo Habilis*

("Handy-man"), who was intelligent enough to make tools probably did not have language or story-making capacities either, or so at least his discoverer, Louis Leakey, thought. However, it is possible that *Homo erectus* had language and also told stories. Unquestionably, there were stories before there were religious myths, and myth probably emerged from story-telling. What began as secular stories sometimes became religious myths because they were regarded as sacred. That process was probably very gradual. Other stories may have been regarded as sacred because they were based on visions, dreams, and other unusual psychic experiences.

Marshack is a science journalist who became a highly competent paleontologist. He thinks that the discovery of fire was a quantum leap in early human culture. He writes:

> For the *Homo erectus* child, fire became automatically a part of his reality, part of his sense of time, his use of time, his sense of place and distance, his kinesthetic awareness of the difference between summer and winter, day and night, rain and no-rain. In some sense, too, fire must have become part of his sub-conscious imagery, an image below consciousness, that meant warmth when he was away in the cold, an image of home and place. It was, then, a kinesthetic reference, a time reference, a geometric reference, and it could be all these without a large use of words.[9]

The child growing up in a camp where there was fire would learn that the same adults that fed and tended him also fed the fire. He would also sense that fire was there before he was. If, when the men were at the hunt, it was the women who maintained the fire, it would be easy to symbolize woman as the "mother" who feeds the home fire.[10]

The specimen found at Choukoutian, with his cranial capacity of some 1200 cubic centimeters, was capable of abstract thinking. He could do more than make tools. He was intelligent enough to tend fire and, for that reason, he had to be aware of temporal duration. Marshack calls it "time factoring," taking time into account. Marshack holds time-factoring to be the basic requirement for story telling since any story must have a beginning, middle, and end. The story teller relates an account of a sequence of events, just as in fire-tending. The fire must be kindled, the kindling blown into flames, tended for a time, fed fuel and coaxed to flame up if it starts to die down, and, finally, it must be allowed to go out or be put out. Marshack writes:

The demands of fire culture are strict. Fire is alive. . . . It must be tended; it needs a home and place out of the great winds, the heavy rains, the deep snows; it must be constantly fed; it sleeps in embers and can die, yet it can also be blown back to life by breath; it can burn a hand; it can sputter angrily and brightly with animal fat; it dies entirely in water; it whispers, hisses, or crackles and therefore has a variable "voice"; it uses itself up, transforming a large weight of wood to gray ash, while climbing by smoke and savor to the sky, at last disappearing in the burning branch or embers to make a second fire. To a man with fire, then, there is a continuous involvement in a complex dynamic process which creates its varying yet "artificial" demands, relations, comparisons, recognitions, and images. Fire ties one down in time and thought because of the constant requirements in maintaining it.[11]

Marshack reasons that story-telling began with subject, predicate, and adjectival statements such as "yellow after snow" for spring flowers. These short, simple statements would have stated the passage of events in time such as the changing seasons. Winter snows, for example, are followed by spring thaw and floods. There could be words for water birds in the time "of the yellow," for example. Marshack argues that to give something a name implies a story because it involves relation and process, the recognition of meaning in time and space.

According to Marshack:

Story is the communication of meaning . . . a certain sort of meaning which is time-factored, relational, and concerns process. Animals communicate primitive elements of "story." At the human level there is a wide, changing, developing and diverse interplay of meaning, understanding, and recognition between a mother and infant *before* words are used intelligibly between them, and this pre-verbal interplay includes the communication of relatively complex "storied" meanings.[12]

Marshack reduces "story" to subject and predicate such as "boy-whose-voice-changes," or "woman-pick-berries." There are also time-factored stories in the seasons. Young animals are born in the spring, the "yellow" time of flowers after the "white" time of snow, thus adding adjectives to subjects and predicates. The young animals grow taller, sleeker, and fatter in the summer when the foliage is lush, the grasses are tall, and the leaves of the trees are green. In the autumn the sere leaves turn russet, yellow, and brown; the days grow shorter; the nights are now longer and colder. The winter is the time of snow, the time when animals grow thin and game is scarce. It is the time of fierce cold winds and when the family huddles by the hearth. Each of these sentences is a story.

Marshack writes:

> All this is assumption and, despite the implication of complexity, it is probably too simple. For *if* language was present, then fire would also be woven with story. If the hunting family was seasonably nomadic, the hearth at the winter cave shelter to which the group always returned may have had a different value or name or story than the temporary campfire, and there may have been a relighting ritual, or simply some effusion of laughter at return to the winter hearth. At this primitive level of possible "story" the details of cultural behavior or telling would probably vary from family to family and area to area far more than would the hard and necessary fire lore. . . . Peking Man was . . . a man with a working knowledge of time, place, and the direction of the bounds of his effective territory . . . he was sophisticated. . . .[13]

Most prehistorians are skeptical of Marshack's theory which is sometimes called "romantic." However, many compliment him for his interesting speculations. Among other problems, there is the question of *Homo erectus* mental capacities. Did this early hominid (humanlike being) have brains enough to communicate? The same questions are asked of Australopithecus and *Homo Habilis*. Since chimpanzees and gorillas are able to communicate simple messages by sign language, and, in one famous experiment, taught to utter a few words, it is sometimes said that all early hominids communicated. Louis Leakey thought that *Homo erectus* may have been able to utter simple sentences and had a limited vocabulary. Other authorities have suggested that communication by gesture may have preceded speech. Indian sign language as well as that of the deaf are sometimes cited as examples of complex non-verbal communication which includes story-telling. Most authorities think that middle pleistocene people, including the Neanderthalers, probably had language. However, it cannot be sufficiently emphasized that we know nothing whatsoever about prehistoric language, including whether each band had its own language or if all spoke variants of an original language.

Between 100,000 and 50,000 years ago, Europe was a frigid, icebound continent. The vast inter-continental ice sheet covered the British

Isles, Scandinavia, northern Germany, northern Russia, and Siberia. The Alps were the center of another ice sheet which reached beyond the mountains to the undulating countryside north and south. Here the Neanderthalers lived.

They probably came north from southerly lands because of game. They, like the woolly mammoths, became acclimated, and stayed. According to Brian Fagan, it took about 50,000 years for the pioneers of our species to make the short distance from the Near East to the Balkans.[14]

Clues to possible Neanderthal religious belief include burials in which the dead are typically found with legs slightly flexed in elongated pits. Near Eastern Neanderthalers were often buried in a tightly crouched position, as though forced into narrow holes. Many were laid oriented east to west, the head to the east, and the body on the right side. Sometimes animal bones and tools are found in the graves. At La Ferrassie in southwestern France, three stone artifacts suitable for adults were found in the grave where three children were buried. One was a new born infant. Some sites have yielded piles of animal bones, artifacts, and reddish fragments. The head of an elderly man at La Chappélle-aux-Saints was covered with large bone plates, and his body was surrounded with pieces of jasper and quartz. An eight year old boy buried at Tashik-Tash in the foothills of the Dianshan in Uzbek was surrounded by a circle of goat horns. A Neanderthal man in the Shanidar cave in Iraq was buried in blossoms as evidenced by seeds which have been identified. Many of the same plants found are used in folk medicine today. In the Alps, poorly excavated caves have yielded cave bear skulls set in niches and deposited in boxes made of slabs of stone. At Monte Circeo in Italy a Neanderthal skull was found in a circle of stones.

These are the earliest evidences of possible supernaturalism as yet found, and are by no means solid proof that Neanderthalers had religious beliefs. It is possible, however, that they believed in life after death and believed in disembodied spirits. If so, they add some credence to E. B. Tylor's theory of animism as the origin of religion. Perhaps they also told stories, some of which may have been religious myths.

As mentioned, the Neanderthalers and Cro-Magnons, the earliest European *Homo sapiens* sapiens co-existed with the Neanderthalers from around 40,000 years ago until around 33,000 years ago when the last of the Neanderthalers vanished. We do not know why they disappeared.

Around 25,000 years ago, the climate worsened in northern Europe after a comparatively mild spell of long duration and there were fierce winters, the last cold cycle of the Würm glaciation. Late Ice Age Europe was a desolate, treeless landscape swept by bitterly cold winds. Away from the upper plains there were sheltered valleys with peri-glacial vegetation and temperate living conditions. Here the wandering hunters wintered, in the Perigord Basin in France and the Danube Basin in Central Europe.[14]

The last and greatest phase of upper palaeolithic culture was the Magdalenian which flourished between 18,000 and 10,000 B.P. This was the age of the great cave paintings such as those of Font de Gaume, Lascaux, and Altamira. There are around ninety such caves in southern France and Northern Spain, a few more in Sicily, and others in the Urals. Engravings and mobile art flourishes from the Iberian Peninsula to Malta on Lake Baikal in Siberia.

The Perigordians, Aurignacians, Magdalenians, and the other upper palaeolithic peoples, ranged over the uplands and plains during the warmer seasons of the year and retreated to the river valleys during the winter. They bartered with one another, traded artifacts, and no doubt traded ideas and myths as well. It was a way of life which flourished for over 30,000 years. Consider that recorded history covers 6,000 years, and that time-span is awesome. We have been mammoth stalkers for most of our existence which is why the sedentary life of cities gives us such problems and the "health nuts" keep urging us to exercise. Biologically, we are not designed for civilized life.

Upper palaeolithic people lived in a highly symbolic world, so much so that John Pfeiffer speaks of a "creative explosion." For the middle palaeolithic, there are a few fragile hints of possible religious belief such as Neanderthal cave burials, and the preservation of cave bear skulls in alpine caves. Then, suddenly it seems, there is a proliferation of mobile art objects such as female figurines as well as parietal art in the caves, the beautiful animal paintings which are so very awesome. One must actually see them to appreciate their beauty. The viewer is struck by the three dimensional effects, the intense realism of design, the details of form. These are not crude, childlike drawings, but splendid works of art which give the impression that caves like Lascaux must have been holy places, cathedrals of the great hunt.

But were they? If anything, there has been too much speculation. Peter Ucko and Andrée Rosenfeldt remind us that the theories which have been spun during the present century are only that. We still do not know why Palaeolithic hunters went into the caves, what the paintings mean, or the abstract signs that sometimes accompany them. We do not know what the female figurines were for either. It is too easy to leap to the conclusion that they are "mother goddesses."

Few of the paintings seem to illustrate narratives. An exception occurs in Lascaux. One composition is of a bison which has been disemboweled by a rhino. Between them lies a dead man, a stick figure. Such compositions, however, are very rare. Usually the engravings and paintings are of animals grazing. There is seldom action. Hunting magic is exceedingly rare. The animals are seldom wounded or maimed. There are no scenes of hunters stalking prey, and very few of animals struck by missiles of any kind. On the other hand, works of art located in very deep recesses of the caves must be associated somehow with mythic themes. They must have had meaning, presumably, though not necessarily religious meaning.

As Ucko and Rosenfeldt suggest, there has been too much speculation about cave art, about the meaning of the many female figurines which occur from southern France to eastern Siberia, the masked dancers such as the famous "Sorcerer of Les Trois Fréres," or the abstract designs and signs. We do not know why palaeolithic people went into the caves, nor why they stopped going into them and abandoned them at the end of the pleistocene. We do not know what thoughts, dreams, and ideals or intentions motivated them to paint the exquisite animal paintings.

Some scholars draw parallels with the myths of contemporary native peoples, for example, the Plains Indians, the San and Kung people of Botswana, and the Australian aborigines. All three had their rock art, stone circles, and petroglyphs. The modern visitor to Font de Gaume, for instance, is tempted to draw analogies. But there is no way to verify anything save how the engravings and paintings were made, the pigments used, the tools, and the probable techniques. What we would like to know most constantly eludes us.

The few nomadic people who have survived in modern times are modern people whose cultures may not give us clues to the prehistoric past. Most ethnologists of the early twentieth century assumed that modern nomadic hunters are members of fossil societies, and that we can know something about primeval peoples from their contemporary descendants. That, however, assumes arrested cultural development and static societies that have undergone little or no development over the course of thousands of years. The little we know of modern American native peoples suggests that this is not the case. For example, the Sun Dance, which was widely practiced by the plains tribes, seems archaic. One easily imagines that it has been practiced for thousands of years. However, there are no reports of the Sun Dance earlier than 1803, even though many European and American travellers had roamed the plains and visited the natives for two centuries before.

Indications are that native peoples live in dynamic, constantly changing cultures, that myths seldom survive more than three generations, and that they are constantly altered as they pass from one generation of story tellers to the next. It is very doubtful that we have any myths that could be traced back to the Ice Age, although Wilhelm Schmidt, Mircea Eliade, and other scholars have made such claims. Both, for example, think that the creation story of the animal which dives into deep water to bring up the stuff of which the world is made originated in central Asia and was brought to the Americas in paleolithic times.

The Ice Age hunters undoubtedly had their myths, legends, and tales about the hunt, their heroes, villains, and lovers. There were undoubtedly animal stories, and it is very probable that animals were regarded as people. Animals were obviously very important to them. That, however, does not justify the theory that the cave artists were motivated by guilt over the slaughter of animals, or that the sculptures or engravings deep in caves were used for the initiation of boys in animal-god cults. The grouping of signs and animals does not justify Léroi-Gourhan's theory of cosmological dualism, nor does the emphasis on animal art verify Abbé Henri Breuil's theory of hunting magic.

The most that can be said is that our upper palaeolithic ancestors probably had myths of the chase and that animals were important to them. Human burials also show probable belief in life after death. We cannot, however, say that they believed that people and animals went to a hidden realm of the dead from which they were reborn in this world again.

It is possible that the ancient Greek myths of Orpheus descending into the underworld or Virgil's *Aeneid* echo palaeolithic journeys into the depths of caves. It is possible that the Styx was originally an underground river reached through a cave. It is possible that palaeolithic hunters made compacts with animals who willingly let themselves be killed. All of this and much more is possible, but we do not know the meaning of these paintings, engravings, nor the meaning and purpose of the female figurines, animal figures, and small objects which are called "amulets."

The visitor to the Natural History Museum in Vienna discovers the Willendorf Venus with some difficulty. She is a plump, ruddy figure, faceless, with huge breasts, a fat belly, and huge buttocks. She has no feet and no arms. Some of the Venuses discovered during the years are shaped like her, but others are slim; still others are very abstract. Indeed, Venuses come in all shapes and sizes and the Willendorf Venus is actually exceptional. We identify her as the typical female figurine because she was the first one discovered. She has become a symbol of the palaeolithic.

The most interesting of the female figurines found is the Venus of Laussel who holds a horn-shaped object marked with thirteen lines. It could be calendrical. However, we have no idea what the Venuses were for, whether or not any of them were sacred objects; nor do we know what myths may have involved them, or what rituals. The Venus of Laussel was probably the deity of a local cult.

In the end we can do nothing with palaeolithic animal art, female figurines, burials, and cave bear skulls except to note their existence. Very probably, at least some of the aforementioned had religious and mythic significance, but we can do nothing but create our own modern myths about them. Of these, there probably have been too many already.

No one knows why there are ice ages, why they begin and why they end. There were several such periods in the history of the earth prior to the pleistocene, and, for all we know, the pleistocene has not ended. We may be in an inter-glacial warming period now.

We do know that the present era, the holocene, began around 12,000 years ago with a warming trend. The ice sheets melted, and the seas rose. The continents assumed configurations closer to their present-day appearance. The climate warmed which meant the desiccation of the grasslands of North Africa and the Arabian Peninsula, the growth of tropical rain forests around the equatorial belt, and the growth of deciduous forests in temperate zones such as Europe, southern Africa, and Australia. Great herds of reindeer moved northward and, with them, some of the reindeer hunters. The mammoths and mastodons vanished, probably hunted to extinction by our ancestors. For unknown reasons, people stopped going into the caves, stopped making animal engravings and paintings, and made far fewer female figurines. This new era is called the mesolithic by the archaeologists. It was a transitional age which is being squeezed with every new discovery of neolithic sites. The time span of this period is being reduced.

Neolithic or "new stone age" refers to the earliest forms of agriculture and stock-breeding on the part of people who used stone implements. There is some possibility that it began in southeast Asia and spread to southwest Asia, but most authorities think that it originated in Turkey and the Balkans. In recent years, sites have been found in these regions which are older than those originally found in Israel and Iraq. In Israel and Jordan there were mesolithic people called the Natufians by the archaeologists, who seem to have supplemented their food supply by agriculture. They may have practiced human sacrifice.

Between 8300 and 6500 B.C.E., neolithic peasant villages appeared throughout the Near East, the Balkans, and elsewhere. Cereals were cultivated, perhaps by women, and animals were husbanded, perhaps by men. There are many evidences of probable religious life such as the special treatment of skulls which suggests a cult of ancestors. The detached skulls and entire skeletons were sometimes buried beneath houses.

Clay figures occur in sites in the upper Euphrates Valley dated to the seventh millennium B.C.E.; horned animals like goats and sheep, and a few figures of women, sometimes realistic and sometimes stylized. Cult centers have been identified at Jericho in Israel, at Mureybe in the upper Euphrates Valley, and at Ganjadareh in western Iran. In one room a niche was found with figurines representing goats and pigs. At Beide in Israel three strange oval figures were found. A room with a niche and ram's skull was found at Mureghet.

Human figures are very rare for the early pre-pottery period. At Jericho, however, there is a family group of figurines, a man, woman, and child. Miniature pregnant-female figures were found at Ain Ghazal. Male figures were found as well.

According to André Dupré, a chasm opened between secular and sacred in the Near East around 6500 B.C.E. Prior to that time there were only household cults. Subsequently, there were priestly cults, shrines, and temples.[15]

The most famous neolithic site in the Near East is Çatal Hüyük which was excavated by James Mellaart. He found fourteen building horizons dating from 6300 to 5400 B.C.E. Each level consists of dwelling rooms, storage spaces, and shrines with sacred reliefs and frescoes. There are figurines and graves of elites of some kind. Certain chambers have wall paintings that were presumably sacred. There are frescoes which depict sacred ceremonies, sacrifices, and rites. There are also scenes which may be of the world of the dead, representations of women who may have been goddesses, of bulls who may have been sacred, and also of family groups which may have had sacred significance.

Çatal Hüyük gives us the first clear evidence of priestly religion, goddess worship, religious rites and concepts, and myths. While there is strong suggestion of palaeolithic and pre-pottery neolithic religious practices and beliefs, none of these evidences are firm. They can all be interpreted in secular terms. Those at Çatal Hüyük and nearby Haçilar in southern Turkey seem distinctively religious, but may not have been.

Anatolia (Asiatic Turkey) declined during the fifth millennium B.C.E., and the important centers of culture and spirituality were transferred to Mesopotamia and the Transcaspian lowlands. There are evidences of migration, metallurgy (copper), and trade. These developments appear to have transformed the region of the Levant and led, by the end of the fourth millennium B.C.E., to the disintegration of all neolithic cultures in the region. The earliest urban civilizations rose about the same time.

Between 5000 and 3000 B.C.E., the world of the living seems to have separated from the world of the dead in the imaginations of chalcolithic (copper age) people. The dead were buried in special cemeteries outside the settlements. Shrines were also found as well as dwellings. Realistic figures gave way to abstract symbols.

These tendencies first occurred in northern Iraq during the first half of the fifth millennium B.C.E., in the Halaf-Hassuna-Samara culture. Here the dead were usually buried outside the settlements. Only children continued to be buried under houses or in household shrines. Anthropomorphic figurines vanished or were transformed.[16]

The Halaf-Hassuna-Samarra culture in Mesopotamia was also distinguished for the appearance of pottery. Among the various designs are the first examples of the swastika. In later cultures this wide-spread symbol represents the cosmos. Its occurrence on Samarra pottery during the sixth millennium B.C.E. indicates awareness of cosmic dimensions. Presumably, the earliest cosmologies were composed about this time, probably by priests and/or shamans. This represents a distinct advance beyond Çatal Hüyük and Hacilar.

An advanced neolithic and early bronze culture developed in Asia Minor and southeast Europe from the seventh millennium to about 3500 B.C.E. "Old Europe" is Marija Gimbutas's name for an area that extends from the Aegean to the Adriatic and north to modern southern Poland and the western Ukraine. Between c. 7000 and 3500 B.C.E., the people of Old Europe developed more complex social structures than those of their neighbors to the west and north. Small towns, crafts specialization, and religious institutions occurred. The people of Old Europe used stone implements in everyday life but also made copper and gold tools and ornaments. They also appear to have invented a rudimentary script before the Sumerians invented cuneiform writing.[17]

Old Europe of 7000 B.C.E. was remarkably advanced. It was cosmopolitan, with widely ranging trade routes along the rivers and across seas. There was a lively trade in obsidian, alabaster, marble, and spondylus shells as early as 6000 B.C.E. There is evidence of sailboats on ceramic designs. The peasants cultivated wheat, legumes, barley, peas, and vetch, they husbanded as wide a variety of domestic animals as in the Near East. Only the horse was absent. Indeed, Gimbutas thinks that Old Europe would have developed into one of the great cultures rivaling those of the Near East and Greece had it not been for the invasions of semi-nomadic aggressors from the northeast, the ancestors of the Indo-Europeans during the fourth millennium B.C.E.

Old Europe was devastated by the barbarians, and the advanced culture only survived in the Aegean by the second millennium B.C.E. Out of it came Cretan, Mycenaean, and Greek Civilizations. The Minoan Civilization of Crete was the epitome of Old European neolithic and chalcolithic culture.[18]

Greek civilization evolved from both Old European and Asiatic origins by way of Minoan and Mycenaean origins. Goddesses were highly important throughout this region and may have been descended from the palaeolithic Venuses. On these grounds, feminist scholars in recent years have created a scholarly myth of goddess-worshipping Balkan and Aegean peoples who were intruded upon and subjugated by patriarchal Indo-European aggressors during the second millennium B.C.E. and after. The latter introduced the predominantly masculine Olympian deities from the homeland of the Indo-Europeans on the North European plains. However, the new people and their gods did not displace the goddesses and goddess worship. Instead, there was synthesis. Hellenic and Old Slavic religions, as well as those of Asia Minor and, to some extent, Mesopotamia, Syria, and Palestine, enter recorded history as religions in which there was both god and goddess worship, priestesses as well as priests. According to the feminist scholarly myth, only the Hebrew Yahwists suppressed goddess worship altogether. The Eden story is regarded by feminist scholars such as Merlin Stone as a mythopoeic metaphor about the rejection of goddess worship. It is believed to have been composed during the late tenth century B.C.E., at the end of the reign of Solomon, and not very distant in time from the prophet Amos who was a fierce opponent of goddess worship.

According to the theory, goddess worship was widespread until the invasion of the Near East and Balkans by patriarchal Indo-European and Semitic tribes which subjugated the goddess-worshippers. The subjugation of women also occurred and was connected to the suppression of goddess-worship. There are, however, archeological evidences of male deity-worship in neolithic and bronze age sites, as well as statuary which could be either male or female. As a result, Gimbutas's theories are suspect.

Throughout the seventh and sixth millennia B.C.E., figurine art was dominated by abstract forms featuring cylindrical, pillar-like necks, hybrid torsos with female buttocks, and birdlike bodies. The archaeologists have also found naturalistic female figurines and evidences of a gradual trend from abstract designs to naturalism.

Clay models of temples dedicated to goddesses have been found. They are rectangular with portals and wide entrances. Some are complex structures made up of three or four inter-connected buildings raised high on sterobate or earthen terraces. The archaeologists have found what appear to be shrines divided into two rooms, one with an altar and the other a sacrificial area. Domestic shrines also occur in house sites. The ceremonial objects included life size bucranes (bull heads), altar screens, and figurines on simple platforms, or in situations that suggest they were votive offerings.

Archaeologists have found many conventionalized graphic designs which presumably expressed abstract ideas on figurines, vases, and house walls. According to Gimbutas, the symbols fall into two basic categories. The first category consists of symbols with single parallel lines, Vs, zigzags, chevrons, meanders, and spirals. Gimbutas thinks that they symbolized the life-cycles of vegetation and animals. This group also include snake, bird, egg, water, fish, moon, lion, and caterpillar symbols. The second group include crosses, encircled crosses, swastikas, and other designs which symbolize the four directions, east, west, north, south.. Some of these designs later became Christian and Islamic symbols with interpretations in terms of those religions. Very possibly, the designs are of neolithic origin, persisted through bronze age times into the classical era, and were utilized by early Christians and Moslems.

According to Gimbutas, the cross has been a universal symbol from the neolithic to the present. It symbolizes the year-journey and also the four cardinal directions, east, west, north, south. Since such designs also occur in palaeolithic cave art, it is probable that circles, crosses, crosses enclosed by circles, are older than the neolithic. According to Gimbutas, the cross evoked whatever powers ensure the continuance of the cosmic cycle, to help the world through all phases of the moon, and the changing seasons. The cross is the symbol of life, a thought which harmonizes both with the older paleolithic calendrical associations explored by Marshack, and with the later Christian idea of the cross as a symbol of Christ's sacrifice for the salvation of humanity. According to Gimbutas, "the fourfold compositions, archetypal and vegetal renewal or wholeness and the moon in the symbolism of Old Europe, are associated with the great goddess of life and death and the goddess of vegetation, moon goddesses part excellence."[19]

The crescents, caterpillars, and horns are symbols of becoming, according to Gimbutas. They depict the idea of continuous creation.

> There is a morpological relationship between the bulls, on account of horns, and the waxing aspect of the moon—evidence of the bull's symbolic function as invigorator. The worship of the moon and horns is the worship of the creative and feared powers of nature. In western Asia of the fourth to the second millennia B.C.E., the cross was usually associated with the lunar crescent as an alternative symbol of the moon.[20]

One speculates on possible palaeolithic prototypes such as the Venus of Laussel with her crescent shaped object marked with thirteen lines, and the proximity of the shelter where she was found to Les Eyzies which is surrounded by numerous decorated caves such as Lascaux. In the latter the bull is prominent as are other horned beasts, some of them fantastic hybrid, horned animals which could have been mythological. In the other direction, temporally speaking, there are abundant evidences of bull cults in Asia Minor, Iran, and the Near East, from the bucranes of Çatal Hüyük in Asia Minor to the Mithraic Cult of the bull in historical times.

Gimbutas draws attention to the importance of bull horns in Old European art. The horns are as large as the whole animal in figures and drawings. She contends that the horn was a lunar symbol of palaeolithic origin, chiefly on the basis of the Venus of Laussel.

> In the mythical imagery of Old Europe, the bull was dominant, as elsewhere in the neolithic world. The schematized bull horn represents one of the basic philosophical ideas of Old European Religion. They are very numerous, especially at Knossos.[21]

The snake was also important, sometimes presented naturalistically and sometimes as an abstract spiral. According to Gimbutas, snake symbolism peaked around 5000 B.C.E. "The snake was mythologized and attributed with a power than can move an entire cosmos." Some compositions on cult vases depict pairs of snakes with opposed heads "making the world roll." The snake was also a symbol of immortality, an idea probably based on its shedding its skin.[22]

According to Gimbutas, the phallus, horns, snake, water bird, and water are interelated symbols in Old European myth and cult. Neolithic and bronze age people probably thought that life originated in deep water, in deep seas, lakes, and rivers. Deities are born from water. Dionysus comes from water, as do the bird goddesses, and Athena and Aphrodite from classical Greece. The universal snake winds around the universal egg like a continuous flow of water. Gimbutas notes the recurrence of this idea in Homer and Hesiod. The island earth is surrounded by Oceanus, the serpentine watery stream. Such ideas also occur throughout the Near East. In Egypt, the gods came forth from Nun, the watery abyss beneath the flat earth. It is source of life, of the Nile, and it is also the land of the dead in some Egyptian myths.[23] The Sumerian cosmology, the oldest recorded, also depicts the earth under the vault of sky floating in the boundless sea.

I think that coincidence is the probable origin of the idea of a bird or snake laying an egg, and, thus creating a world; it is not very mysterious. In modern thought, Mark Twain's Huckleberry Finn and Jim, the runaway slave, floated down the Mississippi on a raft, gazed up at the starry sky and wondered where the stars came from. Jim thought that the moon laid them.

The bird and snake goddess occurs on earth, in the skies, beyond the clouds in the primordial waters. "Her abode is beyond the meandrous labyrinths. She rules over the life-giving force of water, and her images are consequently associated with water containers. The eyes of the bird or snake goddess even stare from the very center of the world, a sphere, with a mythical water stream from the center."[24]

She is sometimes bird and sometimes snake. She is the goddess of water and air, assuming the shape of a snake, a crane, a goose, a duck, a diving bird.[25]

The upper and lower waters which she controlls were represented by labyrinthine meanders and snake spirals. Gimbutas notes sculpted animal-masked women holding large basins on altar tables or women holding bear-shaped cult vessels. Perhaps such symbols were prototypes of later historical deities such as the Egyptian Great Goddess Nut, the flowing unity of celestial primordial Waters.[26]

Old European mythology underwent transformation in response

to the Indo-European invasions during the fourth millennium B.C.E. The bird and snake goddesses of the Old European pantheon re-emerged in the Classical Era in the persona of Athena, who is associated with the owl. According to Gimbutas, she is the direct descendant of the Minoan palace goddess and distant heiress of a neolithic Old European deity. However, she was transformed because of the Indo-European influenced and also by influences from Asia Minor. Aphrodite was associated with geese and, in terracottas of the sixth and fifth centuries B.C.E., she is accompanied by three geese. Homer said that she came from Cyprus, a center of Minoan culture. She was also connected with Ishtar of Mesopotamia who was the Akkadian version of the Sumerian Innana.

Hera, the consort of Zeus, was not Hellenic. She was the rival of Athena, according to Gimbutas, who notes that temples to the two goddesses stand side by side at Paestum. Sanctuaries to Hera were erected at the entrances to rivers, at the seashore, and in valleys surrounded by pastureland over which she was guardian.

Gimbutas notes that the name *e-ra* appears in Linear B tablets. She thinks that Hera was of Minoan and not Indo-European origin as had been thought. Hera was the feminine aspect of the sky, the air and that her archaic features show links with the Old European Snake Goddess.[27]

Gimbutas argues that the Old European Goddesses survived both the Indo-European invasions and Asiatic influences and emerge as the familiar goddesses of Greek mythology. Athena, Aphrodite, Artemis, Hecate, and Diana are all of very ancient descent.[28] From this point of view, Greek mythology was a synthesis, something we have known since the days of Herodotus. As mentioned, Gimbutas's theories are far from substantiated. Even if they are finally disproven, however, they exemplify modern scientific myth-making. In this case, the myth is in service of the contemporary feminist movement.

We are now at the border between prehistory and history. The distinction is based on literacy. Early literate cultures are called "proto-literate." This is the earliest historical era. The oldest protoliterate culture emerged in lower Irak. History began in Sumer.

3

THE MYTH OF ETERNAL RETURN

MYTHS OF SUMER

SUMERIAN THINKERS AND SAGES gave us our first known myths. According to Samuel Noah Kramer:

> On the intellectual level Sumerian thinkers and sages, as a result of their speculations on the origin and nature of the universe and its *modus operandi*, evolved a cosmogony and theology which carried such high conviction that they became the basic creed and dogma of much of the ancient Near East.[1]

This began with the pre-literate bards and minstrels, and was continued by the poets and scribes of the *edubba*, which were schools where the scribes were taught to write.

The schools flourished as early as 2500 B.C.E. They created our earliest known cosmologies. The *dubsar* or scribes were the scientists of their age, also the philosophers: Theirs were primarily intellectual works, highly cognitive and primarily based on linear thinking. They do not seem to be the work of inner inspiration, the recording of visions, or shamanic in character.

The point is important. As Malinowski, Boas, Lévi-Strauss, and many other anthropologists have shown, so-called "primitives" are not so at all. They have their scientists, philosophers, and thinkers, but differ from so-called "civilized" people in that theirs are oral cultures rather than literate. Otherwise, there is very little difference. Written records are the difference between prehistory and history. The only reason why the Sumerians are identified as the first people in history is because they wrote and we can read their writing.

The Sumerians were a round headed people who lived in lower Mesopotamia and founded some two dozen city states. Around 3100 B.C.E. (or a little earlier) they invented cuneiform writing which they inscribed on clay tablets. Thousands of these tablets have been found and are being deciphered.

According to Kramer, the Sumerian cosmology was the prototype for all others in the Ancient Near East including the Hebrew. It is not that in detail, of course, nor are all cosmologies necessarily derived from the Sumerian. It is rather that virtually all archaic cosmologies are like the Sumerian because, to the naive observer, this is what the world looks like. Wherever one is, earth seems concave if not flat; we are all under the bowl of the sky, across which move sun, moon, and planets, through the constellations of apparently fixed stars. The world is also surrounded by a boundless sea. Today we call it deep space, but the effect is the same. One experiences what archaic man does if one stands at Cabo São Vicente on the southwest tip of Portugal and tries to imagine the sea as Prince Henry the navigator did.

According to the Sumerians:

The earth was a flat disk surrounded by a vast hollow space, completely enclosed by a solid surface in the shape of a vault . . . it may have been tin. Between the heaven and earth they recognized a substance which they called *lil*, a word whose approximate meaning is wind, breath, spirit; its most significant characteristics seem to be movement and expansion and it therefore corresponds roughly to our atmosphere. The sun, moon' planets, and stars were taken to be made of the same stuff as the atmosphere, but endowed, in addition, with the quality of luminosity. Surrounding the "heaven-earth" on all sides, as well as top and bottom, was the boundless sea in which the universe somehow remained fixed and immovable.[2]

This is science. It is not religion but a scientific paradigm, the earliest in history. It is also philosophy, a matter of speculation. It is not mystical experience. There is nothing of the numinous in it. To Sumerian philosophers, the sea was the "prime mover" and the "first cause." They never asked what preceded it.

In this primeval sea was somehow engendered the universe *(an-ki)* "consisting of a vaulted heaven superimposed on a flat earth and united with it. Between them came the moving, expanding "atmosphere," which separated the heaven and earth. Out of this "atmosphere" were fashioned the luminous bodies, the moon, sun, planets, and stars. Following the separation of heaven and earth and the creation of the light-giving astral bodies, plants, animals, and human life came into existence.[3]

The Sumerian universe was a tin can floating in a cosmic sea.

In some ways the earliest cosmology known corresponds to our big bang cosmos theory of today; both are based on observable phenomena. In a flat land like lower Mesopotamia, the sky is a blue bowl overhead and to the horizons all around. The land is flat or concave below, and the seas around the land seem to be without limit. This cosmology was a scientific paradigm based on observation and analysis. The luminous heavenly bodies are also visible. The plants, animals, and human beings are obvious physical features of the *ki* or earth. That much of the cosmos is as naturalistic as in our modern theories.

The Sumerians also had their theologians, however. These explained the gods and were concerned with religion. There was, they said, a pantheon of human-like beings, human in appearance but superhuman in power and immortal. These were the *dingir*, the gods. The gods were great luminous beings who were normally not seen but whose manifestations were felt in the forces of nature. It is not certain that they were inwardly manifest in the mind.

Kramer thinks that the Sumerians got their ideas of the *dingir* from analogies with human society. Since human beings manage, tend, supervise, and control lands, cities, canals, fields, and farms, the cosmos and its manifold phenomena must be tended by living beings in human form who are more powerful than we are. They also must be immortal. If they were not, the cosmos would turn to chaos upon their death. As is true of theology in general, these were cognitive interpretations. What we do not know is the inner life of the Sumerians, the nature of their religious experiences.

As Thorkild Jacobsen observes in *The Intellectual Adventure of Ancient Man*, the Mesopotamian cosmos was a heavenly state. The head of the pantheon was king of the gods, actually, a president. However, just as Mesopotamia was a collection of sovereign city-states, so was the pantheon an assembly of individual gods, each of whom had his or her city.

Just below Sky (An) were seven great gods who "decree the fates" and fifty "lesser gods, their subordinates." More important were the distinctions between the creative and non-creative deities. The basic components of the cosmos were heaven, earth, sea, and atmosphere. The deities in control of these components were creative *dingir*. Every other cosmic phenomenon only exists within one or another of these realms. Hence each of the four creative gods created every other cosmic entity.[4]

The Sumerian philosophers reasoned that the *dingir* created by the power of the divine word. This was also probably an analogy with kings. A king commands and it is done. Once created, the various cosmic entities and cultural phenomena operated continuously and harmoniously by a set of rules or conditions, the *me*, the meaning of which is still uncertain,

Our information about the *me* is chiefly from the myth "Inanna and Enki: The Transfer of the Arts of Civilization from Eridu to Erech." It was found engraved on cuneiform tablets of around 2500 B.C.E. In the myth, Inanna, Queen of Heaven and tutelary goddess of Erech, goes to Eridu where Enki, the Lord Of Wisdom dwells in his watery abyss, the *Abzu*. Enki is in charge of the *me*'s, which include such items as "music," "terror," "the truth," and "descent into the nether world." Over a hundred are listed four times in the poem; sixty of these have been deciphered. Like some shamanic tales, the myth is comic. Enki spreads a banquet for his guest who charms him and gets him drunk. Feeling tipsy he gives her a hundred *me* which she promptly loads into her "boat of heaven" and sails off. He sobers up, realizes what he has done and sends sea monsters and a posse after her. An exciting chase follows, in which Ninshubur, Inanna's vizier, rescues her from disaster several times. Inanna finally arrives home in Erech with the treasure to the jubilation of the people.[5]

Although it is about gods, this story probably had no relation to Sumerian religion. Instead it extols civic pride, much like American patriotic lore about Washington and Lincoln.

There were also religious myths, such as the story of the gods who organized the earth in precise detail in accordance with the general principles set forth by Enlil. Ninhursag originally may have been "Mother Earth," the consort of An. She was the mother of all living things. Next in rank came three astral deities: Nanna the moon god, Nanna's son Utu, the sun god, and his daughter Inanna, whom the Akkadians (Babylonians) called Ishtar, the Greeks Aphrodite, and the Romans Venus.

The gods created human beings of clay so humans could do all the work of the world; humans supply the gods with their bodily and economic needs so that they could spend their time partying, travelling about in their sky boats, and otherwise enjoy themselves.[6] Quite obviously, the gods were projections of human beings, very probably of wish-fulfillment fantasies. Indeed, the Freudian interpretation seems convincing.

As with the Greek gods, so too with the Sumerian. They seem to personify sexual yearnings, longings for adventure, travel, and hedonistic pleasures. They have more power than human beings do but they are not on a higher moral plane. Indeed, it is highly probable that the gods were more instinctual and impulsive in their behavior than were either the Sumerian or Greek people. They did as they pleased which is what most of us want to do. In that way they project a kind of hedonistic, primary process. The Sumerian people were probably as hard-working, responsible, and mature as people have been anywhere and at any time in history. Their myths express their regressive longings for a more irresponsible existence in which dreams come true. In that way, the gods were somewhat like film stars of the 1930s or rock stars of today.

A. Leo Oppenheim's statement that "a Mesopotamian religion should not be written"[7] is well taken. We have little real evidence despite the wealth of texts, but the most serious problem is comprehension. We are too far removed from the Mesopotamia of six thousand years ago to know how those people thought, what inspired them, what frightened them, and why they wrote these curiously bawdy stories about their gods. As Oppenheim says, we do not know anything beyond what we can learn from the tablets and temple architecture. According to Oppenheim,

> The monuments of a forgotten cult, of a cult we know only through a few written documents, can reveal, even if perfectly preserved, only a fraction, a dim reflection, of the cultic activities which they served. Their mechanics and functioning, and the meaning which motivated the enactments of the cult, remain removed from us as if pertaining to another dimension.[8]

Turning to the cuneiform religious texts, there are three types: prayers, myths, and rituals. The prayers and rituals are linked. The directions for performing the rituals are carefully described in the rubrics which are presented at the end of the prayers. We know exactly what the priests did when they chanted them. We know what gestures they made, and how they made sacrifices. But there is no correlation between the prayers and rituals on the one hand and the myths on the other. There is no correlation between the temple architecture and the myths either, nor the art work and statuary. Instead, the myths seem to be literary works and, as Oppenheim suggests, should be studied by the literary critic rather than by the historian of religion.[9] Northrop Frye's theory of literary displacement from myth applies better than Eliade's theory of *hierophany*.

Oppenheim thinks that the myths were the works of court poets who probably based their versions on the oral traditions of bards and minstrels. These scribes were originally Sumerian. Later, the same stories were embellished by the Babylonian and Assyrian scribes, and, most of them have come down to us in these later forms. In that way, they belong to the *belles lettres* of the society, as, indeed, Kramer classes them, rather than to the religious tradition. They are not very rich in the numinous or *mysterium tremendum et fascinans*.

According to Kramer, the earliest literary document is a clay cylinder dated roughly 2400 B.C.E. which is inscribed with the text of a myth about the god Enki and his sister Ninhursag, the Earth Mother. The plot is unintelligible. Another fragmentary myth of the twenty-fourth century B.C.E. concerns Enki's son Ishkur, the storm god, who vanished into the nether world. Enlil goes to the sons of the sky god An, the Annunaki for help, and a fox offers to descend to the nether regions to bring Ishkur out.[10]

Kramer thinks that Sumerian literary output exploded toward the end of the third millennium B.C.E. when the *edubba* rose in importance. Were these mythical works? Kramer finds that only some were and that these were actually authored works of literature in a fairly advanced form by the time they were recorded. The same is true of Egyptian literature for the same period. Oral traditions preceded the written texts, and were, presumably, composed by minstrels and shamans. They probably did not rise spontaneously from the people as folk traditions but were the work of elites even in preliterate times.

Kramer denies that Sumerian literary works were religious or composed and redacted by priests for use in the temple cult. There is no evidence to support Sidney Hooke's theory that myth is the content of religious ritual. Kramer thinks that only hymns and lamentations were composed for the temple cult. There seems to have been no relation between the myths and religion.

Most Sumerian literature was written in poetic form. The poems have no meter or rhyme, but the poets did use repetition, parallelism, metaphor, simile, chorus, and refrain. Sumerian narratives, including myths, have static epithets, lengthy repetition, recurrent formulas, leisurely descriptions, and long speeches. Most of them are tedious. There is little feeling for plot. The narratives ramble on in a disconnected way. The structure is very loose. There is little variation in tone. There is also no psychological depth, tension, or characterization.

The myths and epic tales show little emotion and surprise as the story progresses, and the last episode is often flat, no more stirring than the first. Many of the poems seem pointless. The gods and heroes are stereotypes, not flesh-and-blood individuals.[11]

However, the Sumerians were the first to develop the epic as a literary form, and theirs is the earliest literature that we have. The Sumerian story is far less developed than the Akkadian (Babylonian). The Sumerian tales do not have the power and tension of the *Epic of Gilgamesh*, for example. *The Descent of Inanna* is far less dramatic than *The Descent of Ishtar*, its Babylonian descendant. Yet, the reader senses that the earliest written texts are already late versions of early stories. We are nowhere near the origin. This even applies to a few brief literary texts which have been dated around 3000 B.C.E., very close to the invention of writing itself.

The epics are of interest as the earliest versions of the heroic style which also occurred among the Greeks, Indians, and Germans much later. They allow us to appreciate the strong development of the heroic quest myth. The epics were secular works produced by minstrels and bards for the entertainment of royal courts and warrior aristocrats at their banquets. Kramer notes a great many Sumerian firsts but not that the Sumerians seem to have been the first party animals. This is not as facetious as it might appear. Not only the epics but much of the extant mythology, perhaps all of it, was intended for entertainment not spirituality. The same was probably true of the Homeric poems. The latter, however, are far more effective than the Sumerian, which, by comparison are crude and rudimentary.

As of 1963, Kramer had identified and translated nine epic tales, which vary in length from one to six hundred lines. Several are about Gilgamesh, the fifth king of Erech in the lists, the great Mesopotamian hero whose adventures and quests were celebrated by the Semitic Mesopotamians as though he was one of them. Indeed, the surviving Sumerian stories appear to be prototypes of episodes in the *Epic of Gilgamesh* which is far more polished as a work of literature. One hastens to add that we have the epic only in the late Assyrian version. The composition of the epic from final forms probably extended over the course of two millennia, from prehistoric Sumerian times to Ashurbanipal of Nineveh during the seventh century B.C.E. In that way it is comparable to the development both of Biblical texts and, presumably, of Homeric epics, as well although we only have the versions of the eighth century B.C.E.

In the Sumerian Gilgamesh epics, we read of the friendship between Gilgamesh and Enkidu. Their earlier relationship is that of hero and paladin. Enkidu is a servant. In *Enkidu in the Nether World* he dies and Gilgamesh is aggrieved. Utu the sun god releases his ghost through a fissure in the earth and he rejoins Gilgamesh. He is about to tell his friend about the nether world when the story ends.[12] It is unquestionably a work of the imagination, somewhat philosophical and speculative, and also somewhat dramatic as romance. In the *Epic of Gilgamesh*, Enkidu also dies, descends into the underworld, and returns as a wraith to tell Gilgamesh the fate of all human beings. We learn that the land of the dead is a vast gloomy realm where the virtuous and villainous suffer the same fate, a vast Mesopotamian limbo where the spirits perch as black winged birds, feed on filth, and spend eternity in darkness. The bleak picture inspires Gilgamesh to find the elixir of eternal life which he finds and then loses in a thoughtless moment. Both the Sumerian prototype and the later Akkadian form reveal the minds of ancient poets brooding on the mystery of death. They belong in a category with Gray's *Elegy Written in a Country Churchyard*. The poets lament but have no answers. They are not prophets.

In *Pagan Religions of the British Isles* (1992), Ronald Hutton suggests that a prehistoric artwork cannot be presumed to have any single purpose or motive. We cannot assume that they are mythic or religious, for example. He bases this thought on the wide variety of motifs in the art of many contemporary native people such as the Australian aborigines. For that reason, it is impossible to say that this or that wall painting or female figurine were examples of religious art.

This is substantially true of Sumerian texts, also of Egyptian, Greek, and, for that matter, Israelite texts. Archaic people, like the Sumerians, seem to have had a variety of interests and concerns, only a few of which were religious. Indeed, the official Sumerian religion seems to have been a civic religion somewhat like the Roman or Imperial Shinto. We know nothing at all about the inner religious life of the people.

In ancient Sumeria, as in the modern world, most people were undoubtedly preoccupied with the usual economic, social, and political concerns. Their basic priorities were probably much the same as today:

keep your head down and survive. For most Sumerians, the religious myths may have been as marginal as the Christian and Jewish myths are to most North Americans today. In other words, there was probably as much secularism in the ancient world as in the modern. Our notion that people in ancient times were more religious than we are is not supported by the evidence.

GREEK MYTHS

Greek myths are not traditional tales, but literary classics. In the form we have them they are part of the Greek literary tradition. They are *belles lettres*. The result, as G. S. Kirk shows, is a body of myths of an unusual kind. The myths, as we have them, are already part of a demythologizing process which we think is modern. The evidence suggests that rationalist and secularist demythologizing and demystifying processes have been at work throughout the world since prehistoric times.

According to the old story, the Greeks experienced an age of enlightenment during the sixth and fifth centuries B.C.E. This is the Classical Age. It began with the defeat of the Persians at Marathon in 480 B.C.E. and ended with the defeat of Athens by Sparta in 404 B.C.E. Thanks to Greek philosophers such as Aristotle, and other works that have survived, there is an interpretation of Victorian origin which depicts the rise of philosophy in Ionia as a sharp, clear cut departure from myth.

Carl Sagan recently popularized this theory in his PBS "Cosmos" series. According to Sagan, no one in the world thought rationally—until Thales of Miletus around 565 B.C.E. This view is based on the interpretations of early twentieth century Oxford scholars such as Edward Burnet. It was challenged by F. M. Cornford of Cambridge.

According to the old story, mythic thinking predominated until Thales and the rise of rationalism and science. The Greek Enlightenment was very short-lived however, and was undermined by Pythagoras and Plato. By Hellenistic times it had wholly vanished; it was not to reappear until the Renaissance and then only briefly. With the rise of modern science and philosophy during the late seventeenth century, rationalism revived was once more.

Cornford challenged this view in 1914 and argued that the Ionian philosophers were actually mythic thinkers themselves and introduced little that was new. He stressed the continuity of Greek tradition, the view that mythic and rational thinking coincide. He showed that Thales,

Anaximander, and Anaximenes did not write philosophy but held public discourses. They lectured. Their theories were prosaic but based on myth. As Cornford, Kirk and others show, nothing abrupt occurred during the sixth century B.C.E. in Ionia. Instead, the Greek Enlightenment was gradual and highly complex. The three Milesian philosophers whom Aristotle said were first, reasoned independently in part and, in part, adapted myths. The same was true of later Greek philosophers, including Aristotle himself.

As Kirk shows, Greek literature was dominated by Homer, a crucial if ambiguous figure in the transmission of myths. We know almost nothing about him. The Greeks knew almost nothing about him either. He is supposed to have lived somewhere in Ionia, the same seaboard region of what is now western Turkey where the first Greek philosophers lived. He probably lived during the latter part of the eighth century B.C.E. What he wrote was recorded during the fifth century by the so called Homeridae. We really have no idea who wrote the *Iliad* and the *Odyssey*. What we have are the works themselves. This is all. They are not myths but literary epics, presumably based on traditional narratives derived from earlier bards.[13]

The *Iliad* and the *Odyssey* are at the end of a very long oral tradition. Whoever authored the epics, transformed myths and folk tales into literature. Some of the traditional stories may have been very old. Odd details may go back to the thirteenth century B.C.E., which is thought to have been the era of the Trojan War. This was the Mycenaean Age, the late bronze age of the Achaean Greeks who lived in fortified palaces such as Mycenae, Tiryns, Lacedaemon, Pylos, Corinth, Thebes, Archemenos, Athens, Calydon, and Iolcus. Agammemnon of Mycenae and Priam of Troy may have been historical characters.[13]

In addition to legendary and fictional heroes, there were also the gods and goddesses. There is a supernatural dimension in the epic, but more in the sense that the supernatural intrudes in Shakespearean tragedies, like the ghost in *Hamlet*. There is not much concern in the poems for cosmogonies, divine births, or the origins of things. In that way, the Homeric poems do not fit Eliade's category of hierophany nor his thesis that myths are sacred histories and stories about the origins of things. Instead, the poems are literary works and were probably told as entertainment. Like the Sumerian epics, they originated among minstrels and bards who travelled from court to court entertaining the warrior aristocracy. There are frequent references to the gods, especially Zeus, Poseidon, Apollo, Athena, and Hera. They constantly interact with mortals. Unlike the Sumerian gods, they are vividly characterized, and it is from Homer that the Greeks learned of their ancient and hallowed past. Herodotus, for example, writes that Homer and Hesiod provided the Greeks with information about the characteristics of their gods. He said that Homer and Hesiod lived four hundred years before his time. He thought that the Greek gods had been borrowed from Egypt. The stories were works of the imagination and not sacred texts.

The *Iliad* and the *Odyssey* were Greek treasures, just as Shakespeare is a treasure to English speaking people. There were critics like Xenophanes and Euripides who were scandalized by the poems. Xenophanes, an Ionian poet/sage, wrote that Homer and Hesiod attributed everything shameful to the gods: stealing, adultery, and deception. This criticism however, only affected the educated classes. Homer was popular, probably because the epics are fast-paced adventure stories.[14] Greek piety took other forms, such as Orphism, the Eleusinian Mysteries, and Dionysianism as well as the civic cults also existed which, like the Sumerian cults, celebrated with something akin to the kind of ceremonies which used to be held on Memorial Day.

Homer had little to do with religious ideas. What he presents are parodies of the gods and not the deities as they were worshiped in the temples and shrines. The fact that such racy stories were tolerated says much about the changes then occurring in Greek religion. What is more, the official Olympian religion was giving way to Orphism, Eleusinianism, and other mysteries. Of these we know almost nothing. However, the inner side of Greek religion seems to have been expressed in the mystery cults. Their myths, such as the Orphic, *were* religious myths.

Hesiod, the eighth century B.C.E. poet of Boeotia, wrote the *Theogony* or "Birth of the Gods." This was not a sacred text but a literary work. It is not the literary equal of Homer s epics, but it furnished the Greeks with a popular history of their ultimate origins. Herodotus thought that Hesiod had arranged the materials himself, drawing on earlier sources, but also inventing ideas like chaos. There are sensational stories, such as Kronos castrating his father and Saturn eating his children. Herodotus thought that the poems tell us more about Hesiod than about early Greek beliefs and that it was a work of creative writing.

During the sixth century B.C.E., cultured Greeks developed a taste for poems sung to elaborate music on the lyre. Poets such as Stesichorus of Sicily provided them with choral lyrics which were based on mythical themes. There were tales of Helen, Europa, Orestes, Eriphyle, the Calydonian boar hunt, the deeds of Herakles, and the fall of Troy. He told heroic tales in which there was interaction with the gods and added variations of his own invention, such as that the real Helen never got together with Paris. His poems are works of the creative imagination and even further removed from traditional myth than Homer and Hesiod.

Other poets of the sixth and fifth centuries B.C.E. included Simonides who wrote about Danae set adrift with Perseus; Sappho wrote of the marriage of Hector and Andromeda; Pindar wrote choral lyrics. Pindar, who lived during the fifth century B.C.E., was commissioned to write poems to celebrate the victories at games such as the Olympics. They are packed with literary allusions to the gods, but the poems are chiefly about heroes, both warriors and sports heroes.

When we talk about Greek myths, we mean literary traditions. We learn the minds of Sophocles and Euripides, but very little about Greek myths in their original forms.

The most complete literary embodiment of Greek myths is in tragedy of which we have only a small selection. Tragic drama emerged from the choral lyric. Dialogue and impersonation enabled the dramatists to manipulate traditional stories into their own works. Aeschylus, Sophocles, and Euripides all dealt with Orestes's and Electra's vengeance on their mother Clytaemenestra for the murder of Agammemnon. All interpreted myths artistically and conceptually.

Aeschylus and Sophocles explored the implications of the Prometheus story, the former in *Prometheus Bound*. Both politics and theology took drastic new turns by the middle of the fifth century B.C.E., and Aeschylus used the traditional mythic situation as background for exploring contemporary developments in dramatic terms. In other words, the dramatists were writing for people of their own time, concerning issues of their own time. One is reminded of the uses which Eugene O'Neill made of the Electra and Orestes myth in *Mourning Becomes Electra* in which he introduced a Freudian interpretation which Freud, in turn, adapted from Sophocles's *Oedipus Rex*. In that way, there has been a continuing tradition from antiquity to the present, in which Greek tales have been made the basis of literary messages addressed to generations of contemporary audiences.

Sophocles explored current problems of his day in *Antigone*, which he produced in 441 B.C.E. This was a time of crisis in Athens when many were perplexed by the conflict between loyalty to the state and inner conscience. In mythical tradition, Antigone is a secondary character; the issue of Polyneice's death and her burial of him followed by her being immured is a minor episode in the traditional story.[15] As with modern plays such as Anouilh's *Antigone,* the play was a vehicle for the dramatist s message. Anouilh's *Antigone* was a covert protest against the German occupation of France written and performed during World War II.

Sophocles' *Philoctetes* is based on a traditional story in which Philoctetes is abandoned on the island of Lemnos on his way to Troy because of snake bite. It festered and he became a problem to his companions. The prophet Colchas revealed that Troy could only be taken with the help of Herakles's bow which Philoctetes had. In the original story, Odysseus and Diomede went back to Lemnos to fetch Philoctetes and his bow. Sophocles gave the folk tale a completely new dimension. Despite his suffering, Philoctetes became an unselfish example of generosity and kindness. Odysseus, who is the heavy of this story, is a smooth-talking, manipulative villain, and the play explores the contrast between the virtue and expediency.

Myths also occur in prose works such as Plato's dialogues and Herodotus' histories. The latter was naive about myths and used folk-tale themes to fill in gaps in the historical record. As for Plato, it is impossible to tell what is his writing and what is Socrates. Both constantly fell back on myths which they used for their emotive value. Plato's *Phaedo,* with its lyrical myth of immortality in a jewel-studded landscape, is an example. Plato also developed eschatological mythic visions in the *Georgics, Phaedrus,* and in the *Republic.* As with the dramatists, Plato used the myths creatively, and we learn less about them than about him.

The Greeks regarded the myths as didactic stories from the past. They could be used to illustrate situations of ordinary experience. They could be varied and manipulated for effect. They had become ossified by the time we encounter them in Greek literature.

Greek myths have modern counterparts in stories of the American West, such as those of Doc Holiday in Dodge City, or Annie Oakley in Deadwood. One thinks of the inventions of Parson Weems and his story of George Washington and the cherry tree. How he could not tell a lie when he chopped it down, or the stories about the young Lincoln walking miles to return a book. Greek myths were of this same character. As with the Sumerian, we cannot go behind the literary versions to the originals.

Greek philosophy was based on a cyclical view of time. According to the Ionian philosopher Anaximander, for instance, all things have existed before and will again. Some Greek philosophers called this idea "eternal return," a term borrowed by Nietzsche who believed that everything repeated itself again and again. The same idea was held in India. In both Buddhism and Hinduism there is the concept of *yugas* and *kalpas*. Each is an existence of the cosmos. The cosmos, like all sentient beings within it, is born, grows, matures, declines, dies, and is reborn. The Hindu-Buddhist belief in reincarnation is assimilated to the idea of eternal return. The cyclical view of history is based on it as well. Joseph Campbell holds that all world cultures were based on the myth of eternal return until the bronze age, at which time, an alternative appeared in Iran and Israel. This is the linear concept of time in which there is an absolute beginning and and absolute end. Concurrent with this idea of time is the idea of a hero god who wages war with chaos symbolized by a dragon. The hero finally defeats the dragon and history is fulfilled. In my view, all myths are variants either of the myth of eternal return or the Myth of the Hero and Dragon. More will be said on this topic in later chapters.

4

THE HERO AND THE DRAGON

At THE DAWN OF HISTORY all peoples throughout the world probably adhered to religious systems based on the Myth of Eternal Return. According to Joseph Campbell, this is the metaphor of birth, growth, death, and rebirth, the cyclical view of time which was presumably inferred from the diurnal cycle of the sun, the phases of the moon, the procession of the seasons, and the life stages of plants, animals, and human beings. Presumably, this theory was of prehistoric origin. The term "eternal return" or "eternal recurrences" was suggested by Nietzsche who derived it from the Greek classics.

According to the Myth of Eternal Return, there is neither an absolute beginning nor terminus, but instead, infinite regression in the past and eternal recurrence for all time to come. Eternal Return implies monism and the viewpoint that the universe emanates from a transcendental being to which the gods themselves are subject. They, too, experience birth, death, and rebirth in the never-ending process. Eternal Return is the basis of *philosophia perennis* which pervades Greek and Indian philosophy, but the idea is undoubtedly much older and more widespread. Varying forms of this concept are encountered in the mythologies of peoples as widely scattered as the native Americans, the Polynesians, the Australians, and the Kung of South Africa. Presumably, the theory arose during palaeolithic times from the experience of recurring seasons and is based on the observance of the life stages of vegetation, animals, and human beings.

The Myth of Eternal Return was challenged in Sumeria around 2500 B.C.E. About this time, the idea was advanced that the kings of the

Mesopotamian city-states were tenant farmers to the gods, and that the world was created.

This idea seems to have matured among the Semites. According to the Akkadian *Enuma elish*, the hero god Marduk slew the saltwater ogress Ti'amat and created the universe and all living beings from her corpse. Since, however, Ti'amat was not finally slain but periodically revives, the battle must be fought again every year to ensure the survival of the fragile cosmos.

The Canaanite version of the same motif occurs in the Ugaritic texts in the myth of Baal and Mot in which the Lord defeats Death in a battle which recurs each year. The Babylonian Akitu ceremony featured a sacred drama in which Marduk portrayed by the king slays Ti'amat, played by a priest.

The Hebrews rejected eternal return completely. In the first but most recent of the two biblical creation myths, Yahweh creates the world from *tehom* (the deep) once and for all. At about the same time, Amos and Hosea warned Israel of the coming Day of Yahweh, the end time. Subsequently, this idea was elaborated into the Messianic myth of the Day of Judgment. The Hebrew conception of time was linear. Unlike the Mesopotamians and Canaanites, the Hebrews staunchly insisted that there was only one beginning and one end. History is the interval between Creation and Judgment and the ushering in of an eternal divine order. This idea was emphasized by the early Christians who believed that they were living in the last days. The Moslems adopted the idea of Last Judgment from the Jews and Christians. The idea may have originated among the Zoroastrians of Persia. The hero-dragon motif is characteristic of the Hebrews, Christians, Moslems, and Zoroastrians.

THE HEBREWS AND MYTH

The origins of the Hebrews are obscure and controversial. As with other archaic peoples, there are literary and archeological evidences which do not altogether confirm one another. Linguistic analysis is a third approach. The familiar biblical story of the books of Genesis and Exodus are partially confirmed by the archeological evidence. Abraham was a legendary figure who may have lived in Haran around 1900 B.C.E. That city was then a flourishing metropolis of the kingdom of Mari. The palace archives mention the Benjaminites, a Hebrew tribe, as well as many other proper names which also occur in the Bible. The Egyptian historian Manetho records the occupation of Egypt by Asiatic invaders called the Hyksos between 1750 and 1580 B.C.E. This may have been the time of Joseph. However, there is no confirmation of the existence of Joseph in Egyptian texts then or later. Today, most scholars agree that Joseph cannot be listed as a grand vizier of any pharaoh. Whether or not Joseph was an historical character is an open question. He is not mentioned in Egyptian texts.

There is no confirmation for the story of Moses either. He is also a legendary hero. There is no mention in Egyptian records of the New Empire period of the Hebrews or their captivity, the plagues, or the drowning of pharaoh's army in the Red Sea. Most historians think that Moses was an historical character and that he flourished around 1230 B.C.E., that the pharaoh of the exodus was Rameses II. Most scholars also think that it was the Sea of Reeds rather than the Red Sea which the fleeing Hebrews crossed. The Sea of Reeds was a marshy area near the present Suez Canal. It is possible that the lightly laden Hebrews got through safely while the Egyptians with their heavy chariots were bogged down. Various speculative explanations have been advanced, but we have no other record than the Book of Exodus itself. There is no archeological documentation and no relevant Egyptian texts. Most biblical scholars think that there was an exodus, that there were far fewer Hebrews than the exodus accounts mentions, but that they did go to Sinai. Although there is a monastery and tourist camp at what is called "Mount Sinai," it is not actually known where the Sinai of the exodus was located, save that it was somewhere in the Sinai Peninsula. There is no confirmation for the fall of the walls of Jericho which, at that time, was a tiny village, according to the archeological records. Jericho had been much larger much earlier. The conquest of Palestine is also controversial. Archeologists have found charred ruins of ancient Canaanite towns, but there is no certainty as to when they were destroyed or by whom. The fact that Ugaritic, the language of the Canaanites, and Hebrew are almost identical strongly suggests that the Hebrews were originally Canaanites who became a distinctive people with their own language around the eleventh century B.C.E. The traditions of wandering, captivity, and the conversion event at Sinai were certainly part of their tradition at an early date, and are probably based on legends of the southern tribes. The northern tribes appear to have had very different traditions of their own.[1]

During the nineteenth century, Julius Wellhausen of Tübingen University and other German biblical scholars identified at least three distinct strands in the Hebrew text of the Pentateuch, the first five books of the Bible. They called these the J (for Jahvist) text, E (for Elohist) text, and the P (for Priestly) text. Of them, J is oldest and goes back to the ninth or tenth century B.C.E. E is slightly younger, P is post-exilic, probably of the fourth century.

The conquest of Palestine is a controversial issue. While Hebrews may have penetrated and settled the highlands of Palestine, beginning around 1200 B.C.E., it is not clear that it was a sudden conquest. Some scholars think that it was a gradual infiltration. Everything concerning the early history of the Hebrews is highly speculative. However, the history of Israel from the time of David, around 1000 B.C.E., is well-founded. We are on very sound historical grounds from the time of David on.

The linguistic evidence shows that Hebrew is very close to Ugaritic, the language of the Canaanites. A person with a knowledge of Hebrew can easily master Ugaritic. This suggests that the Hebrews were originally Canaanites, the same people as their neighbors. Hebrew appears to have developed as a distinctive language about the time of Saul and David. There was a remarkable literary outpouring in the neighborhood of Jerusalem during David's reign which continued through Solomon's into the time of the two kingdoms. The oldest texts of the *Tanakh* or Old Testament seem to have been written during this era. There are a few earlier fragments such as the "Song of Deborah" which some scholars attribute to the thirteenth century B.C.E.

The J and E writers were probably temple scribes. According to one recent study, J may have been a woman. The scribes probably composed their texts from folk-tales, legends such as the Joseph stories, and from oral traditions about the captivity in Egypt, the exodus, and the Sinai experience. Both the J and E writers reflect the issues of their times and, indeed, biblical scholars use those references in dating them. J, the earliest of the two, probably lived during the latter days of Solomon's reign and perhaps into the era that followed. Because of acute discontents between the northern and southern tribes, the kingdom split into Judah (from which we get the term "Jew") and a northern kingdom which is sometimes referred to as Israel, and sometimes simply called the Northern Kingdom. The northern tribes always had been in Palestine. The southern tribes preserved nomadic traditions. Their hero was Moses. Their deity Yahweh (I Am) revealed himself to Moses in a typical shamanic visionary experience. Yahwism, or the worship of Yahweh, seems to have been a minority cult at first.[2] Thanks to the energetic proselytizing of its adherents, what originally had been a tribal religion became Judaism which gave rise to two daughter religions, Christianity and Islam.

Most scholars think that J was of the ninth century B.C.E., and the E writer of the eighth century B.C.E. The reason for the terms Yahwist and Elohist is their usage of terms. The Yahwist called the deity Yahweh, a name so sacred that Jews seldom utter it. Most Jews use the term *Adonai* or the Lord. The Elohist used the terms Elohim which is plural, or El which is singular. It simply means "god" or "the gods" and is linguistically related to the Arab term Allah. The Priestly writer is believed to have lived after the Babylonian Exile. He or she perhaps flourished during the fourth century B.C.E. Some time later redactors integrated the three texts into the form we have today in the Old Testament.

The Elohist, who was a contemporary of some of the early prophets, shows his concerns over the Hebrew worship of Canaanite fertility deities and mother goddesses. The Yahwist epic showed how Yahweh created the world and humanity and that, beginning with Adam and Eve, they defied him. He chose a people Israel to be his witnesses in the world, led them out of bondage in Egypt, made a covenant with them at Sinai, led them through the wilderness and to the promised land. Still the people refused to obey him and, being a jealous god, he punished them for their iniquities with natural disasters and by bringing powerful enemies down on them to scourge them. He warned them that he expected righteousness of them and that he hated vain sacrifices and empty rituals. The Elohist epic is another version of the same story. The P writer adapted a cosmogony to his purposes and focused on ritual matters. He flourished during post-exilic times.

During the era of the two kingdoms, great seers or *nabim* arose such as Isaiah, Micah of Yahweh, and Jeremiah. They were religious reformers who preached variations on the same theme: Has not Yahweh brought you out of bondage and to a new land? Has he not kept his promises? But you have deserted him and whored after strange gods. He is a jealous god, a god of wrath and vengeance and, in time, he will punish his people Israel in a final day of judgment, Day of Yahweh. Yahweh was the hero-god who wages war against the black forces of evil both cosmic and human. History moves toward an end-time when he will triumph over all adversaries.

An older generation of scholars emphasized the discontinuity between the pre-exilic and post-exilic eras. The pre-exilic religion was formerly called Hebraism in some scholarly quarters, referring to the national religion of a people who lived in a particular geographical location. In 586 B.C.E., when Jerusalem fell to the Babylonians, Nebuchadnezzar had the leaders of the Hebrew community taken in bondage to Mesopotamia where they were allowed to settle and live in peace but not return to Palestine. A similar fate had befallen the Northern Kingdom in 721 B.C.E., and the ten tribes had been carried off to Assyria. There is no mystery about their fate. They were simply assimilated by the Assyrians. On the other hand, the Judean exiles kept their identity and transferred their allegiance to the portable scrolls of the law, *Torah*, the first five books of the Bible. Henceforth, the scattered people were known as Jews, a peculiar people who were led by teachers called *tannaim*. The rabbis or teachers emerged from the *tannaic* as the authorities on Torah. They interpreted and expanded upon the law in terms of everyday life and, in so doing, founded Judaism as a legalistic religion. Most modern scholars stress the continuity with the pre-exilic era and do not regard post-exilic Judaism as being different from pre-exilic.

Rabbinical commentaries collected in *mishnah* and *gemara* made up the basis of *Talmud*. Other teachers in Israel focused on the coming day of the anointed one or *messiah*. The Greek word for *messiah* is *christ*.

The messianic hope was based on the idea that some day a king like David would come and free the Jews from foreign oppression. He would found the Jewish state once more in Palestine. In time, the messianic idea became elaborate and universalized. The messiah will come just before the God brings about a calamity. The old world and all that pertains to it will pass away and a new world will come into being. The messianic teachers spoke in metaphorical terms. Indeed, Messianism is a myth derived from the Hero-Dragon theme. In the beginning God created the heavens and earth and also created humanity. In the fullness of time not only the Jews but all humanity will be tried and appropriately punished or rewarded. In the last days, the hero-god will vanquish the dragon of chaos.

During the exilic and post-exilic eras, the scribes, priests, prophets and rabbis held certain writings in such high regard that they were regarded as divine revelation. The process of canonization whereby certain texts were deemed authoritative was chiefly based on community consensus. No books were held in such high esteem as the writings of the J, E, and P writers. Another text, that of the Deuteronomist, was also greatly esteemed. Altogether, there were five books or scrolls made up of these writings as pieced together by the redactors. This was *Torah*, a term which means law or wisdom, and which also has spiritual connotations which cannot be readily translated. Torah and Talmud became the basis of Judaism during the early centuries of the common era. The chief center of Judaism was in Babylon. The Palestinian Jewish community was almost completely annihilated in 132 C.E. Those Jews who lived in the Mediterranean world, and especially in Spain, were called Sephardim. Those who migrated to Germany, Poland, Lithuania, Russia and other northern European countries were called Ashkenazim. These two Jewish communities developed their own peculiar customs and traditions including mythologies.

The Jews carried the scrolls of the law wherever they went. They were copied with great care and, when any became tattered or worn, they were burned. Over the centuries, the esteem for these particular texts rose. Other texts were canonized or authorized to make up *Tanakh*, the Jewish Bible which Christians call the *Old Testament*. Other books were highly respected but, for various reasons, were not considered to be divinely revealed. These were books of the Apocrypha, meaning "secret." Still other writings, such as the voluminous Books of Enoch, were classed as *Pseudepigrypha* or "false texts." There are also the books of particular sects such as the Essenes. The Dead Sea Scrolls are Essene books. They include an almost complete Hebrew version of *Tanakh*, the oldest extant. The scrolls were discovered in 1948. Most of the messianic texts are in the *Apocrypha*, *Pseudepigrypha*, and Essene texts. Jewish and Christian mystics at the beginning of the Christian era composed books now called the gnostic texts.

The apocryphal, pseudepigryphal, Essene, and gnostic texts are highly mythical. There is also a mythic component in some of the rabbinical writings in *Mishnah* and *Gemara*. The mythic element in *Tanakh* (or the *Old Testament*) is severely reduced. For example, in the first of the two creation stories in Genesis (Gen. 1:-2:4a), the Hebrew term *tehom* or "the deep" is clearly related to the Akkadian term *Ti'amat*, the salt water ogress. However, the priestly writer who composed this story used the term in an impersonal sense. There are also mythic metaphors in some of the prophetic writings as well as in the wisdom literature which includes the Book of Job. Zechariah 3 and Job 1, 6 refer to a celestial court in which Yahweh presides over an assembly of angels. In fact, the very mention of angels introduces a mythical dimension. Satan, or the opposer, is one of them. However, he is only mentioned in three texts (2 Chronicles 21, Zechariah 3 and Job 1, 6). In none of them is he the Devil or even demonic, but a kind of prosecutor who acts on behalf of Yahweh, sometimes, as in Zechariah, with excessive zeal. The war in heaven, fallen angels, and other mythic themes are rarely alluded to in *Tanakh* but often appear in the apocryphal and pseudepigryphal texts. The latter are the chief sources of angelology and demonology in later Judaism, Christianity, and Islam.

Robert Graves and Raphael Patai identify many mythical components in the Hebrew scriptures.[3] There are monsters such as Behemoth and Leviathan, demons such as Lilith, angels, the talking serpent in Eden, the story of Cain and Abel, the deluge, the story of the tower of Babel, of Sodom and Gomorrah, the seven plagues, passover, much of the exodus story, and the miraculous events which occur during the wandering in the wilderness, the conquest of the promised land, and events during the wars against the Philistines. Most of the mythic events occur before the founding of the kingdom by Saul. This, in my view, confirms the impression that the J and E writers recorded orally transmitted traditions. In that way, they were much like Homer and Hesiod, their near contemporaries in Greece.

Around 200 B.C.E., rabbis in Alexandria translated the books of the Hebrew Bible into Greek. Because there were seventy rabbis it was called the Septuagint. It is our oldest version of the Bible, older than the version included among the Dead Sea Scrolls, the ninth century C.E. Sinaitic text, or any others in Hebrew.

MYTH AND REVELATION

Orthodox Jews, Christians, and Moslems deny that biblical religion is mythological. However, all three acknowledge that there is Jewish Christian, and Islamic mythology. By that they refer to folklore, and stories such as the Hassidic tales and Haggadah in the case of Judaism. The Christian equivalents are the Arthurian cycle, the quest for the Holy Grail, and the lives of the saints. There are Moslem saintly myths and legends, as well as folklore and stories such as those known in the West as *The Arabian Nights*. There are also the Jewish and Christian apocryphal, pseudepigraphal, and gnostic texts which are considered to be of entirely human authorship, non-canonical, and mythological. Jews, Christians, and Moslems distinguish between the myths and legends surrounding Judaism, Christianity, and Islam, and essential doctrines and dogmas.

Orthodox Jews and Christians regard the Bible as infallible scripture, inerrant, because it is divinely revealed. It is the Word of God. Moslems acknowledge the revealed character of the Bible but hold that it is superseded by the Koran, which is made up of the oracles received by Mohammed from the angel Gabriel. The Zoroastrian Avestas are also considered to be revealed by adherents of that religion, and the Vedas, *srúti* or revelation to Hindus. In certain other religions, such as Buddhism, there is no concept of divinely revealed scriptures, there being no concept of God in the Western sense.

Modern liberal Christians and Jews acknowledge the revealed character of the scriptures but are not literalists. Instead they speak of the "truth of the myth," the idea that God has sometimes revealed himself in the context of stories that are fictional. In earlier times, this viewpoint was seldom encountered explicitly. Spinoza was among the first to attempt a rational interpretation of scripture. However, Jewish and Christian mystics often regarded biblical stories as allegories, or else, as in the *Kabbala*, looked for the hidden messages. Some Protestants, such as the Friends or Quakers, rejected the literal authority of scripture and instead held that God reveals himself in the Inner Light. The Quakers are among the most radical of Protestants since they take justification by faith to its ultimate conclusion and reject the authority of church and clergy as well as scripture. The same was true of the pioneer Unitarians of the sixteenth and seventeenth century. They emphasized the authority of the individual conscience rather than tradition, creed, and dogma. Though biblical until the mid-nineteenth century, most Unitarians rejected the literal inerrancy of Scripture and insisted on rational interpretation. Most twentieth-century Unitarian-Universalists are humanists. Many deny that they are Christians and stress individual freedom of belief and hold that science is the best way to discover truth.

In Abbassid times, some medieval Moslems, such as the Mutazilites, were also rationalists and rejected koranic literalism. The same was also true of most Islamic mystics, the Sufis, for whom inner spiritual experience took precedence over revealed texts, tradition, and the authority of the *ulema*, a sort of supreme court of Moslem doctrine and law.

During the nineteenth century, German scholars known as "higher critics" studied the documentary origins of the Bible. They became convinced that there had been a process of recording and revision over time, so that what had been regarded as the Books of Moses, for example, actually had been written by several authors over the course of many centuries. The final texts as we have them in various modern translations are based on earlier Hebraic and Greek versions, of which the earliest is the Septuagint or Greek Old Testament which was translated from Hebrew around 200 B.C.E. No other text, not even the Dead Sea Scrolls, is as old.

Julius Wellhausen and other higher critics were believing Christians who had no intention of undermining faith in the authority of the scriptures. That, however, was the consequence, and by the end of the nineteenth century, many educated Europeans and Americans had become "modernists." That term referred to Christians who rejected biblical literalism and attempted to reconcile traditional Christian doctrine with modern knowledge. The same occurred in Judaism, in the movement known as *haskalah*, the Jewish Enlightenment. It resulted in Reform or Liberal Judaism. It has not occurred as yet in Islam, although there have been individual liberal Moslems, such as the Indian Iqbal, one of the rare modernists in Islam.

Some Christian and Jewish modernists or liberals have concluded that the scriptures are entirely of human authorship. Scriptures are fallible, archaic, and subject to revision and interpretation. Certain texts are acknowledged to be mythical. These include the Creation and Flood stories and the New Testament birth stories, as well as the Book of Revelations. Rationalist Moslems consider the Night Journey of Mohammed to be a myth. In this story, briefly mentioned in the Koran, the Prophet was taken up by an angel and deposited on the site of the temple in Jerusalem.

From the humanist viewpoint, the Bible is mythical. This includes all references to the acts of God, angels, demons, and other supernatural beings, theophanies, miracles such as the parting of the Sea of Reeds (probably not the Red Sea), and the various posthumous appearances of Jesus to his disciples, and, the Ascension. The most controversial issue for Christians is the Resurrection of which there are four distinct versions, as the discerning reader of the Gospels discovers. There is no biblical support for the ascension of Mary which, to non-Catholics, is entirely mythical. Many secular humanists argue that almost nothing is known about Jesus, and that Christianity was founded by Paul.

From the humanist view, the stories of the patriarchs, the Joseph stories, and the stories of Moses are legendary. That is to say, there is a probable kernel of historical and biographical truth mixed with fiction. The same is true of so-called historical accounts such as 1 and 2 Kings and 1 and 2 Chronicles. There is probably a kernel of history, much embellished and altered, however, by the redactors or editors. The Book of Job is probably pure myth, as is the Book of Ruth. Humanists regard the Bible as an anthology of Hebrew and early Christian *belles lettres*. Most humanists appreciate it as literature but reject it as canon or revealed scripture.

Judaism, Christianity, and Islam are based on variant readings of the Bible which, to all three faiths, is the revealed Word of God. All three faiths are ethical monotheistic religions based on the premise that the cosmos was created in the beginning by the Supreme Being, a spirit, who continuously reveals himself through various modalities, and who acts in time/space to bring cosmos out of chaos. Jews believe that God chose them at a certain moment in history and revealed his will to them in terms of a covenant in which he champions them in return for their obedience. He became their God. They must have none before him. He rewards them when they obey and punishes them when they stray. They are his witnesses in the world. Through that witness, all humanity will someday acknowledge him as the one and only deity.

The Day of the Lord will be heralded by the anointed one or messiah whom Christians say is Jesus Christ. By his obedience to God, Jesus has fulfilled the conditions of the covenant, paid the price for humanity's sins. God became man in him, died on the cross, rose from the dead, and ascended to heaven to sit at the right hand of God the Father. In the fullness of time he will come again to judge the quick and the dead and will reign forever.

But the errant Jews and Christians failed to keep God's commandments, and so God revealed himself again through the angel Gabriel to Mohammed. The words of the prophet are recorded in the Koran of which there is a heavenly archetype. The Koran supersedes the Old and New Testaments. In the fullness of time the *mahdi* or messiah will come to proclaim that the Day of Judgment is at hand. On that day, the dead will be raised and judged. Iblis (the Devil) will be cast into hell with all who follow his ways. The faithful will be rewarded in the Garden of Allah where they will enjoy everlasting bliss.

All three readings of scripture are variants of the Hero-Dragon Myth. The Hero-God wages war against the Evil One and his minions. In the end, God will triumph and the Devil will be vanquished. This interpretation, of course, is humanistic and is not as the faithful interpret sacred history. From the humanistic point of view, myth and sacred history are the same, and all theology is derived from myth just as, in literature, epic, romance, high mimesis, low mimesis and irony are derived from myth. Frye's system of displacement applies. Finally, in the humanistic view, to which I personally subscribe, Jewish, Christian, and Islamic theologies are all elaborate wish-fulfillment fantasies. They are illusions. By all definitions of the word, they are myths.

From the eighteenth-century Enlightenment on, a minority of scholars explicitly rejected the idea of biblical uniqueness, finding no reason other than familiarity and prejudice to hold onto it. The essence of this argument is that there is no more reason for believing in Yahweh's reality than for that of the Canaanite El, the Sumerian An or Enlil, or the Babylonian Marduk. In fact they are all ethnic variants of the Sumerian cosmos and its mythical *dingir* or gods, assimilated and modified by the Semitic peoples who came into the Fertile Crescent from the desert. This is the historical point of view which is essentially human-istic or secular.

The Ugaritic and biblical texts part company on issues concerning fertility and the fecundity of both the land and of human beings. The gods are nature deities. In the Ugaritic texts, Baal dies in summer and descends into the nether regions. As he does so, the earth becomes bar-ren. He revives in the autumn with the refreshing rains. Yahweh is not a nature god and cannot be equated with Baal or El in that sense. Instead, he is a tribal god who has a covenantal relationship with his people.[4] As such he is like Marduk, the tutelary deity of the city of Baby-lon. His functions in the natural world are less important than his divine leadership of a particular people. He is the Lord God of Israel who will have no gods before him. This does not mean that these gods are nec-essarily illusions. To the contrary, the older texts of the *Tanakh* strongly suggest that the rival gods exist. When Israel wars against the Philistines, Yahweh, as Lord God of Hosts, wars against Dagon, the Philistine deity. They both exist, but, as a condition of the covenant of Sinai, Israelites are pledged to give exclusive devotion to their jealous deity because they are his people.

The Bible is unique, as is the God of Israel. However, both are unique in the way that every religion is unique. Every deity is unique as well, and, for that matter, every snowflake. There is no deity quite like El of the Canaanites nor Marduk of Babylon, even though parallels can be drawn. All peoples consider their gods to be the true gods, partly because of familiarity but also because most peoples consider them-selves to be chosen peoples. This idea, like virgin births, the resurrection of gods and heroes, or their bodily ascension to the celestial regions, is a common mythic theme. As myth it is a metaphor for revealed truth to believers, Those who do not believe regard such stories as myths in the common sense of illusion and fiction. They are not lies because those who believe the stories are invariably sincere; rather, they are illusions.

Christian missionaries in Hawaii taught the natives that Kane, Lono, Ku, Kanaloa, and other traditional Polynesian gods were hea-then idols. God, they said, is not a concept but absolute. He is the only deity. All the others are myths. Most Hawaiians, however, like native peoples elsewhere, did not embrace Christian exclusiveness but instead synthesized their traditional beliefs with Christianity. Most Hawaiian converts to Christianity did not think that their forbears had been wrong but rather that they saw through the glass darkly. The Bible made clear what their ancestors always had known but had known indistinctly.

Abstract, intellectual concepts of the universe, as well as meta-physical theories of all kinds, do nothing for the human spirit. They offer no comfort or consolation, no hope of life after death, no support for human values, no assurance that the heart of the universe is justice or love. From time immemorial, people have embraced the apparently absurd mythical versions of reality because of inner needs which are not met by science and philosophy. Critics disparage such needs as childish, but, in point of fact, almost no one matures completely. The frightened child is always there. For that reason, people throughout the world sur-render to the myths precisely for the reasons that Freud gave. They are wish fulfillments. For some people, at least, they work. In that way, the biblical myths have been special to people throughout the world. Some-how the Bible conveys authority, especially to those who decide that sci-ence and philosophy are irrelevant. The biblical message crashes through into consciousness and people are changed because of it. Those of us who are secular humanists acknowledge these inner transforma-tions but interpret them in psychological terms. We find no need to invoke the supernatural nor the metaphysical. However, there is no doubt but that certain scriptures such as the Bible, Koran, and Bha-gavad-Gita, have had exceptional impact on humanity, so much so that they are acknowledged to be revealed or *srúti*, regardless of philosoph-ical beliefs and scientific theories. In this way they are myths as metaphors of truth and not myths as metaphors of illusion. Psycholog-ical need is the origin of revelation.

Islam is based on the same premise. The Koran proclaims the com-ing day. Both Christianity and Islam, moreover, owe something to Zoroastrianism, a Persian religion, with its dualist theology of warfare between Ahura Mazda and Ahriman which will finally end in the tri-umph of Ahura Mazda. Thus, while the *Enuma elish* is a compromise between Eternal Return and the Myth of the Hero and Dragon, Zoroas-trianism, Judaism, Christianity, and Islam are founded on a dualist the-ory which repudiates both monism and Eternal Return.

THE QUEST FOR THE HOLY GRAIL

The medieval search for spiritual fulfillment is well symbolized in the quest for the Holy Grail. The Grail appears to Arthur and the knights of the Round Table at Pentecost. It hovers in mid air before them and then vanishes. The knights want to see it again and four set out. Each goes alone and plunges into a different part of the wood. Parzival discovers the Grail Castle and glimpses the mysterious vessel again when he is served a bountiful meal by a beautiful maiden, the Grail Bearer, and sees the Loathly Damsel. Sir Galahad beholds the Grail as well, and goes on to the Eastern lands, his quest just begun. But neither Sir Gawain nor Sir Lancelot see the Grail again because they have sinned, nor does the simple-minded Sir Bors, who is the only knight to return to Camelot.[4]

The Grail Quest is a fifteenth-century monkish allegory based on a number of earlier bardic tales, and especially Chrétien de Troyes's *Conte del Graal* which was written between 1175 and 1190. He was a Breton *conteur* or bard in the service of Count Philip of Burgundy. The wandering Breton *conteurs* were court entertainers who recited old tales of the legendary King Arthur and the Knights of the Round Table which had circulated in Brittany for six hundred years. Stories like *Tristan and Iseult* were Cornish and Welsh stories from the fifth and sixth centuries. When the Saxons overran Britain, Christian British Celts fled to Brittany, which was then called Armorica, taking with them Welsh, Cornish, and Irish lore.[5]

The *conteurs* also told older tales about heroes like Conn of the Hundred Battles and Brân the Blessed. Conn was an Irish king of the second century; Brân was an ancient British sea-god. In the story of "The Phantom Horseman," Conn is invited to dine at a gold and white palace where his enthroned host reveals that he is Lug, an Irish deity of the Tuatha de Danaan. He is served by a beautiful maiden who suddenly turns into an ugly hag. She is Eriu, the Irish fertility goddess in her alternately wintry and spring March-day moods.

In Celtic lore, the *graal* was a deep dish, platter, or cauldron which produced food. In Chrètien's story it is a vessel which magically offers hot and cold dishes to some and refuses others.

During the fifteenth century, Cistercian monks rewrote Chrètien's story as the *Queste del Graal*. It is an allegory of salvation and mystical vision. As Loomis puts it, "To behold the Grail openly is not to see a sacred vessel in an earthly castle, but the Beatific Vision, vouchsafed by God's grace only to those who have fitted themselves by discipline and contemplation for the ineffable experience.[6]

Celtic mythology is based on the Myth of Eternal Return. The pre-Christian Celtic cosmos is born, dies, and is reborn again in eternal cycles. The Celtic Christian bards revised the traditional Celtic stories to accord with Christian doctrine and introduced the knight errant who goes forth to confront the dragons, giants, and demons. The goal of the quest is salvation. There is one creation and one end time, one God, one Christ, one birth, one death, and one salvation.

The Myth of Eternal Return is profoundly pessimistic. If existence is an eternal round of death and rebirth, nothing matters save the attainment either of Nirvana or the dissolution of the self in World Soul. By presenting life as a dramatic confrontation between the good god and the evil demon, the Myth of the Hero and the Dragon introduces moral purpose as an existential imperative. Life is a quest. From this point of view, the Grail Quest dramatically exemplifies the Myth of the Hero and the Dragon, par excellence.

The underlying motif of the Hero and the Dragon fascinated a number of scholars early in the twentieth century, especially Frazer, Rank, and Lord Raglan. The latter set forth a paradigm of the hero which he applied to certain myths and legends. According to Raglan, there are prophecies at the birth of the hero and an attempt is made to kill him, often by his father. But he is spirited away and reared by foster parents in a far away country. We are told nothing about his childhood. On reaching manhood, he wins a victory over a king, giant, dragon, or wild beast. He marries a princess, often the daughter of his predecessor. He becomes a king. For a time he reigns uneventfully and prescribes laws. Later he loses favor with the gods and his subjects. He is deposed and exiled. He dies mysteriously soon after, often at the top of a hill. His children, if any, do not succeed him. His body is not buried, but, nevertheless, he has one or more holy sepulchers.[7]

Raglan analyzed this typical biography, identified twenty-two elements, and scored both divine and human heroes by it. Moses scores twenty-one points, Oedipus and Theseus twenty, Dionysus nineteen, Romulus seventeen, Bellerophon and Perseus sixteen, Zeus, Pelopes, and Jason fourteen, Asclepius and Joseph twelve, Apollo eleven, and Elijah and Siegfried nine. The low scores of the last named are chiefly because little biographical data is given.

Raglan thinks that the heroic biography is manipulated so as to be paradigmatic and exemplary. The incidents of the model hero story fall into three life stages, birth, initiation, and death, which are further subdivided. The hero myth has been discussed most fully by Joseph Campbell in *The Hero with a Thousand Faces*. Campbell, too, thinks that the saga originated in ritual initiation. He reduces its essence to the formula separation-initiation-return. Campbell calls this the "monomyth":

A hero ventures forth from the world of common day into a region of supernatural wonder; fabulous forces are there encountered and a decisive victory is won; the hero comes back from his mysterious adventure with the power to bestow boons on his fellow man.[8]

Some chance happening, a blunder, perhaps, sounds the call to adventure. For example, the princess's ball rolls into a pool in Grimms' fairy tale "The Frog King," or the Angel of the Lord speaks to Moses from the burning bush. If the call is heeded, the curtain is raised on the mythological journey. The call "signifies that destiny has summoned the hero and transferred his spiritual center of gravity from within the pale of his society to a zone unknown," symbolized as "a distant land, a forest, a kingdom underground, beneath the waves, or above the sky, a secret island, lofty mountaintop, or profound dream state. . . ."[9] A guardian may appear, a helpful crone, a fairy godmother, a wizard, shepherd, smith, teacher, ferryman, or helpful animal. The guardian shows the way and also provides the hero with "amulets against the dragon forces he is about to pass."[10] Thus, Ariadne provides Theseus with the ball of thread to help him find his way out of the labyrinth and the Sibyl told Aeneas where he would find the golden bough.

Soon the hero encounters the "threshold guardian" who stands "at the entrance to the zone of magnified power." These are the custodians of the four directions (and also up and down), who stand for the limits of the familiar world of ordinary experience. Beyond lies darkness. The hero must go through the magic threshold into the eerie region of the deep forest, desert, jungle, or deep sea. He may descend into the depths and be swallowed by a sea monster. Descent into the belly of the whale symbolizes death to the old self. As the hero is disgorged, he rises reborn.

> The disappearance corresponds to the passing of a worshiper into a temple—where he is to be quickened by the recollection of who and what he is, namely dust and ashes unless immortal. The temple interior, the belly of the whale, and the heavenly land beyond, above, and below the confines of the world are one and the same. . . . Once inside he may be said to have died to time and returned to the World Womb, the World Navel, the Earthly Paradise. . . . Allegorically, then, the passage into a temple and the hero-dive through the jaws of the whale are identical adventures, both denoting, in picture language, the life-centering, life-renewing act.[11]

The regenerated hero now enters a road of trials where dragons must be slain, and enemies outwitted or defeated. As the hero strives and succeeds, he or she transcends the narrow bonds of ego and achieves self-realization. Here, at the "nadir, the zenith, the uttermost edge of the earth, the central point of the cosmos, in the tabernacle of the temple, or within the darkness of the deepest chamber of the heart," the hero encounters the Queen Goddess of the World and experiences the *ieros gamos*, the mystical marriage.

The mystical marriage symbolizes the assimilation of the feminine aspects of the soul. According to Campbell, "The meeting with the goddess (who is incarnate in every woman) is the final test of the talent of the hero to win the boon of love (charity: *amor fati*), which is life itself enjoyed in the casement of eternity."[12] The mystical marriage with the Queen Goddess of the world symbolizes the hero's triumph. Woman symbolizes life and the achievement of self-knowledge.

The sacred marriage prepares the hero to meet the father who, at first, is terrible. But when the hero has opened his soul to the terror of the father he discovers that he is

> ripe to understanding how the sickening and insane tragedies of this vast and ruthless cosmos are completely validated in the majesty of Being. The hero transcends life with its peculiar blind spot and for a moment rises to a glimpse of the source. He beholds the face of the father, understands—and the two are atoned.[13]

The goal is apotheosis in which

> Those who know, not only that the Everlasting lies in them, but that they, and all things, really are in the everlasting, dwell in the groves of the wish-fulfilling trees, drink the brew of immortality, and listen everywhere to the unheard music of eternal concord. These are the immortals.[14]

The hero has achieved the ultimate boon. He is "a superior man, a born king."[11] Having won, the hero makes the perilous flight home, meeting and overcoming new perils along the way, as the master of the two worlds.

Thanks to the interpretations of medieval theologians throughout the world, the prophets and founders of the world religions fit the saga pattern well. Moses is called when the Angel of the Lord confronts him in the burning bush; he goes down to Egypt and leads the Children of Egypt out. He is aided by angelic helpers and miracles. At Sinai he becomes atoned with the Father. He is a king in the sense that he leads his people. As leader he gives them laws. But he dies before he can cross Jordan and enter the Promised Land.

The Buddha is the son of a king. He leaves home when he is a young man. He undergoes many trials and privations. Eventually he experiences apotheosis under the Bodhi Tree after overcoming all temptations. He becomes the wandering teacher who gives a new law.

Zoroaster has a miraculous birth, obscure childhood and youth, and, when he is grown, sets out on a journey. On the way home from his travels, he pauses by the River Paiti and experiences an epiphany in which he is taken up into the celestial court of Ahura Mazda. He is mutilated and restored, a symbolic motif of spiritual death and resurrection. He is tempted by Angra Mainyu, the Opposing Spirit, and overcomes. He goes out into the world to teach the new law. He is rejected but, eventually, he brings about the conversion of the royal family. In his old age he is slain defending a temple.

Jesus has a miraculous birth. He is the Holy Child born of the Virgin Queen of Heaven and of royal descent and is destined to be the anointed king, the Messiah or Christ. His father is a god. His childhood and youth are obscure. He heeds a call, leaves his home, and sets out on a quest in which he encounters demonic and human opposition, meets helpers, and overcomes many trials. He proclaims a new law. He is the dying and resurrected god who gives eternal life. He challenges and triumphs over the Prince of Darkness who is ruler of this world. He descends into hell and ascends into heaven. His church is his holy bride. In the last days he will return to reign forever.

Christian theologians incorporated all Hero and Dragon myths into the Christian myth during the first three hundred years of the Christian Era, proclaiming, as they did, that Christ was not only the fulfillment of Judaism but also of Greek philosophy, the Hellenistic mystery religions, Mithraism, and Zoroastrianism. As Christianity expanded throughout northern Europe, the Celtic and Teutonic traditions were also incorporated. During the high middle ages, the myth was systematized by the scholastics and deepened by the mystics.

During the Reformation, the myth underwent reductionist revision. With the rise of modern science and philosophy it underwent further reduction and rationalist reinterpretation. We continue to encounter the Hero and Dragon myth today in conservative Jewish, Christian, and Islamic circles, but, what is more interesting, is how the Hero and Dragon myth flourishes in disguise in literature, the fine arts, and the popular arts.

Northrop Frye's suggestion that Western literature is displaced from the Bible and the Graeco-Roman classics has merit, as does Robert Graves's opinion that the derivation is chiefly because of education. There is nothing very mysterious about it, nothing that requires elaborate psychological explanations such as Jung's theory of the archetypes of the collective unconscious. The latter, however, is a useful interpretation of the subtle ways in which the Hero and Dragon myth surfaces in postmodern culture.

The much-commented-upon influence of myth on literature is easily accounted for. Poets like T. S. Eliot and W. B. Yeats, as well as novelists like James Joyce, who are famous for their mythic motifs, were deeply immersed in classical culture from their earlier years and were also much influenced by Frazer's *The Golden Bough*. This was true of most European and American poets and novelists up through the first half of the twentieth century. It is no longer true today. Few study Greek and Latin anymore and few read Frazer. The classical influence has all but vanished.

In some cases, the continuing impact of the Hero and Dragon myth on works of literature, art, and music is deliberate and intentional. In others, where there is no intention to draw upon a mythic theme, the discerning reader recognizes the underlying mythic motifs anyway. In the novel, for example, one encounters the epic hero, the tragic hero, the comedic hero, and, above all, the *eiron* or ironical character. The hero invariably confronts the dragon, the very nature of story being the need to have a central character with a problem to overcome. At the same time, the Myth of Eternal Return occurs in those novels which offer "a slice of life," and in which there is no definitive story line. The very essence of the Hero and Dragon myth is that life is a story. The essence of the Myth of Eternal Return is that it is not and that life goes from anticlimax to anticlimax.

In the archetypal myth, the hero defeats the dragon, rescues the maiden, and inherits the kingdom. In the Christian version of the myth, Christ confronts Satan, ransoms humanity, and founds the Kingdom of God. This, the comedic mode, supplanted the tragic mode of Greek drama in which the hero falls because of his own error and, by so doing, brings ruin on his society as well as himself. As a literary mode, comedy is not funny but fulfilling. The hero is challenged but wins. In tragedy, which is not just any sad story, the hero achieves much but errs because of a flaw. He falls and in his fall brings down a society. The comedic mode has been superseded in our time by the ironic mode in which the anti-hero is a victim. He is a bungler and we look down on him with pity and contempt. From the demonic perspective, in comedy the dragon loses; in tragedy he is severely challenged but ultimately wins; and in irony he is not even challenged. All three are variants of the archetypal Myth of the Hero and Dragon, but the ironic mode is a very recent development. We do not encounter irony in traditional Western literature or art. Today, we encounter little else. In itself, the predominance of the ironic version of the Hero and Dragon myth is a moral commentary on our age since it is the dragon who is really the hero. Only the dragon acts with courage and determination, but, of course, he is bound to lose as well since there are no winners or losers. The Hero and Dragon myth has been reabsorbed into the Myth of Eternal Return. The latter is very compatible with the scientific world view whereas the former is not. As in Hindu-Buddhist thought, the whole of human history from the scientific perspective is but a fraction of a second in the cycles of eternity.

By the thirteenth century, the world religions peaked. The era was distinguished by cathedral building and monasticism in Christendom, the flowering of Jewish mysticism and rabbinical wisdom, and Islamic art, science, literature, and mysticism. The great Hindu and Buddhist eras of philosophy mysticism had just passed. During this same era, the cultures and religions of the Mayans, Aztecs, Mississippians, and Hopewellians also flourished in the Americas. This, too, was the era of marae-building in eastern Polynesia and when the black civilizations of Zimbabwe and Mali flourished in Africa. Subsequently, the world religions declined all over the world. They continue to decline today despite ephemeral revivals.

5

WHERE IS MYTH
IN THE MODERN WORLD?

THE FIRST PLUNGE INTO DEEP SPACE

THE DISCOVERY OF AMERICA BY COLUMBUS IN 1492 provides as good a date as any to mark the beginning of the modern age, that and the Portuguese explorations and Italian Renaissance. All were fifteenth-century developments. That was simultaneously the last medieval century and the first modern one. Columbus typifies the age. He was medieval in some ways and modern in others. He and almost everyone else in 1492 thought that the cosmos was geocentric. Contrary to the conventional idea, most educated people of the day knew that the earth was a globe, but few thought it revolved around the sun. Columbus's cosmos was essentially the same as Dante's of the thirteenth century, and Dante's was based on the geographical writings of Ptolemy, the Alexandrian geographer, astronomer, and mathematician of the second century C.E.

Ptolemy was a scientist, and his theories were scientific theories, not myths. He based them on scientific research and observation, not on mystical experiences, creative imagination, or anything else of a nonrational nature. His *Geographike syntaxis* and *Almagest* were authoritative scientific works which went beyond the works of Aristotle. His geographical data was not challenged until the Portuguese and Spanish explorations of the fifteenth century. His cosmology persisted until the revisions of Copernicus during the sixteenth century and those of Galileo during the seventeenth century.

These comments are necessary in order to correct the old notion that medieval people were all monks and that science was in a state of stasis. It was not. There were medieval scientists as well as medieval mystics, medieval naturalism as well as medieval mythology and theology. Like the modern scientist, the ancient or medieval scientist was an observer and, when possible, tested his hypotheses, and verified them as best he could by rational/empirical techniques. The techniques, of course, were very limited and flawed. The medieval era was no more an age of faith than ours is today. It was also a scientific era. All eras are.

Prince Henry the Navigator and Columbus were medieval scientists whose geographical discoveries resulted in important geographical revisions which were of such a profound nature that most historians more or less arbitrarily decide that the medieval era ended in 1500. In many ways, the medieval era persisted until the French Revolution in western Europe. In southern and eastern Europe it persisted well into the nineteenth century. In Asia and North Africa it persisted into the twentieth century. Some parts of the world are quite medieval today. In other words, the modern did not happen everywhere at once.

It began in Portugal with the founding of the first national state after the battle of Aljubarrota in 1389. Portugal became a nation-state before Spain, France, England, or any other, the first nation-state in history. Since the nation-state is a modern phenomenon, Aljubarrota could be regarded as the beginning of the modern in the realm of politics. The English enclosures of the late fifteenth and early sixteenth centuries were another modern step, this one in economics. The enclosures refer to the consolidation of manorial lands into grazing lands for sheep under private ownership. The typical medieval manor was made up of strips of land tilled by serfs or vassal freemen. The enclosure movement marked the beginnings of modern agriculture. Another modern economic development was the joint-stock company, forerunner to the capitalist corporation. The new commercial houses were founded in England, Holland, and France during the sixteenth century. They gradually displaced the old medieval guild which was a medieval institution. The guild assumed full social responsibility for its members from cradle to grave, regulated trade, and also regulated the standards of craftsmanship. The joint-stock company was competetive, invidualistic, and chiefly for profit. The new era was characterized by the rise of entrepreneurs who competed with one another and who assumed full responsibility for themselves and their families, and no one else. Medieval Europe was in a way socialist; the Renaissance was capitalist.

In 1492 Columbus sailed across the ocean sea to discover new lands. In that way he was a modern entrepreneur and scientist. Columbus died in 1506 thinking that he had been very near the Garden of Eden on his third voyage when his sailors drew up buckets of fresh water at one spot when they were well out of sight of land. They were off the mouth of the Orinoco River which Columbus supposed was one of the rivers that flowed from Eden. In that way he was medieval. Like Dante, he thought that Eden was an actual geographical place, just as he and virtually everyone else in that time thought that if one was able to ascend high enough in the sky one could go beyond the fixed stars to heaven. Like most people throughout the world, medieval Europeans assumed the continuity of the natural and supernatural realms. God was in an actual astronomical location just as Satan was either in outer darkness or else imprisoned in the bowels of the earth. Angels ascended and descended from heaven to earth. There were spirits of the dead and elemental spirits. Those who made compacts with Satan or his demonic agents could sell their souls in return for supernatural powers which they could use to work their will. Medieval people believed that witches, fairies, and elves were real. These supernaturalist beliefs did not die among the educated classes until well into the eighteenth century and they still survive today among peasants in remote parts of Europe.

The effect of the geographical and astronomical discoveries of the fifteenth and sixteenth centuries were to push back the borders of the old traditional mythologies. In their place, new mythologies were composed by the scientists and scholars in the form of theories. Both the old and new theories, however, continued to be myths in the sense of being interpretations of the universe founded on the best evidence available at the time. Like the old, however, the new myths were subject to revision in the light of new discoveries, and so the process has gone on into our own times, just as it has been proceeding since prehistoric times. Mythmaking continues in the modern age, and it is no less a characteristic of our times than of any other in the past. Since the days of Prince Henry and Columbus, the form of the new myths has changed. Both Prince Henry and Columbus wrote prose rather than poetry, and were less prone to metaphor and symbol than were their predecessors. But both were still myth-makers in the sense that they invented paradigms. The major change in mythmaking in the modern age has been in the *style* of mythic expression. The archaic myth is a metaphor; the modern myth is a theory. Both are models or paradigms.

Christopher Columbus and Dom Henrique (better known to English-speaking people as Prince Henry the Navigator), typified fifteenth-century science. Their chief interest was geography. Thanks to Ptolemy, both knew a great deal about the European landmass and something about Africa as far south as the Guinea coast. Arab and Tuareg camel caravans regularly crossed the Sahara between what was known as Guinea and North African ports such as Ceuta and Tangier. They brought gold and, as Europe shifted from the medieval subsistence economy to the capitalist money-economy, that metal became important. It was useful to know about Africa south of the Sahara on that account. Consequently, it was of interest to the Portuguese to discover a way to get at the gold directly rather than through the Arab middlemen. That was one important Portuguese motive for sending ships down the coast of Africa. The Venetian galley was adequate for the Mediterranean trade, just as its Roman, Greek, and Phoenician predecessors had been. Galleys were rowed by slaves and their rowing was augmented by sails. Viking *knorrs*, or trading vessels, were also rowed but had the help of a single large, square sail. These ships had proved their worth in oceanic voyaging. However, they seldom went very far out of sight of land. An island chain connects Scandinavia and the British Isles with Iceland, Greenland, and the coasts of Labrador and Newfoundland. Deep ocean voyaging well out of sight of land demanded improvements in both navigation and marine engineering. These were undertaken by the Portuguese who developed an ocean-going sailing ship which they called the *caravela*. We know it better by the Spanish name *caravel*.

Prince Henry, who was a member of the Portuguese royal house of Aviz, had a keen interest in navigation. Early in the fifteenth century, he built a navigation institute at Cabo São Vicente (Cape St. Vincent) on the rugged southwestern tip of Portugal where steep bluffs rise above the sea. The visitor to Cape St. Vincent easily can imagine Henry's curiosity and awe. From here, as from other European promontories such as Land's End, England, the modern visitor gazes out to sea as did the ancient and medieval ancestors of modern Europeans. There is still a feeling of mystery, much like gazing up at a starry sky. To ancient and medieval people, the ocean sea, as they called it, was deep space, and it had the same significance to them that outer space does to us. They were on the shores of a vast sea which, for all they knew, stretched into infinity. Prince Henry was certain that it did not. He knew the world was round, and also that if his ships sailed far enough they would reach the further limits of Africa. The Portuguese could then sail east and eventually reach India. Europeans had known about India since the days of Alexander the Great if not before. Thanks to

Marco Polo in the thirteenth century, they also knew about China and the prosperous sources of spices in the East Indies as well. To Prince Henry, the African landmass was, in part, an obstacle. It was in the way. On the other hand, because of the Arab gold trade from Guinea, Mali, the Songhay Empire, and other West African kingdoms, Prince Henry was also interested in West Africa as a source of gold. He had another motive, and this was a typically medieval one. There long had been rumors of a powerful Christian kingdom located somewhere in Africa. If the Portuguese could reach that kingdom and form an alliance with it, they might outflank the Moslems and capture Jerusalem by coming up from the southeast. Prince Henry was not wrong. The Christian kingdom of Prester John was Ethiopia, a Coptic Christian state. However, Ethiopia was not nearly as powerful as the Portuguese had hoped. They finally made contact with it during the sixteenth century.

Spain was also in the process of becoming a national state. Throughout medieval times, the Christian states in the north had been pressing south in what Spanish historians call *La Reconquista*. In 1492, the last of the Moslem strongholds fell. Mighty Castile, the most powerful of the Spanish kingdoms, was about to forge a national state. It was at that moment in Spanish history that the Genoese adventurer Columbus appeared with his interesting proposal. Unaware of America, and having underestimated the width of the ocean sea, Columbus finally persuaded Ferdinand and Isabella to subsidize his famous voyage.

Columbus, as mentioned, was a man who was both scientist and medieval Christian. *The Santa Maria* and *Pinta* were square-rigged caravels of the latest state-of-the-arts design. The little *Nina*, which was lateen rigged with triangular sails, was a bit old-fashioned. All three were a distinct improvement over the Venetian galley but not over the *caravela* of the Portuguese navigator Bartolomeu Dias who finally reached the Cape of Good Hope in 1486. Dias, Columbus, Vasco da Gama, Magellan, and the other Spanish and Portuguese navigators not only discovered new lands and proved that the world was round, but also pushed back the frontiers of fantasy, the medieval equivalent of our modern science fiction. They did not, however, dispense with myth. Instead, new myths replaced old.

FROM MYTH TO HISTORY

There have been historians since prehistoric times, and there have been historians in every culture in the world. In archaic times, in so-called primitive cultures, they were story-tellers. To cite an example, nine-teenth-century scholars in Hawaii, such as Judge Alexander Fornan-der, collected and published ancient Hawaiian *moo'lelo*, a term which refers to stories, myths, legends, or histories. The same word applies to them all. It is, as mentioned earlier, typical of usage in all archaic lan-guages. Fornander published the story of Paao in *An Account of the Poly-nesian Race: Its Origins and Migrations*. It was a traditional story which was transmitted from one generation to the next but not written down until the nineteenth century. It was traced back to the late fourteenth or early fifteenth centuries on the basis of geneological data, assuming thirty years to a generation. According to the story, Paao was the last navigator to sail to Hawaii from *Kahiki* by which, Hawaiians, meant any south sea island. It was not necessarily Tahiti. Paao was an actual person who lived several hundred years before Captain Cook discov-ered the islands. His story is a legend. As such, it is presumed to have a kernel of truth, but it is based on traditions which cannot be verified.

History is based on documents and is much more reliable than legend. We know much more about Columbus than we do about Paao. Both, however, were human beings who acted in a natural landscape. Columbus's sailors never saw any of the mythical monsters that they were afraid of.

Paao did not interact with the *akua* or gods or any other supernat-ural elements. Instead we hear of the heroic exploits of a great Polyne-sian seaman, much as the journals of Columbus record the latter's nau-tical exploits and achievements. The supernatural element is reduced to the minimum. Yet there is a mythic watermark in both Columbus and Paao. Both are heroes. They are persons of great stature, and there is a mythic element in the structure of their respective stories. They both embarked on quests. Campbell's heroic formula, departure→initia-tion→return, applies. In that way, mythic motifs are inherent in scien-tific historiography. However, it is implicit rather than explicit, and we are not supposed to think of either Columbus or Paao as supernatural beings.

The historian may aim at complete objectivity, as Leopold Ranke did early in the nineteenth century, but the historian is yet to be born who has achieved it. Instead, all historical accounts are highly colored by the personal bias and prejudice of the historian, and he or she is invariably affected by the milieu in which he or she lives. It cannot be otherwise. Historical writing is heavily compromised. The most objec-tive historical writing is still subjective despite the best intentions of the historian. There is no such thing as historical objectivity. The best that can be managed is balance and judiciousness. There is all the difference in the world between implicit slants or perspectives which arise despite the best intentions of the objectively-minded historian and the deliberate distortion or knowing falsifying of history. We call the latter propaganda.

In the ancient world there were few scholars who attempted to write objective history. The earliest of these was Herodotus who severely reduced the supernaturalist element in his historical writings without eliminating it altogether. Thucydides was much more secular. However, Thucydides' version of the Peloponnesian War is implicitly mythic in that it is subjective. Thucydides wrote an Athenian version. In some ways, it is even more so than that of Herodotus who wrote concerning the Greek wars with the Persians. The Greek author was very fair to the Persians. In that way he was balanced and judicious. Medieval European historians were mainly chroniclers. Those, however, who wrote historical accounts of the Norman Conquest of England, for example, were highly subjective, very biased on the side of the Normans. The opposing Saxon viewpoint, that of the losing side, was suppressed. The Norman historians wrote history to justify the conquest and subjugation of England; their accounts are mythic in the sense of being highly interpretative and subjective. They wrote propaganda. What is more, mythic motifs are discernible in all historical writing. It is unavoidable. All histories are written in terms of the two basic alternative myths. Cyclical history is based on the Myth of Eternal Return and the linear historical is based on the Hero and Dragon Myth. All historical writing is based on one or the other, sometimes on combinations of both.

During the early eighteenth century, historiography was profoundly influenced by the Enlightenment. For that reason, Gianbattista Vico (d. 1744) is sometimes cited as the founder of modern historiography. However, that does not mean that Vico wrote detached, objective history. Instead, he wrote history from the perspective of what many modern historians call the "age of reason." The implication is that no one did any thinking until the eighteenth century. That is a highly slanted viewpoint, and, in that sense, a myth. Vico saw history in terms of progress from a dark age of priests through a somewhat brighter era of kings to a modern age of the science and reason school of thought which he thought was about to dawn. Since Vico's time, most historians have been of the Enlightenment viewpoint and have embraced the idea of progress, a mythic idea of modern times. During the closing years of the twentieth century, a new viewpoint called "postmodern" has appeared which challenges the assumptions of the Enlightenment. According to the deconstructionists, the objectivity of reason and science is a modern myth. This is historical myth-making in the present day. Both the Enlightenment and deconstructionist positions are subjective interpretations rooted in the milieu of the times, the personalities and psychologies of the historians, and many other factors. For these reasons they are all more like the myths, legends, and story-telling of archaic times than they are not. The whole process has been in continuity since antiquity and probably will continue to be so in the future.

Modern historiography is mythic in other respects as well. Certain mythic themes are detectable in historical writing, usually they are unintended. These include the myth of the hero, the messianic myth of the New Jerusalem, and of origins. Indeed every mythic theme which has been mentioned plus many others that could be occurs today disguised as historical interpretation, political ideology, or scientific theory. We seem predetermined to think this way. It is of our nature to think in these terms.

Of all the various mythic themes, two strike me as being basic to all others: the Myth of Eternal Return and the Myth of the Hero and Dragon. We do not encounter these stories directly in modern historical writing, but they are detectable as the basic foundation on which schemas are built. In many instances, the two themes are combined, though one is inevitably subordinated to the other. Eternal Return is the basis of the cyclical view of history. The Hero-Dragon myth is the basis of the idea of progress.

Among modern historians, only a few have attempted to write general history. These bold attempts are inevitably flawed because of the magnitude of the task and are anything but objective. Each is a speculative attempt to view the human enterprise as a whole by integrating historical events into grand patterns which the historian intuits. Unless we give that credit to Herodotus or Augustine, Vico was probably the first to attempt to write world history. Those who have come after him have unwittingly been affected by him. They include Oswald Spengler, Arnold Toynbee, and Karl Jaspers, to name but three twentieth-century historians of what is often called *Weltgeschichte* or world history. Most professional historians fault the world historians very severely because of the gaps in their knowledge as well as their distortions. Indeed, most professional historians deny that world history can be written at all. Most historians prefer to write the specialized historical monograph or, at best, national histories. However, even the specialists fail to realize Ranke's ideal of complete objectivity just as he failed to himself. The mythic element is always discernible.

There is another sense in which history is mythic. This is the symbolism which certain historical events hold for later generations, as well as the emotional associations which accumulate around them. A few well-known modern examples illustrate this idea: the battle of Gettysburg, the sinking of the *Titanic*, and the bombing of Pearl Harbor.

Frank Haskell's account of the battle of Gettysburg, written by a participant a few weeks after the event, is very different from twentieth-century histories of the battle. It is not merely a matter of fact. It is a matter of mood. Haskell tells about dead and dying men and horses, of carnage. It reads very much like a recent account of Vietnam or the Gulf Wars to which we are much closer in time and which, as yet, have not been transformed into myths. Today, the battlefield at Gettysburg is a national shrine and there, beside the bronze men and the guns, we sense a larger-than-life titanic struggle between legendary heroes, culminating in Pickett's heroic charge up Cemetery Ridge. Terms like "high-water mark of the South" convey the same heroism we encounter in the *Iliad* which was composed by Greeks but in which the Trojans are heroes. In many historical accounts and nearly all novels about Gettysburg, the heroes are the Confederates, especially to northerners. But this was not as the battle was experienced at the time by the participants in either the Confederate or Union armies. Their experience was like that of Haskell.

The same is true of the sinking of the *Titanic*. At the time, the event was an appalling marine disaster, and newspaper readers were horrified at the loss of life. In retrospect, novelists, film-makers, and even historians transformed the *Titanic* into a symbol of the hubris of the old world which went down during World War I which broke out two years after the ship sank. The *Titanic* has undergone yet another transformation since the discovery of the ship by divers and the recovery of the ship's safe and other artifacts. Now that we know where the ship is and have thoroughly studied the history of the event, the *Titanic* seems to be losing some of its mystery and therefore its symbolic aura. We hear less about *hubris* than we did a few years ago.

The bombing of Pearl Harbor, which I survived, is another case in point. None of us who were in Hawaii at the time viewed this event in symbolic or mythic terms. Later many of us have done so, both on the personal and historical level.

Film versions of the bombing made during World War II were crude propaganda films intended to vilify the Japanese and justify the war effort. Later films, such as *From Here To Eternity*, actually captured some of the mood of Hawaii just before Pearl Harbor as well as the raid itself. This is probably because the film was made during the early 1950s when memories of the actual event were fresh. *Tora Tora Tora* was the epic film of Pearl Harbor but was produced many years later. It is mythic. There are heroes and villains. Admiral Yamamoto who master-minded the raid and Lieutenant Commander Fujita, who led it, are presented sympathetically. They are among the heroes. Admiral Kimmel and Short are again made the heavies. Admiral Halsey is among the American heroes because he does what he can with what he has. There is *hubris* and *nemesis*, all the elements of Greek tragedy, in fact. When I saw the film for the first time, I had the odd and very disconcerting feeling of watching events which I knew very well from personal experience, but which were not as I had experienced them. The film was well researched in the process of its making, and was very accurate in all but a few minor details. Yet the whole effect was wrong. It was not the way it was, but I cannot say explicitly *why* it was not, only that it did not feel right. What was wrong was the mood. Also, events which I had personally experienced as real-life situations had been transformed into a story.

Historians of Gettysburg, the *Titanic*, and Pearl Harbor try to tell the stories as they were since they write from historical documents. However, once the historian, *any* historian, makes use of a document, he or she necessarily introduces interpretations which flow from various conscious, subconscious, and unconscious psychic levels of that person's being. For that reason, there is an unavoidable myth-making element in all historical writing.

Vico, Marx, Spengler, Toynbee, Jaspers and every other historian or philosopher of history who has ever lived are myth-makers. They are not really different from the archaic Hawaiian *kahunas* who composed the original story of Paao. Historical writing and myth-making are intimately related.

Vico was one of the founders of secular history. His intellectual descendants include Marx, Spengler, and Toynbee. In turn, Vico's philosophy of history derived from Augustine. He presupposed a beginning in time as well as an end-time toward which all things move. Vico reduced the mythic element in the sense of divine myth, but produced a secular myth in the process.

Vico was among the first to write *Weltgeschichte*. In part, Vico derives from Descartes and the Enlightenment, and, in part, he is in opposition to it. Descartes broke with tradition but also thought the study of history a waste of time because the sources were so unreliable. "The overcurious in the customs of the past are generally ignorant of those of the present. Besides, fictitious narratives lead us to imagine the possibility of many events that are impossible. . . ."[1] The trouble with history is that most histories tend to provide poor models. Vico did not agree. He thought history could be written and that it was a worthy enterprise. He did not, however, think that the historian could be completely objective.

In his *Scientia Nuova Vita*, Vico asserted that there is a universal law of history, a pattern, and it is reflected in the histories of particular peoples. The pattern is a spiral, as mentioned, a *corso* or *ricorso*. There have been three great periods of history: the Age of Gods, Age of Heroes and Age of Men.[2] The first refers to theocracy, the second to warrior aristocracy, and the third to democracy. Vico suggests that there was movement from the age of gods to heroes to men in Greece and that this same pattern was being repeated in European Civilization. The Hellenic Age of Gods was the Homeric Age, the Age of Reason, the era of Pericles. In turn, the Periclean Age was followed by the Hellenistic Era with its mystery religions which, in turn, culminated in Christianity.

Christian Sacred History is very discernible in Hegel's secular history-writing. According to his *Lectures on the Philosophy of History*, the human spirit has evolved out of the *Welt Geist* whose essential nature is that of freedom. "All worth which human history possesses—all spiritual reality, he possesses only through the State." Man only realizes himself through the state. The state is thus the Hegelian hero, the *Welt Geist*, the Hegelian god. "The state is the Divine Idea as it exists on earth." The ultimate goal of history is the realization of human history within a national state. spirit works through the totality of blind drives, passions, and the interests of men. Individual men are unimportant. Only the universal state is real. In the oriental civilizations of the past the state was absolute monarchy. Freedom was only potential. In the Mediterranean civilizations democracy emerged and, with it, some measure of individual freedom. In the modern world, and especially Prussia, the particular forms of freedom of the past emerge for the first time into an unprecedented example of universal freedom.[3]

Hegel's philosophy of history is an epic displaced from the Christian Myth and rooted in Augustine and Vico. It was later restated in dialectical material terms by Marx. Some modern philosophies of history emerge from myth and come down to us in a sequence: Augustine→Vico→Hegel→Marx→Spengler→Toynbee.

Marx points out in *The Communist Manifesto* that the whole history of mankind has been a history of class struggles, contests between exploiting and exploited, ruling and oppressed classes. In ancient times, the class struggle was between slaves and slave owners; during the Medieval Era, feudal lords exploited serfs and land was the basis of wealth. During modern times, capitalism arose; the bourgeoisie made the commercial and industrial revolutions and became the ruling class on the basis of their exploitation of the working class. Marx and Engels called the latter "proletariat" because they were a class which had no rights or position within society, and because their labor was alienated in order to serve the interests of the capitalists. Marx's schema of history combines cyclical and linear perspectives. It is cyclical in the repetition of the life and death struggle of the ruling classes, and linear in the inevitability of the final revolution toward which history inexorably moves. In Campbell's schema, Marxism is assimilated to the Myth of the Hero and Dragon. The collective hero is the proletariat. The dragon is capitalism..

As Marx wrote in 1843, the Old World is ruled by philistines who are masters of slaves who do not want to be free and "who do not feel themselves to be men, who cleave to their masters like a breed of slaves or horses." They are neither free nor are they persons because they are not inner directed, maturer responsible individuals. Like children they are dependents for whom all major decisions are made by others. "Human self-feeling, freedom would first have to be reawakened in the breasts of these people," Marx wrote. His conversion to socialism at that time occurred because of his Enlightenment-influenced rational conviction and romantic intuition that the great mass of people had vast creative potentialities which would emerge once alienation was overcome.

Marx's first historical observations appeared in 1844. He envisioned history in Viconian terms modified by Hegel. History, he said, is the collective self-realization of humanity. This idealistic view was frankly mystical. In his younger years he was imbued with humanistic idealism. In his later years, having become chastened concerning the "lumpen proletariat," he saw history as process subject to natural laws. In his *Economic Political Manuscripts*, Marx asserted that "History . . . is a real part of natural history, of nature developing into man." The "Whole of so-called world history (is) nothing but the engendering of man by human labour, natural becoming leading to the production of man." *Man* is in a state of becoming. The real history of man is the gap between "society that is becoming and society that has become. The human essence must be reduced to his absolute poverty that its inner worth may be born of it." Helmut Fleischer sees mythological implications in this. In his words, "a deep necessity seems at work, as a result of which the road to the kingdom of heaven runs through the vale of tears."[4]

In the young Marx's apocalyptic vision, the communist movement is the "necessary form and the energetic principle of the immediate future," but communism as such is the goal of human development, which is the formation of human society. By passing through and beyond it, "the positive elimination of private property as human self-alienation" leads to the "acquisition of true human nature through and for men." Communism completes the process of naturalization and humanization, and is the "ready solution of the conflict between man and nature and with men, the true abolition of the conflict between existence and being, between objectification and activity of the self, between freedom and necessity, between the individual and the species. It is the solution of the riddle of history and knows itself to be that solution.[5]

The young Marx interpreted history as a "uniform process with a recognizable beginning and end knowable in advance," a goal toward which the whole of humanity were directed. It was a deeply humanistic but also apocalyptic vision with religious overtones, an "ethical-religious system of thought—the lost paradise regained." As Marx wrote in his *Paris Manuscripts* of 1844, "The whole historical process—reflects the general pattern of the Judeo-Christian interpretation of history as a providential process of salvation leading to a meaningful final goal." Fleischer notes that these early apocalyptic statements are often interpreted as *the* Marxist theory of history. They are not. Marx revised his views between his twenty-sixth and twenty-eighth years, during 1845 and 1846. He rejected the apocalyptic vision he had adopted from Vico, Feuerbach, and Hegel and subsequently all hypostatization of history. "History does nothing"; he wrote after 1848, "it owns no tremendous wealth . . . and it fights no battles." Man does all that. There is no such person as "History"[6] who uses man to attain his goals. History is "nothing but the activity of man pursuing his ends." Marx consciously rejected historical teleology before he wrote his Communist Manifesto and never returned to the earlier position. Marx denied that there is any process in which a plan is being unfolded. There is no normative essence in man which history realizes. As Fleischer puts it, "History is no longer a uniform trend toward the realization of an anthropogenetic programme, but is, in many respects, the contingent result of a highly complex synthesis."[7] Subsequently, after rejecting the Hegelian view of history, Marx turned to historical empiricism. Out of this came the mature Marxist theory of history. "In broad outline, Asian, ancient, feudal, and modern bourgeois methods of production can be described as progressive periods of economic social production."[8] The goal is the classless society. Marx was an optimist. He believed that capitalism would collapse because of its internal contradictions and that the hero workers would slay the dragons and usher in the new world of the classless society. His vision was a secular version of the Hero-Dragon myth. All optimistic interpretations of history are. They are comedies.

With the outbreak of World War I, optimism gave way to gloom and doom. During July, 1918, as Ludendorf hurled his weary troops against the Allies east of Rheims in the Second Battle of the Marne, a sickly teacher took satisfaction at the appearance of his recently published book in local Munich bookstores. Oswald Spengler conceived of the book during the year of the Second Morocco Crisis in 1911; the episode convinced him that Europe was about to plunge into a fratricidal war which would be the ruination of Western Civilization. Yet it was not the anticipation of war that inspired him to write his pessimistic philosophy of history but the intuition that Western Culture already had died. The war would do no more than dispose of the remains. Spengler's myth was Eternal Return, which, like Buddhism, is profoundly pessimistic. It is not tragic because there are no heroes to fall. It is ironic because all existence is suffering. It is pointless.

Spengler moved from chilly Hamburg to Munich the year the war broke out. He was in ill health, impoverished, and alone. His mother, who was his only friend, had just died. His doctoral dissertation on Heraclitus had been twice rejected by the professors at Halle because it was inadequately researched. Rejected for military service during World War I, he taught high school by day and at night wrote his great book by candlelight. When it was written he sent the huge manuscript to a Viennese publisher.[9] With the central Powers going down to defeat, perhaps the title itself persuaded the editors to accept it. It was *Das Untergang des Abendländes: The Decline of the West.*

Spengler was deeply impressed by Nietzsche and expanded upon the philosopher's contention that "culture" is the vital, dynamic, and creative stage of a society s growth while "civilization" is the decadent corpse which already has expired. In turn, the Nietzchean view of history has its ultimate origins in the myth of eternal return, the view that all is constant cyclical change, birth and rebirth, just as the year moves from spring and summer to fall and winter.

Spengler wrote secular history in the context of mythic themes.

They exemplify the transition from myth to secular history. In doing so he corresponds to Herodotus in the ancient world whose secular history emerges from myth and retains the mythic watermark.

According to Spengler, each of eight historical cultures which he identified was an organism which emerged mysteriously "with primitive strength from the soil of a mother-region to which it remains finally bound throughout its entire life-cycle."[10] For each there is a dawn, morning, and noontime during which its unique images, passions, and ideas are realized. As the day lengthens into afternoon, these innate energies are expended. Toward the end of its millennium, each culture ripens, decays, and descends into twilight and finally expires at nightfall. Spengler wrote, ". . . I see world history as a picture of endless formations and transformations, of the marvellous waxing and waning of organic form. . . ."[11]

To read Spengler is to enter the world of myth in which the gods and heroes are displaced by nations but in which the mythic vision is still apparent. At his best, Spengler reads like a poet. He evokes moods and imagery; he constantly employs symbols, most of which immediately derive from the Classical-Christian mythic inheritance. *Untergang des Abendländes* is an epic and, as such, is displaced from myth. Thus Faustian Man is an heroic abstraction of a mythic being. His visions are mysterious, transcendental, and teleological. The Gothic cathedral, with its upward-thrusting spires, arches, and flying buttresses, express Faustian Man's aspirations, his reaching up into infinite space. Faustian Man's typical literary form is the biography and the novel. The Faustian tragic hero is a Hamlet or Lear inwardly driven by a demonic will-to-power which brings about his own destruction. Faustian Man is historically minded. He invented the clock. His political form is the nation state and the dynastic monarchy. Faustian Man is inventive. He is the experimental scientist. His landscape is dark and misty; his is a world of deep woods, lofty heights, and deep valleys. The rays of the pale Northern sun gleam faintly on the plains and filter through the opaque coloured glass of the stained glass windows of the dark cathedrals.[12]

According to Spengler, religion is the most basic expression of the *Welt Anschauung* of a culture. All other facets of a culture emerge from its religious vision. Apollinian religion was humanistic and rational. Magian religion (that of the Semites) is monotheistic and ethical. Faustian religion is mystical and apocalyptic, and emerged from both Apollinian and Magian roots, but, since the origins of every culture are mysterious, the precise nature of that emergence cannot be explained. Faustian Man's religion is called "Christianity," but it is really "Marianism." Spengler not only doubted the historicity of Jesus himself but thought that the early Christians did as well. He was impressed that Mary was a much more vivid figure to early medieval Christians than was Jesus. "Thus, presently arose beside Jesus a figure to which he was Son, which transcended his figure—that of the Mother of God . . ." which figure expressed Faustian Man's "primary feeling for infinity in Time . . ." and also his "sense of the succession of generations." Thus the Mater Dolorosa and not the Suffering Redeemer became "the pivot of German-Catholic Christianity of the Gothic Age."

The Faustian religion attributed the doctrine of *agape* to Mary and erotic love to satan. It was a dualistic religion in which the Mother of God wars against the Devil. It was also a religion which emphasized personal religious experience. Marianism is the source of Faustian individualism.

> *To be able to will freely*, at the very bottom is the one gift that the Faustian soul asks of heaven. . . . Every confession is an autobiography. . . . This peculiar liberation of the will is to us so necessary that the refusal of absolutism drives to despair, even to destruction.[13]

Faustian Culture was born around 900 C.E., just after the disintegration of the Carolingian Empire in which Apollinian Civilization had finally expired. The Faustian noontide was the High Middle Ages. Its sun declined toward the West with the outbreak of the Protestant Reformation which shattered the medieval synthesis. When Gothic "bliss" and Marianism gave way to Protestant individualism and puritanism, the West entered the twilight of the Enlightenment which, to Spengler, was only apparently an era of progress.

The twentieth century is a time of dissolution in which Faustian culture has already perished. It died around 1900, leaving the rotting corpse. Spengler's apocalyptic vision was not a prophetic warning of impending doom. It was an obituary. Western culture had died. In a short time the war-making Caesars would appear. Like carrion crows they would dispose of the remains. In time a new culture would germinate from the soil fertilized by the demise of the old. Spengler says little about what is to come. He died in 1936 while the Caesars were still rampant. In time, a new culture will grow from the corpse of Faustian. But it doesn't matter. Life and death are pointless.

Spengler's name is often coupled with Arnold Toynbee's since both were general historians who attempted to write world history in terms of teleological schema. Both were literary world historians, humanists rather than scientists, and prophets of doom. Both had a cyclical view of history, based on the birth, death, and rebirth of cultures. Thus, in both Spengler and Toynbee, we encounter the Myth of Eternal Return.

Toynbee was an Oxford don in August, 1914 when World War I broke out, a professor of classical history.

It "flashed on my mind," he later wrote

> that the fifth century B.C.E. historian Thucydides had had already the experience that was now overtaking me. He, like me, had been overtaken by a fratricidal great war between the states into which his world had been divided politically. . . . I now saw that Classical Greek history and modern Western history were, in terms of experience, contemporary.[14]

After the war, while riding the Orient Express from Constantinople, Toynbee jotted down headings which he called "parts." Between 1927 and 1939 he produced his monumental, multi-volume *A Study of History* which is the most comprehensive attempt of any historian to write world history in this century.

According to Toynbee, "past civilizations have met their deaths not from the assaults of an external and uncontrollable assassin, but by their very own hands. . . ."[15] They are not organic growths doomed to perish when they have lived out their life-spans, nor is there inevitability in their decline. They die because of the hubris of ruling elites, creative minorities which become dominant minorities.

What Toynbee calls the "creative minority" is the hero of his epic. The villain is the demonic "dominant minority" which is what the "creative minority" becomes when it has lost its élan and vision. Civilizations grow because of the release of vital energies and decline because of "a loss of harmony which leads to the forfeiture by a society of its power of self-determination." As declining civilizations enter their terminal "times of trouble," schisms occur which break societies into warring states beset with class struggle. "Thus the social schism which is the outward criterion of the disintegration of a broken-down society is not just a schism and nothing more." The "creative minority" gives way to the "dominant minority" which tries to "hold by force—against all right and reason—the position of inherited privilege which it has ceased to merit; and then the proletariat repays injustice with resentment, fear

with hate, and violence with violence when it executes its act of seces-
sion." By "proletariat" Toynbee means any significant segment of the
population alienated from society and deprived of rights. "Yet paradoxically this explosive process of disintegration ends in positive
achievement—the creation of a universal state, a universal church, and
barbarian war lords."[16]

> [During decline] the spirit of creativity . . . is not utterly over-
> whelmed. . . . Enough creativity survives in the dominant minor-
> ity to enable it to embark on wars of imperial conquest which give
> the false impression of vitality, and which are accompanied by
> the emergence of universal religions which are highly institution-
> alized, conspicuous for missionary activity, ecclesiastical power,
> and doctrinal orthodoxy.[17]

These, too, give the false impression of vitality. In point of fact, both the
universal state and church are on the brink of collapse and the apparent
vitality is actually because of terminal illness such as those in which
there is a surge of energy just before the patient dies.

Toynbee showed how Christianity synthesized the religious traditions of the Mediterranean World and became a universal church.
According to Toynbee:

> [Churches] are the institutional embodiments of higher religions,
> and the true mission of higher religion . . . is to enable human
> beings to enter into a direct personal relation with a trans-human
> presence in and behind and beyond the universe.

As he pointed out,

> A human being is not simply a social animal: he is also a person-
> ality seeking a directing relation with an ultimate spiritual reality.[18]

Toynbee was perplexed by the religious paradox. The church preserves
tradition and reaches millions of people but all too often stifles creative
individuals in the process. Religion is the means by which people are
brought into a relationship with the transcendental. Yet the transcendental invariably gives way to the secular in the process of mediation,
and, in particular, by the missionary efforts to reach as many people as
possible too often stifle free thought and persecute heretics. Toynbee
took particular note of the moral dilemma. The nemesis is a spiritual

tension that is proportionate in its acuteness to the degree to which the process of institutionalization is carried. In a highly institutional church there is likely to be a conflict between the individual conscience and the ecclesiastical "Establishment." The conscience asserts itself to its peril; yet society cannot afford to let the conscience be intimidated and coerced, [because] conscience is a personal, not a collective faculty. The spiritual level of a society cannot be higher than the average level of the participants; the collective level can be raised only on the initiative of the individual; and when an individual does rise above the level of his social environment, this is the fruit of a previous victory over himself in his own spiritual life.[19]

Toynbee held that "Human emotions, consciousness, and will are not collective; they are faculties of an individual human being; and the inner spiritual life of a person . . . is the field in which the spiritual mastery has to be fought." This is Man's most urgent and difficult task. "Because he is a natural living being, his instincts are egocentric, but he can only survive as a social animal. He "cannot contract out of society"; thus, as mentioned, self-centeredness cannot be tolerated. The founders of the great religions perceived that "salvation must be sought not in the field of social relations, but in the field of a person's inner spiritual life, and that, in this field, salvation can be won only by self-mastery." Thus the great founders of religion have "taught that self-mastery is the indispensable pre-requisite for the establishment of a right relation between a human person and the ultimate spiritual reality."[20] The problem arises when, as is usually the case, the priest interjects himself between the individual and the transcendental as the authority figure to be obeyed as representative of the divine. At this point a subtle transition occurs from religion to secular ideology.

Spengler and Toynbee are in the tradition of the great Greek historians such as Thucydides and Herodotus and share the cyclical view of history which, in turn, emerges from the Myth of Eternal Return. In their histories this mythic schema is quite explicit since Spengler and Toynbee wrote history with mythic motifs consciously in mind. Most modern and post-modern academic historians, however, reject teleology and confine themselves to narrowly circumscribed topics which are rigorously interpreted in terms of the canons of modern scientific historiography. Even so, the teleological implications lurk in the background as unvoiced implications. What has occurred has been a descent of myth to the underworld, like a river that plunges underground. Myths which are consciously rejected persist sub-consciously and unconsciously in post-modern historiography.

Karl Jasper's schema is displaced from the Judeo-Christian apocalyptic vision of the New Jerusalem. It is optimistic and is derived from the Myth of the Hero and Dragon. The Enlightenment myth emphasizes the rise of science and philosophy during the seventeenth century, the great watershed of modern history. Prior to Descartes and Newton, according to this view, mankind stumbled through the darkness. Since then he has lived by reason though with catastrophic eruptions of the irrational, as during the Reign of Terror and, most recently, in the Third Reich. With setbacks, however, the general development has been progressive. I would say that Jasper typifies the liberal view of history.

According to Jaspers, mankind emerged from prehistoric darkness into the light of archaic civilization which exploded into brilliance during the Axial Era which refers to the half millennium preceding and succeeding the year 500 B.C.E. which Jaspers calls the "axis" of history. During this time, Classical Philosophy was founded in China, the Upanishads were composed in India; the Buddha appeared; Zoroaster flourished in Iran; the Prophets of Israel from Elijah to Deutero-Isaiah flourished, and the Ionian philosophers emerged in Greece followed by the great tragedians, Plato, and Aristotle. What follows is the Post-Axial, during which time Christianity and Islam arose on the foundations of the Hebraic and Hellenic creations. The next great era was the Enlightenment which began during the seventeenth century, and which has made the world what it is today.[21]

According to *The Origins and Goals of History*:

From the dark world of a prehistory lasting for hundreds and thousands of years . . . ancient civilizations emerged . . . in Mesopotamia, Egypt, the Indus Valley, and along the banks of the Huang Ho. . . . From the midst of the ancient civilizations...during the Axial Period, from 800 to 200 B.C.E., the spiritual foundation of mankind arose in three mutually independent places, in the West—polarized in Orient and Occident—in India and in China. Since the end of the Middle Ages, the West has produced in Europe modern science and with it, after the eighteenth century, the age of technology—the first entirely new development in the spiritual and material sphere since the Axial Period. . . . The contemporary world, with its great American and Russian blocs, with Europe, India, and China, Asia Minor, South America, and all other regions of the earth, has in the course of a slow process dating from the sixteenth century, become a *de facto* single unit of communication . . . so that only just now has it been possible to talk about world history in a meaningful sense.[22]

According to Jaspers, the history of religions is best understood in terms of the Axial.[23]

In Spengler and Toynbee we encounter irony, the view of history as a bleak process in which cultures and civilizations, like the people who compose them, are doomed, and in which their life and death is absurd. This view contrasts sharply with the romantic optimism of the Marxist view of history as well as with the equally optimistic liberal idealism of Karl Jaspers.

The mythic image is less explicit in the specialist studies of the professional historians but is by no means absent. It occurs in basic assumptions which are seldom explicitly expressed but which are discernible as implications. For example, the American frontier historians of the school of Frederick Jackson Turner evoke the American Dream, and in that mythic image we encounter a version of the Christian apocalyptic myth of the New Jerusalem. Indeed, virtually all American history is written from this particular perspective; it is inherent in the very nature of American democracy. The mythic image occurs in other histories as well, wherever, in fact, we encounter the idea of national mission or destiny. The histories of Britain, France, Spain, Italy, Germany, Austria, and Russia all exhibit mythic image in this latter sense. They are all based on the Myth of the Hero and Dragon.

Thus, most postmodern historical interpretations are variants of the Christian apocalyptic, since most are written in terms of future expectations, with the view in mind that the nations are moving toward some ultimate destiny. Moreover, since the expansion of Europe has created a single global village, global history itself is now written in terms of Christian sacred history. The myth provides the paradigm.

Post-Modern historiography plays the same role that myth did in archaic societies. It explains origins, how the world and its various nations, classes, institutions, movements, customs, skills, and arts came to be and how it is that the world is as it is today. Consequently, history is the equivalent of cosmogony. All particular origins, moreover, are subsumed in the larger view of human evolution which, in turn, is a phase in the vast cosmology of the expanding universe which originates in the big bang some fifteen to twenty billion years ago. The fact that the cosmological and historiographical views are founded on well-verified scientific evidence does not alter the situation. Archaic myths are all founded on the best available evidence and are discredited when the evidence no longer substantiates them. At the same time, there is always a transition from the old myths, which have been superseded, to the new. The latter invariably emerge from the former, first as modifications and revisions, and ultimately as independent species, something new and different.

Today we are in the midst of just such a transition. Western Civilization was an archaic, parochial culture until the seventeenth century. Throughout the long era from earliest prehistoric times until the rise of modern science, revelation was the acknowledged source of knowledge and, as hierophany, or disclosure of the sacred, myths were authoritative. The discrediting of myth during the Enlightenment shattered the authority of Christian sacred history because science challenged revelation. The Bible was shown to be wrong about the origins of the universe, the world, mankind, and the various facets of human culture. That this is not universally acknowledged is only to say that in some quarters the archaic views persist, founded on the archaic authorities. But the very hysteria with which science is resisted by conservative Christians only proves the point. Their world view has been discredited and such cannot occur without causing great distress. At the same time, even in those circles in which the new world view of science is wholly accepted and the old Christian myth rejected, the myth persists underground in the unconscious and surfaces in ideas, images, and fantasies. The myth is discernible, as we have seen, in post-modern historiography.

Indeed, it also occurs wherever scientists formulate general theories, as in the case of evolution and cosmology. It cannot be stressed enough that in such cases the occurrence of myth is entirely unconscious. However, people who are agnostic or atheist, who totally reject traditional religions, have been conditioned from birth in societies permeated with traditional values and their attitudes and ideas have emerged in a context in which such influences are inescapable. It is not that the ideas are inherited. No evidence suggests that they are. It is rather that, in the scheme of things, conscious ideas and images invariably constitute a superstructure which emerges from the unconscious which is, in turn, universal, being grounded in instincts which are inherited as basic aspects of our biological nature.

Until the turn of the century, though the unconscious was acknowledged by philosophers, poets, and novelists, few attempts had been made to study its nature in systematic fashion. These efforts began with Charcot's experiments with hypnosis, then Charcot's discoveries awakened the interest of Freud. In turn, Freud's discovery of the personal unconscious aroused the interest of Jung, who discovered the collective unconscious. They completely revolutionized our views of myth and showed that it was akin to dream and fantasy. They also showed that, far from vanishing with the Enlightenment, myth continued to persist in our civilization, disguised though it usually is, in literature, art, and popular culture.

Some modern philosophies of history are founded on the Eden-New Jerusalem motif, that is to say, the idea of primitive innocence corrupted by civilization but redeemed through fire. This vision is ultimately based on Judeo-Christian Apocalypticism. Those modern philosophies of history which focus on the rhythmic rise and fall of civilizations derive from the more archaic Myth of Eternal Return. Thus, while the Spenglerian philosophy emphasizes decline and disintegration and Toynbee sees a "time of troubles," both anticipate the New Age which will dawn day after tomorrow. A new culture will arise. But that culture, too, will one day wither and die and give rise to yet another culture and another as long as humanity lasts. The only conceivable end-time is either a nuclear holocaust on such a scale as to totally annihilate humanity or an astronomical catastrophe.

Other philosophies of history are based on the Hero-Dragon motif. Marx looked far beyond to a brave new world of freedom and abundance, while Jaspers looked to the future as it seemed to be in post-World War II Europe. The democracies had triumphed over totalitarianism, and a new age of freedom and democracy seemed about to begin. Spengler anticipated a Post-Faustian age, Toynbee hoped for the revitalization of Christian Civilization. But while Marx saw world communism as universal fulfillment, Spengler and Toynbee see no end-time but only continuing episodes in the unfolding drama of humanity's sojourn.

Both views of history are mythic, the first being Judeo-Christian and the second classical Greek. All other views of history, including those of the specialists, partake of one mythos or the other, imply either and the New Jerusalem or Eternal Return.

---————— 6 ——————---

SECULAR MYTHS IN NOVELS

MYTH AND THE ARTS

N̲O̲ ANIMAL CREATES A WORK OF ART BUT MAN. Why do we? Captain Cook noted in his journal that the natives of Tierra del Fuego "... are content to be naked but ambitious to be fine."[1] Cook was a no-nonsense practical sort of man, and it puzzled him that these exceptionally primitive inhabitants of a savage land of rocks and freezing winds preferred to make ornaments of the bolts of red cloth he gave them rather than clothe themselves. As Cheney says

> In the childhood of art the creator was nearer to God, expressed himself with clairvoyant directness and inspired vividness. Primitive art, in the right sense, is that golden time when the soul is near the Great Source, when an harmonious order is divined in nature, when the shaping hands obey an inner feeling of rhythmic progression and cosmic rightness.[2]

Volumes have been written trying to make sense of art, why we have it at all. Why did Assyrian kings and Dutch merchants employ artists? Why did the Church? Even the most crass and philistine of Babbitts exhibit aesthetic sensibilities in the showroom of a car dealer. Is it possible that we are not as functional and practical-minded as the utilitarians among us insist? The things of the mind and the spirit have always been of central importance, at least as important as making a living or raising a family. Every society since the upper palaeolithic has had its art, including those which have been most impoverished. Any animal can find food and shelter and procreate. Only man is an artist and to man art always has been a basic and fundamental need, as much a need for his soul as food is for his body.

Although we do not know the myths, there is a mythic aspect in at least some palaeolithic cave art, and a great deal in neolithic and bronze age murals and mobiles throughout the world. Temple art and architecture emerged before secular in the great archaic civilizations. For a time, from the Hellenistic through the Roman eras, the secular arts flourished. In the early medieval, there was a return to the religious motifs once more. During the Renaissance, secular art and architecture emerged; they became predominant from the Enlightenment to the Industrial Age, and continue to prevail through the twentieth century. But, from the Industrial Revolution on, we encounter ideological art and architecture, the factory, sky-scraper and high rise in the capitalist West and the monumental architecture of the countries of the former Soviet bloc.

In the former socialist countries, we encountered remarkable conservatism, exemplified by the mandatory preference for Soviet Realism (Stalin's taste) throughout the Stalinist Era, and the reconstruction of war battered cities like Warsaw and Leningrad as *Alte städte*; these were cities rebuilt in their original styles. This, too, is symbolically significant. Soviet socialism was remarkably conservative.

Paradoxically, capitalist architecture is more explicitly ideological than was Soviet. This is especially true of the great financial towers of modern Western cities. Wall street is traditionally the most explicit example because the financial buildings tower so impressively over Trinity Church in their midst.

To quote Cheney:

> In one way or another all plastic art is an expression of how a man feels in the universe, set down in images visually affective to other men, who feel and enjoy that something too. Expression on one side, pleasure on the other. A bit of order in a disordered world; a hint of controlled rhythm among the endless casual motions and vibrations and shocks that make up life.[3]

Indeed, as Eliade points out, art begins with archaic man's rendering of cosmos out of chaos, imitative of the creative acts of the gods. If this is so, there is a direct relationship between myth and the plastic arts just as there is a relationship between myth and literature.

The starting point of art, as with myth, is the symbol. The impulse, idea, image, or plot, which is in the conscious mind, can be expressed in any of the languages of which the human mind is capable. Thus, there is a very well-marked path to the epic poem and from the epic to all other forms of oral and literary expression in which the essence is logos. There is, too, some relationship between story and music, since both are holistically structured, as Lévi-Strauss points out. Both are rhythmic; both are structured.

For reasons difficult to explain, we have a propensity to miniaturize. One of the earliest examples of human art is a small Aurignacian horse head from around forty thousand years ago. The panther in La Mouthe is an image, and if, to the artist, it expressed something beyond representation, it was a symbol. The same is true of the polychromatic cave paintings at nearby Font de Gaume and Lascaux. The shaman who painted the horses, bison, and mammoths, and the people of the clan who viewed it experienced something, though we can only guess what these paintings and engravings meant to them.

A story, too, is a miniaturizing of landscapes, persons, animals, and vegetation. Something happens. If we tell what has happened we invariably add, delete, shape, manipulate, refine, distort, and alter. In the process of such alterations we become myth-makers. In the plastic arts the story is not narrated, save in the comic strip or the Victorian popular painting in which the picture tells a story. If we except those works of art and programme music and ballads, what is created is a feeling which speaks to the soul. The vehicle of communication is the symbol which is an image endowed with hidden meaning that is inferred, implied, sensed, and felt. Art is the language of the soul.

According to Freud, in "Creative Writers and Daydreaming," the artists, poets, novelists, and playwrights are persons who are in touch with the inner child. Freud writes: "Should we not look for the first traces of imaginative activity as early as in childhood? The child's best-loved and most intense occupation is with his play or games." Freud goes on to ask,

> Might we not say that every child at play behaves like a creative writer in that he creates a world of his own, or, rather, rearranges the things of the world in a new way which pleases him?" It would be wrong to think he does not take that world seriously, Freud contends. "Indeed, on the contrary, he takes his play very seriously and expends large amounts of emotion on it."[4]

Freud asks, what is the opposite of work? Surely not child's play. It is too serious to the child. Indeed, children know very well what play is and what it is not. Both fantasy and play are categories which are very real, but they are different categories of reality. Fantasy and play are categories which are as real as so-called realistic pursuits.

The child creates a world of fantasy which he takes very seriously and in which he invests a great deal of emotion, time, and thought. Yet it is a make-believe world in that he is the creator of it. He has made it up and believes in it in the sense that he is committed to working out its various aspects.[5] A novelist is a god who creates a world, populates it with paper people and gives them life. Indeed, one learns more theology from creative writing than from the study of religion. The child does the same in his fantasy play. He creates his own world and populates it. Frequently, this created world will be more important to the child (and creative writer) than the so-called real world. To both that other world is banal and ephemeral.

Freud's comments also apply to myth-making. The mythic vision is akin to that of the child; myth, creative art, and child's play are of the inner world of the soul. This inner world is not a chaos but an order in which there is a strong sense of the possible. The child as well as the novelist (and the myth-maker) knows what can be done and what cannot be done. There are always the unspoken rules. There can be magic, but it must be both appropriate and conform to certain principles.

By child's play Freud had in mind the fantasy psycho-dramas of latency aged children. The child's imagination is sparked by something he has heard and seen. He miniaturizes in a drama acted out with one or two playmates. In such games toys are props. The creative writer no longer needs the props as physical objects but translates them into mental images.

As Freud points out, "As people grow up, then, they cease to play, and they seem to give up the yield of pleasure which they gained from playing. . . .[6] What appears to be a renunciation is really the formation of a substitute or surrogate. In the same way, the growing child, when he stops *playing*, he now *fantasizes*. He builds castles in the air and creates what are called *daydreams*.

Freud contends that people never give up anything which is pleasurable but make substitutes. Thus, "A child's play is determined by wishes; in point of fact by a single wish—the wish to be big and grown up." The child always plays at being grown up, and in his games he imitates what he knows about the lives of adults.

On the one hand, he knows that he is expected not to go on playing or fantasizing any longer, but to act in the real world; on the
other, some of the wishes which give rise to his fantasies are of a
kind which it is essential to conceal. Thus he is ashamed of his
fantasies as being childish and as being unpermissible.[7]

Far from being stereotyped and unalterable, "the various fantasies, castles in the air, and day dreams" integrate into the person's view of reality and continuously change with every change in his case. Thus, past
present, and future string together with the thread of the wish running
through them. Both day dreams and night dreams arise from wishes of
which we are ashamed. Both are wish-fulfillments.

The creative writer is a "dreamer in broad daylight," when he
authors novels, romances, short stories, and dramas:

> One feature above all cannot fail to strike us about the creations of
> these story-writers; each of them has a hero who is the center of
> interest, for whom the writer tries to win our sympathy by every
> possible means and whom he seems to place under the protec-
> tion of a special Providence. . . . If our comparison of the imagina-
> tive writer with the day-dreamer, and of poetical creation with
> the day-dream is to be of any value, it must, above all, show itself
> in some way or other. . . . A strong experience in the present awak-
> ens in the creative writer a memory of an earlier experience (usu-
> ally belonging to his childhood) for which there now proceeds a
> wish which finds its fulfillment in the creative work; the work
> itself exhibits elements of the recent provoking occasion as well as
> of old memory.[8]

The reason that creative writers draw so heavily on childhood memories is because "a piece of creative writing, like day-dreaming, is a con-
tinuation and a substitute for what was once the play of childhood."

> We must not neglect to go back to the kind of imaginative works
> which we have to recognize, not as original creations, but as the
> refashioning of ready-made, and familiar material. Even here, the
> writer keeps a certain amount of independence which can express
> itself in the choice of material and in changes in it which are often
> quite extensive. In so far as the material is already at hand, how-
> ever, it is derived from the popular treasure-house of myths, leg-

ends, and fairy-tales. The study of contributions of folk psychology such as these is far from being complete, but it is evident that myths are distorted vestiges of youthful fantasies of whole nations, the *secular dreams* of humanity.[9]

Child's play and the creativity of the artist are intimately related to myth-making, the artist, poet, novelist, and the playwright are the shamans of the postmodern era. They are the individual voices which also articulate that which emerges from the psychic depths of the race.

CLASSICAL AND CHRISTIAN MOTIFS IN MODERN LITERATURE

As Lilian Feder shows in *Ancient Myth in Modern Poetry*, Graeco-Roman, Teutonic, and Celtic mythic themes constantly occur in modern literature. William Butler Yeats, T. S. Eliot, Ezra Pound, and W.H. Auden were steeped in *The Golden Bough* as well as the Classics. "Throughout Yeats' prose and poetry—from his earliest writings to his last ones—he finds analogues in Celtic, Greek, and Eastern myth and in mystical doctrine. . . ."[10] All of Yeats' adaptations of myth indicate a need to impose order and unity on an apparent anarchy in his romances. It was so with the other afore-mentioned poets. Their use of myth was deliberate and intentional. In his *Essays and Introductions*, Yeats wrote:

> I think profound philosophy must come from terror. There is an abyss beneath us into which our inherited convictions drop. Whether we will or not we must ask the ancient question is there reality anywhere? Is there a God? Is there a soul? Why cry with the Indian sacred book: "They have put a golden stopper into the neck of the bottle; pull it; let out reality.[11]

Since World War II the classical myth has been far less apparent in modern literature than before. There are occasional exceptions, John Updike's fantasy tale *The Centaur*, for example. But, even indirectly and in disguise, the Classic mythic theme is rare. On the other hand, the Christian Myth occurs frequently, as in the novels of John Updike, John Cheever, Jack Kerouac, and William Burroughs, always disguised but discernible. It is proof once more that the Classical mythic heritage is much less significant than the Christian, that the latter is the dominant Western myth. There is a strong Christian imprint in the novels of J. D. Salinger, for example. His Holden Caulfield in *The Catcher in the Rye* yearns for purity. Purity drives Holden to embark on his Manhattan odyssey: he seeks to recover the innocence of childhood since only the child supposedly has clarity of vision, unclouded by shame. In Holden's dream, "Jesus curses the man who caused kids 'to stumble' so that they may continue unspotted. Holden longs to keep them all in their innocence and for none to stumble. What Holden means by 'phony' is hypocrisy." "Theirs is the darkness of the double-eye which deceives others in the same state. Holden is "a sort of atheist" because he is repelled by conventional Christianity which he recognizes as sham piety. But Holden, 'a sort of atheist', is really a pilgrim on the way himself. In *Franny and Zooey*, Franny and a friend are lunching in a cafe. She has been reading a Russian novel called *The Way of a Pilgrim* and tries to learn the "Jesus prayer" she finds there. suddenly she becomes ill because of the meaninglessness of modern life. She is found in a faint in the ladies room, murmuring the Jesus prayer. In the Zooey story the Glass family tries to bring Franny through her spiritual crisis. Zooey reminds his sister how their brother used to tell them to polish their shoes for the Fat Lady who is really Christ. The strange allusion is to the "humble brother" who is only seen by the spiritually perceptive, never by the conventionally pious. "My God! He's the most intelligent man in the Bible," Zooey exclaims. "Jesus . . . realized that there is no separation from God . . . who in the Bible besides Jesus knew—knew—that we're carrying the Kingdom of Heaven around with us, *inside*, where we're all too goddam stupid and sentimental and unimaginative to look? You have to *be a son of God to know that kind of stuff*."[12]

In Jack Kerouac's *On the Road*, Dean Moriarty is the "holy goof."

> In their blind flight in fast cars, high on Benzedrine . . . they do not experience life around them. Rather they experience the exhilarating danger of roaring through towns down a seemingly endless road where speed is almost an end in itself. Kerouac coined the term "beat" in 1940 while "trying to think of the meaning of the Lost Generation and the subsequent Existentialism."[13]

In 1954, he had a vision while in a Catholic church in Lowell, Massachusetts, his home town. In the vision he was told that the meaning of "Beat" was "Beatific" in the sense of converting "alienation into splendid spiritual transcendence."[11] In *On the Road*, Sal and Dean roam America in quest of the flash of ecstasy "that erases one's rational preoccupation with the world and gives him a sense of oneness with the All-Knowing God."[14]

The persistence of myth in literature has been noted by the archetypal school of critics. These derive their mythic interpretations from Frazer and Jung but are by no means necessarily Frazerians or Jungians. Indeed, most of this school resist classification since they frequently disagree with one another. What justifies the term "archetypal critic" is their discernment of recurrent patterns in literature and culture or "archetypes." The archetypes are not always perceived as tendencies or energies emergent from the collective unconscious, the Jungian view, but are usually attributed to cultural experience. Archetypal criticism, which has its counterparts in other disciplines, is actually a line of thought which includes scholars as diverse as Northrop Frye and Joseph Campbell.

The relationship to Jung in both Frye's and Campbell's cases is indirect and with many reservations. As Campbell has said, Jung's view of myth has a "cookie mold" aspect and, in any case, Jung devoted far less attention to myth than to his theory of archetypes.

Abrams holds that archetypal critics identify the death-rebirth theme which Frazer evoked as the monomyth from which all others are derived. They accept Frazer's theory that the dying and resurrected god is derived from the cycle of the seasons and the death and rebirth of vegetative and animal life. The heroic ideal of the saga is assimilated to this theme. The critics find this mythic theme of the god who dies and is reborn in Near Eastern and Greek myth, the Bible, Dante's *Divine Comedy* and certain poems such as Coleridge's *Rhyme of the Ancient Mariner*. The death and rebirth theme is assimilated to others, such as the *descensus ad inferos, ascensus ad paradiso*, the search for the father, the Paradise-Hades image, the Promethean rebel-hero, the earth goddess, the *femme fatale*.[15]

According to Maud Bodkin, a Jungian, archetypes are psychic residues which originate in repeated experiences over many generations. They are inherited in the brain structure.

> It is like a deeply graven river hid in the psyche, in which the waters of life, instead of flowing along as before in the broad but shallow stream, suddenly swell into a mighty river.[16]

When this occurs, there is always acute emotional intensity

> as though chords in us were struck that had never resounded before, or as though forces whose existence are never suspected were unloosed. When an archetypal situation occurs we suddenly

feel an extraordinary sense of release, as though transported or caught up by an overwhelming power. At such moments we are no longer individuals, but the race; the voice of mankind resounds in us.[17]

According to Bodkin, the

archetype is the *participation mystique* of primordial man with the soil in which he dwells, and which contains the spirits of his ancestors. The impact of an archetype summons up a voice that is stronger than our own. Whoever speaks in primordial images speaks with a thousand voices; he transmutes our personal destiny into the destiny of mankind, and evokes in all those beneficent forces that ever and non have enabled mankind to find a refuge from every period and to outlive the longest life.[18]

Novels such as Conrad's *The Heart of Darkness*, Thomas Mann's *The Magic Mountain*, and James Joyce's *Ulysses* are often cited as modern literary examples of the quest. Some critics also find this motif in more recent works such as John Updike's *Rabbit Run* and William Burrough's *The Naked Lunch*. Not all modern novels are quests by any means but some are.

Frye has explored the archetypal approach to literature most profoundly. As an Oxford student, Frye rebelled against the current idea that literary criticism should be a science akin to linguistics. He "avoided the Ph.D. . . . by sheer accident" and went to work on a study of William Blake which convinced him that the Bible was the frame of Western myth and that Christianity absorbed the whole of Classical and Teutonic tradition, that ". . . it is a historical fact that our literature is most directly descended from the Biblical myth."[19]

As Frye writes,

. . . the Bible preoccupied me, not because it represented a religious "position" congenial to my own, but for the opposite reason. It illustrated the imaginative assumptions on which Western poets had proceeded. The poet is taken over by a mythical and metaphorical organism, with its historical roots in the Bible, and the integrity of that organism is his Muse, the mother that brings to life a being separate both from herself and him.[20]

In the course of studying Blake's "private mythology," Frye realized that the Bible had a mythological structure from creation to apocalypse in time, from heaven to hell in space, and that this universe
formed a framework of imagery for all European poets down to his
own time. It either had destroyed or absorbed other mythological structures including the Classical, Celtic, and Teutonic, and provided the
basis for the cosmologies of Dante and Milton. The mythological universe is a model of the constructed world of civilization and culture. It is
a world built on human desires and anxieties and preoccupations.[21]

By Blake's time, astronomy had made it clear that the Christian
universe was imaginary. Blake was the first poet to realize how drastic
an imaginative change the Scientific Revolution was. In his *Prophecies* he
tried to restructure the "discarded model" and see it as human rather
than divine. He "wanted to recover the mythological universe for the
human imagination, and stop projecting it on the objective God. Only
Goethe made a similar effort, in the second part of *Faust*. But Goethe did
not construct so firm an articulated skeleton of the imaginative cosmos
as Blake."[22]

Blake's mythic universe had four main levels. At the top was the
sky father who made the world. The second level was the "unfallen
world" of innocence; below that was the fallen world of "experience."
Below that was the chaotic, demonic world. The crisis of history was the
descent of God into the fallen world of experience, the dwelling place of
man.

Frye completed *Fearful Symmetry* in 1947. He then turned to the
study of Spenser's *Faerie Queene* "only to discover that my beginning
was my end."[20] He had become deeply involved in myth and Biblical
typology. As a result he embarked on a much more ambitious enterprise and produced *Anatomy of Criticism* (1957), the most complete study
of criticism since Aristotle's Poetics.

Frye showed that Western literature moved from myth through
romance, high mimesis and low mimesis to irony during the course of
the past fifteen hundred years. "In the pre-medieval period literature is
closely attached to Christian, late Christian, late Classical, Celtic or Teutonic myth."[23] At the outset of the medieval, European literature had
absorbed Christian, late Classical, Celtic, and Teutonic Mythology and
moved toward their incorporation into the tradition. The whole of literature is a series of displacements from myth.

In his third essay of *Anatomy of Criticism*, Frye discusses the theory
of plot. Myth is at once extreme, naturalism at the other. The Bible is the
mythic source.

The city, the garden, and the sheepfold are the organizing metaphors of the Bible and of most Christian symbolism, and they are brought into complete metaphorical identification in the book explicitly called the Apocalypse or Revelation, which has been carefully designed to form an undisplaced mythical conclusion for the Bible as a whole.[24]

In the rotary of *mythoi* (plot), tragedy and comedy contrast and so do romance and irony. They roll like the seasons: comedy, spring, romance, summer, tragedy, autumn, irony, winter. In the myths of spring, the hero's society rebels against the society of the elders *(senex)* and reverses the order; summer is the romantic quest in which the hero goes forth to find the Grail; autumn is the tragedy in which a whole society goes down in the fall of the hero; winter is the ironic time of meaningless death. Bodkin and Frye, in the tradition of Frazer, state the romantic thesis of hidden depths.

According to Frye, there is a process of meaning-displacement whereby all Western literature derives from the Bible and, to a lesser degree, from the Graeco-Roman classics. Frye derived this view from his study of Blake and expanded upon it in *Anatomy of Criticism*. It has been given further clarification and expansion in *The Great Code*.

Frye held that all literature is displaced from myth which, in the case of Western tradition, is first of all the Bible, and secondarily the classical, Celtic, and Teutonic elements which have been incorporated. Frye defines myths as stories about gods, which he identifies as supernatural beings whose powers are qualitatively greater than human beings. Both the gods and the landscapes in which they enact their dramas are of a wholly distinctive order from anything in the natural world. Power is the basis of displacement. If the central characters of a work of fiction are less than godlike but more powerful than ordinary human beings, they are heroes and their stories are epics or romances. Myth displaces to epic and romance. Frye contends that the literatures of India, China, and other Eastern civilizations displaced no further from myth than romance. In the West, however, the picaresque novel appeared during the sixteenth and seventeenth centuries; in it the characters are larger than life yet not of heroic stature. Frye calls literature of this type "high mimesis" or imitation of a superior order, a designation for which many critics entertain reservations. Since the beginning of the eighteenth century, the novel has appeared in which the characters mirror ordinary people in ordinary landscapes, they are familiar figures who are anything but heroic, but who cope reasonably well with life's exigencies. Avoiding the term "realism," Frye chooses to identify literature of this sort as "lower mimesis."

The ironic mode predominates in post-modern literature. The ironic character, like Willie Loman in *Death of a Salesman*, is hapless and ineffectual. His story is often sad but lacks the dignity and significance of tragedy. He does not cope as well as the average person. We pity him. Since such characters sometimes take on the aspects of the holy fool, (or holy goof, as Kerouac puts it), there is a fantasy element in them which distinguishes them from real-life characters. We look down on them, they are less than life. In a sense, they seem mythical. They do not behave like ordinary people but seem to be dream figures even though they usually enact their dramas in a familiar setting. In *Anatomy of Criticism* Frye suggests that irony marks the return to myth, but he does not elaborate. If Frye is right, there is a grand cycle in the history of Western literature from myth to irony through the various modes such as romance and high mimesis to low mimesis at the opposite pole from myth, and back to myth once more.

As Ursula La Guin, Harold Schechter, and other scholars of popular literature point out, the mythic motif is very apparent in genre literature, especially science fiction and fantasy. Here they constantly occur, both explicitly and implicitly. They are very discernible in the detective story, the western, the war story, the romance, and the gothic tale. Indeed, since those who produce such stories are usually formula writers, there is little of the author's personal vision and much that is derived from the mass culture which is the market. On that account the popular culture is much closer to its mythical roots than the high culture.

According to Campbell, all of the mythogenetic zones have vanished. By "mythogenetic zone" he means geographical regions where recurrent experiences over long periods of time have produced certain themes and motifs which give rise to myths. According to him, all the mythogenetic zones vanished during medieval times. The modern and post-modern mythogenetic zone is the psyche of the creative artist, poet, novelist, playwright, and short story writer. Since the artist (to use that term in the broadest sense) is in touch with the inner depths from which fantasies and dreams emerge, he plays a role in modern and post-modern society akin to that of the shaman in archaic societies. He is the medium of the psychic underworld. In a figurative sense, he communes with spirits. Poets and novelists, such as W. B. Yeats, T. S. Eliot, Thomas Mann, Ezra Pound, and James Joyce, in brief, the literary giants of the postmodern era, have been inspired by the mythic vision to an exceptional degree. Through the poems, novels, and plays of such writers, the myths have been communicated to us. Children's literature is a case in point. Lewis Carroll's Alice books are good examples.

THE DESCENSUS AD INFEROS OF ALICE*

On July 4, 1862 (which was either "cloudless blue above" or "cool and rather wet"), a party of picnickers strolled through Christ Church Meadows, Oxford to Folly Bridge where they boarded a gig on the Isis and rowed upstream to a spot where they spent a pleasant afternoon. While Robinson Duckworth rowed stroke, a pale Anglican divine who was also a learned mathematician entertained little Alice Liddell and her two sisters with a fantasy which he made up as they drifted along.[25] The story was about a girl named Alice who chased a waistcoated rabbit down a hole and plunged into a strange underground wonderland where everything was topsy-turvy. At Alice's request, Dodgson wrote *Alice's Adventures Underground* which was published three years later as *Alice's Adventures in Wonderland*, under his pen-name Lewis Carroll.[26]

Alice's Adventures in Wonderland and the sequel *Through the Looking Glass* have flourished as masterpieces more pleasing to adults than to children because of their remarkable symbolism and profundity. Wonderland is the inner chaos of the human psyche and Alice is the archetypal heroine who descends into hell. She is a Victorian Inanna and her story is in the tradition of the sixth book of Virgil's *Aeneid* and Dante's Inferno in *The Divine Comedy*. While there is no suggestion of conscious derivation or adaptation of this descent theme on Carroll's part, it is interesting that the story occurred to him during the Late Romantic era when considerable attention was being given to the idea of unconscious mind, especially in the Germanies but also in Britain.[27] This preoccupation was to culminate at the *fin de siecle* in both psychoanalysis and C. G. Jung's theory of collective unconscious.[28]

The *descensus ad inferos* or descent into the nether regions occurs in Sumerian mythology in *The Descent of Inanna* and is also the theme of Orpheus and Eurydice; it is the story of Psyche and Amore in Apuleius, and of Balder's ride into Hel in Norse mythology. As Eliade shows, Siberian and North American shamans frequently make a psychic descent during trance states.[29] Among Altaians, for example, the shaman makes a psychic journey across desert and steppe, a perilous quest

---

* Published in *Dalhousie Review*, January 1983.

which eventually leads to the pit down which he plunges into Erlik Khan's kingdom of the dead. Eliade also notes the cosmogonic dive myth which he believes was brought to North America from Siberia by paleolithic migrants. In the typical myth an animal is commissioned by the creator god to dive down to the bottom of the sea and the soil from which the cosmos is created. In many Asiatic versions the animal is actually a man in the shape of an animal. He seeks to set himself higher than the creator god and is punished for his pride. Thus, in an Altaic version, Erlik Khan is Lord of the Underworld because he was the first man to die, a consequence of his sin. He was the adversary who defied the creator god by attempting to be creator himself instead of agent.

> In the beginning when there were only the Waters, God and a man were swimming together in the shape of black geese. The "man" tried to rise higher than God and fell into the water. He begged God to help him and make a stone rise from the waters and God sent him to fetch it. The man kept a little in his mouth and the silt began to rise. He had to spit thus producing the marshes. God said, "You have sinned, and your subjects will be evil. My subjects will be pious; they will see the sun, the Light and I shall be called Kurbystan. As for you, you shall be Erlik."[30]

Eliade suggests that this story is typical. The theme is cosmogonic and the high god creates cosmos from the chaos of primordial waters much as Elohim forms the firmament out of *tehom* in the Genesis cosmogony, or Enlil creates cosmos from the body of the saltwater ogress *Tiamat* in the Akkadian *Enuma elish* and its Sumerian antecedents. Primeval waters also stand for primordial chaos from which cosmos is formed in the *Theogony* of Hesiod. Stories of the cosmogonic dive as well as of primordial waters can, of course, be found in many cultures throughout the world and ranges through Polynesia, Australia, the Americas, and Eurasia. It appears to be encountered less frequently in Africa. In some mythologies the descent is into the belly of a sea monster, as in the Finnish Vainamöinen stories, in others the descent is sub-terrestrial. The myths vary. Inanna descends into the subterranean land of the dead to challenge her sister, Orpheus and Psyche go down into Hades to revive their lovers, the Siberian creator animal dives to the bottom of the sea to bring cosmos out of chaos; Vainamöinen is swallowed up and imprisoned. There is, in other words, the risk of comparing oranges to apples in any attempt to find a common theme in *descensus ad inferos* stories. At the same time, just as oranges and apples are all fruit, so do descent stories share the category of the quest myth. Whatever the purpose or goal, the hero or heroine descends into the depths to emerge wiser than before. While wisdom is by no means the only motive of the journey, it is the one most frequently encountered. For example, the Altaian shaman seeks the wisdom of the dead; Odysseus sailed to the distant land of the Cimmerians to seek the spirit of the blind Teiresias, the Theban sooth-sayer whom Persephone had given occult powers of comprehension. Aeneus descends into the depths of Orcus to find his dead father Anchises and learn his own destiny. Thus, while the descent may be an underground plunge, a dive into the depths of the sea, a swallow-ing up by a sea monster, or a flight into outer darkness, the journey is usually a quest for wisdom.[31]

C. G. Jung refers to the descent story as the *Nekyia* from the title of the eleventh book of the *Odyssey*. The *Nekyia* is the journey into the Land of the Dead by the living even if, geographically speaking, it is still part of the same world. Jung was intrigued by the recurrence of the *Nekyia* in the dreams of some of his patients.

> In the sea lies a treasure. To reach it he [the dreamer] has to dive through a narrow opening. This is dangerous, but down below he will find a companion. The dreamer plunges into the dark and discovers a beautiful garden in the depths, symmetrically laid out, with a fountain in the center.[32]

Jung interprets "the treasure hard to find" as the self which lies hidden in the ocean of the unconscious and which only can be reached by the plunged into the depths. The descent into the depths motif is archetypal.

Dante is highly important as a medieval link between archaic mythology and modern thought, especially where the *Nekyia* or *descensus* is concerned. Dante embarks on his journey *nel mezzo del cammin di nostra vita*.[33] He first plunges into the Dark Wood in thee mist of which lies the entrance into Inferno (the necessary preliminary to the Vision of Hell), and here encounters the shade of Virgil, who guides him into the depths. There are seven concentric rings which spiral down through rocky gorge and alpine crag to the frozen pit where Lucifer, buried up to the waist in eternal ice, devours sinners.

In grand design Inferno is the ante-chamber to Purgatorio, via which those who persevere eventually attain Paradise and the Beatific Vision. At the gates of Paradise Virgil can go no further but passes Dante on to the angelic Beatrice. Dante would not go on until he had fully explored the significance of the Dark Wood, nor could he enter Purgatorio until he had descended into the depths of Inferno.[34] The imprint of the Sixth Book of the *Aeneid* is clear in the *Divine Comedy* just as, in turn, Virgil's *descensus ad inferos* has its thematic antecedents all the way back to Homer, and possibly to archaic shamanism.

As a literary theme, the *descensus ad inferos* first appears in the archaic myths such as *The Descent of Inanna* and was given epical form by Virgil and Dante. While the way thereafter is not quite as clear, it is generally accepted that T. S. Eliot's *The Waste Land*, for example, bears an ironic relationship to Dante's Inferno and it is also sometimes suggested that Joseph Conrad's *The Heart of Darkness* is a descensus ad inferos.

Without attempting to follow the various possible stages of the *descensus* in terms of transitional literary modes, I suggest that such an examination by competent literary scholars would probably disclose romantic and mimetic expressions of this theme and a schema in which there is an evolution from the predominantly sacred mythical modes to the modern secular forms of literature: In other words, a great deal of modern fiction and poetry gives voice to the *descensus ad inferos* motif.

Children's stories are possibly closer than any others to the mythical mode, especially those classics of the nineteenth and early-twentieth centuries, one such as Hans Christian Andersen's stories, Collodi's *Pinocchio*, and Frank Baum's *The Wizard of Oz*. These were invented just after the disappearance of the fairy tale and folk-tale. Once the Grimm brothers had collected, recorded, edited and published German fairy tales, that tradition became frozen, a process which occurred with mythology in the ancient world with the classical writers. Considering the close relationship between the folk tale and myth, it is possible to see at least some of the children's literature of the nineteenth century as bearing a relationship to myth. While Andersen is believed to have drawn on Danish folk-lore, the writers of late-nineteenth-century children's literature invented their tales. Still, they could not possibly be immune from the cultural heritage as well as from fashions and currents of their times. Therefore, what was created invariably bore the watermark in form and substance of both tradition and contemporary literary modes.

Lewis Carroll belongs in a category with Collodi and Baum as a creative writer of children's stories rather than a collector and adaptor like the Grimms. Most critics find the sources of Carroll's imagery adequately explained in terms of the author's early years in a Yorkshire parsonage. The first Alice story is also supposed to have been inspired by the sight of a rabbit leaping down its hole during the upstream row that July afternoon. Dodgson and the children saw the rabbit and the don started the story, making it up as he went along, and as it occurred to him. It was an improvisation. At the same time, he necessarily gave expression to both subconscious and unconscious motifs the way that story tellers do after the excursion when he retired to his chambers and composed the tale more or less as he had told it. Frye refers to the Alice stories as poems which implies even more where symbolism and imagery are concerned, and, to say something further, the poems are ironic. As such they bear a particularly close relationship to myth.

The Alice stories are also dreams and, from the Freudian point of view of A. M. E. Goldschmidt, they abound in psychoanalytic symbolism. Alice is penetrating the depths of id. In her dream, Alice leaps down the rabbit hole and chases the white bunny down a labyrinth through a "low low hall" round which are locked doors.[35] While no evidence of physical pedophilia has been found for the highly repressed and moralistic Dodgson, it has certainly been read as an underlying motivation, however subconscious or sublimated. The stories abound in sexual symbolism. What is more interesting, however, is the recurrence of the *descensus ad inferos* theme with or without sexual implication as a motif of an inner journey into the depths of psyche and the discovery of inner chaos barely contained by the fragile ego. Further, what is implied for the self is also voiced for humanity in general, the comment that law, order, and the conventions are appearances which cloak the hidden realm of violent disorder and absurdity. The Alice books, and especially *Wonderland*, offer bleak observations concerning the fragile and largely illusory character of rationality and morality and all other ego functions, as well as reality testing itself. Is reality the surface world of common sense order or the psychotic inner world of absurdity, impulse, and intense hostility.

The Alice stories also lend themselves to Jungian analysis. Alice is Carroll's "anima," archetype of the feminine principle, "who moves from innocence to experience, unconsciousness to consciousness," his Beatrice who conducts him, however, through Purgatorio to where he

glimpses Paradiso. Wonderland is the Shadow realm which corresponds to the Freudian id. It is the psyche underground and Alice is the
Child Archetype who unites opposites, the healer who makes all things
whole and who is also symbolically speaking, roundness, the circle,
sphere, quaternity, mandala, and, therefore, both the archetypal self
and the God-Archetype. This interpretation is much more optimistic
than the Freudian and sees Wonderland as a potentiality which Alice
herself transforms into wholeness as Child Archetype, because "the
child is all that is abandoned and exposed, and, at the same time,
divinely powerful, the insignificant beginning and the triumphant
end."[36]

While the foregoing interpretation of Judith Bloomingdale is not
without considerable interest, it is perhaps too explicit. The same can be
said for Goldschmidt's Freudian analysis. Both are pat, and, in both,
the effort to force Carroll and his stories into depth psychological theories and modes is suspect. Still without specific application of either
Freudian or Jungian theories in detail, however, there can be little question but that the concept of the unconscious is implied. I prefer the
approach of Joseph Campbell, in which the implications are allowed
as such but without insistence on sexual symbolism on the one hand or
specific archetypes on the other.

What does follow is the recognition that Carroll's Alice books are
examples of modern literary creations which echo archaic mythology.
They also exemplify the way certain works of children's literature
closely resemble myth even though they are not authentic fairy tales but
works of creative writers.

Alice's Adventures in Wonderland is a quest myth which employs
the *descensus ad inferos* motif. Alice plunges down the rabbit hole on
impulse, and, by so doing, follows a particular mode in which the
adventure is leaped into by chance rather than intent. Beneath the tiny
door she glimpses "the loveliest garden you ever saw" and after much
fumbling because of her awkward size (either too big or too small), she
manages to find her way into the strange underground world with its
hostile creatures. Here, in the course of her encounters with the rude
caterpillar, the Mad Hatter and his crazy guests, the screaming Duchess,
and the capricious Queen of Hearts, she discovers that the flowers in
what she thought was a beautiful garden are painted. By the time she
attends the tea party and meets the Cheshire Cat she has almost reached
the bottom of her descent into the abyss. The Cat is the one creature
who offers any explanation of pandemonium but he cannot be relied on
as an ally.

"How do you know I'm mad?" said Alice.
"You must be," said the Cat, "or you wouldn't have come here."

Alice is bemused. Her plunge underground is a dive into Unreason, a demonic realm full of wildness and peril, ruled over by a mad queen who constantly shouts, "Off with their heads!" a command never obeyed. All the elemental forces are freed, their secrets held by the playing-card royals. In truth they are a sham within a sham since the initial above-ground perspectives are also illusory. In fact Alice discovers what she has been given reason to suspect from the first encounter with the Queen at the croquet game. The dream ends in a crazy trial. Alice grows gigantic, until she towers over the court and its creatures. In exasperation she shouts, "Why you're nothing but a pack of cards!" The words have magic effect because her tormentors turn into the cards they have been all along and the wind blows them away.[37] Neither they nor any of the other denizens underground ever had substance but were always illusory. Alice ascends from her Wonderland dream, awakened by her sister, and runs off to tea. In *Through the Looking Glass*, the sequel, Alice enters a different kind of quest, one in which she is eventually crowned Queen in the world of the chessmen.

What has she (and Carroll) learned? Like the shaman in his journey down into the Land of the Dead, Alice has braved the ordeals and perils and has been rewarded with wisdom both about herself and the world. Life is not really as it seems in terms of conventional wisdom, what at first appears to be hell is actually redemptive being composed of phantasms without substance. They really are nonsense, not reality. This realization is the beginning of her salvation. Appropriate from a Victorian clergyman, Carroll's Alice books are soteriological in implication and, as such, are far more effective than his later didactic stories which were both sentimental and highly explicit in their Christian orthodoxy. While Carroll did not intend the Alice books to be such, they are gospels of a sort, addressed to children but with nuances which can only be grasped by adults. In their imagery and drama the stories have charm which has made them classics but they also convey deep insights which are of a religious character and which belong in the ancient tradition of the archaic quest myth. In the *descensus ad inferos* of his heroine Carroll, inadvertently or not, voices universal truths and was, in that sense, a prophet.

In Jungian terms, the Alice books express Dodgson's anima, but that is the feminine image in a man which is not the same thing as being feminine. Frank Baum is another example. He was fond of children of both sexes, was very childlike himself, very able to go into the child's world. He had never left it. His constant business failures and unhappy marriage suggest that he found little compensation in having had to grow up.

Neither Dodgson nor Baum had a particularly happy childhood. However, both had very rich inner experiences as children and were in love with their fantasy worlds. These are what they revealed in their books. Beatrice Fairfax is a woman writer who was like them. Her childhood was narrow, hedged about with restrictions. She had, however, a rich inner life which flowed from her fantasies about animals. All three contrast with Louisa May Alcott, whose Meg and Jo in *Little Women* are young women growing up. Hers *is* a feminine myth, and so are most of the books written by women for girls such as *Anne of Green Gables*. Dodgson's Alice, however, and Baum's Dorothy are modeled on little girls whom the writers knew. Dodgson wrote about Alice Liddell and Baum about a little girl named Dorothy who died in her childhood.

Theirs is the mythic theme of the *puer aeternus* who lives in Never Never Land. Barry's Peter Pan is an excellent example. They took life-long delight in the inner world of the imaginative, introverted child. They did not relate to the boisterous, gregarious child who goes out for sports, but the quiet, dreamy child who makes up stories. Today such children are probably computer nerds. In Dodgson's day, and Baum's, they were solitary kids who were never lonely because they lived in their own worlds among imaginary companions. Having never left that world, Dodgson and Baum revealed it to the world through their art, something which no child can do. We really only know the inner world of the child from the testimonials of regressive adults like Dodgson and Baum, even today. The kind of child who lives in Never Never Land seldom reveals much of its landscape to teachers and psychologists, and, almost never, to parents. For this reason, and others, Jung never attempted to analyze children and indeed held that adults should not intrude in the child's inner world.

In recent times, Walt Disney captured the child's world to a remarkable degree, essentially because he, too, had never left it. For that reason, Disneyland, which he designed and built himself, reveals the inner world of the child who grew up during the early years of the twentieth century. I doubt that it reveals the inner world of children today. Like the authors of *Alice in Wonderland* and *The Wizard of Oz*,

Disney drew upon his own inner child. In that sense these particular stories about children (they are not really children's stories) express a mythic theme. That theme is of the *puer aeternus* and *puella aeterna*, the pre-pubertal, inward looking, dreamy child for whom childhood is the Eden from which the boy or girl is expelled when life forces him or her to grow up. Charles Dodgson, Frank Baum, Beatrice Fairfax, and Walt Disney are like Adam and Eve after the Fall, banned forever from the garden of innocence to which they long to return.

7

THE MASKS OF MICKEY MOUSE

JUNG WAS PROFOUNDLY INTERESTED in popular novels such as Rider Haggard's *She* and the Sherlock Holmes stories because the archetypes manifest themselves in purest form in this type of literature. The serious novelist, poet, artist, and composer reveal the depths of themselves, and draw upon the personal unconscious. The film director, cartoonist, popular songwriter, and writer of popular, commercial literature, however, produce what they think will sell. Their eyes are on the public taste and for that reason, they do not draw upon their own creativity or originality. Instead, they are the mediums of public attitudes, fashions, and modes which emerge from the collective unconscious. As a result, the popular arts are closer to traditional folklore than are the literary and artistic productions of gifted individuals. They are our nearest equivalent to folk art. The popular writer or film producer tries to give the public what it wants and, in so doing, caters to popular moods. He or she is the modern equivalent of the minstrel or bard who also had his audience in mind; or the village bard who did not invent stories but told stories which he has learned from others. The difference perhaps lies in the focus. The artist, poet, and composer articulates a personal vision, draws upon his or her own imagination, and expresses his or her own soul. He or she is like a mystic in religion. The popular artist is like the shaman or popular preacher. He or she articulates what other people think and feel. Popular art is collective in that sense, a collective rather than an individual voice.

In our times, the film has been one of the most important vehicles for popular expression. From the turn of the century until after World War II, the cinema was the chief vehicle of popular entertainment; it was followed by radio during the era roughly between 1930 to 1950. Since then the chief vehicle has been television. However, contrary to Marshall McLuhan's belief, the medium is of less importance than the message. That message is collective.

The film has been one of the chief vehicles for popular culture during the twentieth century, whether in the form of cinema or the television program. Some films deliberately exploit mythic themes; they do so consciously. In others, however, archaic mythic themes occur in spite of the scenario writers and directors. Their motives are to entertain and, above all, to sell the film as a box-office hit. Such motives are usually uppermost in mind. The writers and directors deliberately pander to the public taste, only constrained by what is legal or by what may offend the public and therefore keep audiences away. Their own personal standards, artistic ideals, and tastes are irrelevant; they have nothing to do with it. The goal is to make money.

The wartime film *Casablanca* is such an example. The film was made in the first place because Hollywood had gone to war, and most of the film producers were fervently patriotic, genuinely so. But it was also good business. It was good public relations as well. During the war years, films in which the good Allies defeated the bad Axis powers were profitable; politicians and bureaucrats liked them, and they led to contracts of various kinds; they also enhanced the public images of the studio.

At the same time, however, the very act of pandering to the masses and to mass taste involved the articulation of commonly held ideas and deeply felt emotions. These in turn had their appropriate psychic aspects, which were not individual or personal but universal and archetypal. *Casablanca* touched a responsive chord in most people and went far beyond the intent of the film producers.

MYTHS AND MOVIES

Casablanca was produced by Warner Brothers in 1943. Though it had some prominent actors in the cast, *Casablanca* was a low budget film in which the story line was improvised in the course of production. *Casablanca* was one of the propaganda films which Hollywood churned out during World War II. There was nothing special about it.

Everything was chaos. An irritable Humphrey Bogart chain smoked and complained to the director because the production was so makeshift. It promised to be a disaster, and he wanted no part of it. Yet

Casablanca has become a classic, a perennial favorite of Cinema Sixteen Clubs and now a popular videocassette. There is even a *Casablanca* film club at Harvard University where the film is shown every week. Clips from *Casablanca* sometimes turn up in current films, and phrases from *Casablanca* have become folklore. There was public outrage when a colorized version was issued. Many regarded it as sacrilege, like painting a moustache on the Mona Lisa. *Casablanca* lovers celebrated the film's fiftieth anniversary in 1993.

Today, a half century after the film appeared, successive generations of filmgoers are still moved by the song "As Time Goes By" (which was written during the 1920s), and everyone knows the moment when Ilse appears at Rick's *American Cafe*, when Sam is at the piano. Rick doesn't say "Play it again Sam," but everyone thinks he does. There is also the sentimental moment at the end of the film when Rick and Louis walk off into the night to join the Free French at Brazzaville, Louis with his *kepi* at a rakish angle.

Why has *Casablanca* endured? In part, it is because of Bergman and Bogart, archetypal romantic lovers who evoke "hearts and flowers." For all his cynicism, Rick is a sentimental slob. He sneers at high mindedness and lets desperate refugees win at roulette, he hides resistance leaders, and, in the end, gives up the woman he adores to his rival out of love. Anything but the misanthrope he professes to be, Rick is a knight of the Grail.

Samuel Goldwyn's *The Wizard of Oz* is another popular film which became a classic. It was produced in 1939, a significant year for films. Unlike *Casablanca*, *The Wizard of Oz* was expensively produced and was expected to do well at the box office. The studio was not disappointed. It did do well. In part, the film was popular because of the surprise when Dorothy is swept up from a drab, black-and-white Kansas into a technicolor Munchkin Land. In part, it was because of songs, such as "Over the Rainbow" sung by Judy Garland and "We're Off to See the Wizard." A few years later, Australian troops marched into battle singing it. At the time it was made, however, no one anticipated that *The Wizard of Oz* would be enjoyed a half century later.

Today, *The Wizard of Oz* is a perennial Christmas and Easter feature on television and a popular videocassette despite the fact that much of the effect is lost when it is seen on a small screen. Since its first appearance, moreover, the film has appealed more to adult audiences than to children. Its sequences are well known to people throughout the world, and are even more familiar to people today than when it was released. Everybody knows Dorothy, her ruby shoes, her three companions, her dog Toto, the wicked witch whom she outwits and kills, and the humbug wizard whom she exposes. Indeed, to this day, viewers continue to find subtle meanings in *The Wizard of Oz*, more so than in Frank Baum's children's book.

Critics note the film's undoubted artistry and high dramatic qualities. There is also the appeal to nostalgia which, in large measure, accounts for the film's continued popularity among people of the older generation. Like *Casablanca*, *The Wizard of Oz* is archetypal. It is a modern fairy tale. Dorothy, the archetypal princess, answers the call to adventure. She embarks on a road of trials in which she encounters helpful animals and guides. After reaching the Emerald City, she and her friends are tried. They must bring back the witch's broom. They confront and defeat the witch and go back to the Emerald City. There, Dorothy and her friends discover that the hard-to-find treasure was in themselves all along. Dorothy returns home a changed person.

The year 1939 was an epic year for the Hollywood dream merchants. *Gone With the Wind* and *Stage Coach* were released, as well as *The Wizard of Oz*. These three films were highly mythic. *Gone With the Wind* was so long that the Civil War and Reconstruction sequences were separated by an intermission when the film first appeared. Both *The Wizard of Oz* and *Gone With the Wind* also delighted movie audiences with the use of color. All three evoked the mythic vision of America on the eve of World War II when the beleaguered European democracies seemed to be very fragile and decadent in the face of German, Japanese, and Soviet totalitarianism.

Gone With the Wind evoked the romantic vision of the gallant South. Ancient Confederate veterans were deeply stirred when they saw the film at its opening. They remembered the siege of Atlanta. Romanticized as the film was, it still conveyed the true story to those who had experienced the Civil War. Its mythic theme was redemptive.

Rhett Butler, played by Clark Gable, is apparently a cynic, a profiteering blockade runner. But, when the lost cause really is lost, he bids Scarlett (played by Vivien Leigh) goodbye and asks her to embrace a soldier of the South who is going off to join the army of a staggering Confederacy. He is like Hector in the siege of Troy. He engages in desperate battle in what seems to be a hopeless cause. He can do nothing else because he is a man of honor. That the film was produced and released when Chamberlain's appeasement policies were failing to "bring peace in our time" unquestionably underscored the heroism of the old South with its foolish but gallant lords and ladies. They fought against overwhelming odds—as overwhelming as the democracies faced in 1939.

Stage Coach with John Wayne evoked the spirit of the old West and the legendary hero with his six-shooter. Wayne, like Gable, played the role of a knight who appears to be a villain. The stage coach passengers show their true character when the Indians attack. The heroes are rejects: the saloon girl, the drunken doctor, and the wandering cowboy. The real villains are the banker, the southern gentleman-gambler, and the proud southern lady. John Wayne is a bold Siegfried. The banker is cowardly as Hagen. *Stage Coach* reminded Americans of the courageous frontier people who built America in the face of great odds. *Casablanca, Gone With the Wind,* and *Stage Coach* are all based on the Hero-Dragon Myth. So is *Star Wars* among films of more recent vintage.

During the 1970s and 1980s, the Western gave way to the science fantasy, sometimes called the "space opera." There are many parallels between them. Both the "space opera" and the "horse opera" are adventure stories based on archaic mythic themes.

Shortly before his death, Joseph Campbell spoke at considerable length about the archetypal significance of George Lukas's and John Dykstra's *Star Wars* which was directly influenced by Campbell's *The Hero With a Thousand Faces.*[1] Luke Skywalker, the obscure young hero from an out-of-the-way planet, leads the war of liberation against the evil Empire and the Dark Lord. The evocation of The Force, the wickedness of the Empire, the heroism of Luke and his paladins, the captive Princess Leia whom they rescue, and the great foes whom they overcome after great struggle recapitulate the Myth of the Hero and the Dragon once again.

Casablanca, The Wizard of Oz, and *Star Wars* disclose the same archetypal themes in three distinctive contexts: modern romance, fairy tale, and science fantasy. Of the three, *The Wizard of Oz* is mythic in a familiar fairy land setting. Like Odysseus, Dorothy travels from the ordinary world of everyday life to a land of wonders where there are fantastic beings in a magical landscape. There she and her friends slay the wicked witch. In *Star Wars,* the viewer easily recognizes the hero, the wise old man, the captive princess, and the demonic adversary in the guise of beings on distant planets in outer space. In *Casablanca* the hero, princess, and the dragon are clad in plain clothes and the action takes place in an actual geographical locale in an actual historical moment. While the characters are larger than life, the hero is the owner of a bar; the heroine a refugee; and the villains are the Nazis.

In *The Wizard of Oz* the mythic is deliberate and intentional. Frank Baum is supposed to have made up *The Wizard of Oz* to entertain the little girl named Dorothy. He invented the Oz stories the way Samuel Dodgson (Lewis Carroll) made up *Alice in Wonderland*.

Casablanca, on the other hand, was improvised. Yet, the very process of improvisation evoked archetypes of the collective unconscious. The studio film crew act as a team. Even the grips and gaffers have their role. Yet the archetypal images are realized to an even greater degree than when a creative artist is at work.

The director is the film maker but he is manager rather than artist. A film, like a cathedral, is a social product, and articulates the dreams, ideals, values, fears, hopes, and enthusiasms of society because it must meet the demands of the box office.

Often a studio buys rights to a book that a team of hack writers exploit. Their scenarios are kitsch, yet they frequently turn a work of individual art into a myth in modern dress because in the very process of creating a box office hit, they strive to reach the lowest common denominator of public taste.

Reels of film are edited with much attention paid to technical effect and little to artistic merit. What emerges bears little resemblance to the original script let alone the book on which it is based. What is finally produced is a collective enterprise. The film differs sharply from the short story, novel, or play which originates in the imagination of the individual artist.

While the serious novelist or artist plunges deep into his own psyche and produces a work of individual self-expression, the popular writer paradoxically draws from deeper wells, those of the collective unconscious. The commercial writer does not reveal his soul. He is a craftsman who uses his technical skills to perform a pragmatic function. The aim is to entertain. The process is impersonal and does not draw on his life experience, affects, yearnings, hopes, and fears. Yet, precisely because the professional writer works from formulas, he reveals the archetypes of the collective unconscious. His stories are mythic. To be sure, the novelist plunges far deeper than his own psyche, but since all he says emerges through the medium of his consciousness, the archetypes are camouflaged.

Popular genre includes the gothic, mystery story, Western, science fiction, fantasy tale, horror story, romance, and historical romance. In the gothic, for example, an innocent young woman finds herself in the eerie surroundings of an old mansion. She is threatened by a dark sinister man, and rescued by a light complexioned young hero. In the

Western, a stranger on a white horse and wearing a white hat rides into a town that is being terrorized by villains who ride dark horses and wear dark hats. The hero slays the villain in a street duel and restores order. In the romance, a plain young girl is attracted to a handsome young man who, in turn, is bewitched by a beautiful but unscrupulous rival. The heroine outwits her and wins the young man and the story ends in their marriage.

In the popular genre the archetypes are obvious. Readers quickly identify with the characters and live in the stories because of their universality. In the serious novel the reader must study as one does a text of sacred scripture. Serious reading is exegetical and hermeneutical. One may be moved by the style and beauty of language and to be fascinated by the author's insights, but the story line rests on the surface of something profound and complex. Great works of literature are seldom "page turners." The popular story is like the popular film. The viewer identifies with the hero or heroine and feels his or her anger, frustration, hopes, fears, and love. One feels virtuous, kindly, or heroically courageous. When the viewer emerged from the theatre during the 1930s and 1940s, he or she often went home feeling heroic or compassionate.

Today the central character is often an anti-hero, sometimes a villain. According to Harold Schechter, "the true hero of popular culture is neither the goody-goody nor wild, but represents the ideal integration of the civilized and premature ego and shadow." Tarzan is both a savage and a gentleman. Superman has the strength of Hercules and the wisdom of zeus. In motion pictures, especially, the archetypes constantly recur in the context of stories which are more mythic than realistic. They are acted out by characters who are mimetic rather than ironic. Unlike the realistic novel, the film seldom mirrors real life but, like a fairy tale, it creates a Never-Never land in which the good are rewarded, and the wicked punished and in which the heroes are plausible enough by their fragility for us to identify with them but they are far wiser and more competent than most of the viewers. Also, the themes of most popular films are thinly disguised mythologems which those familiar with myth immediately recognize. In Donald J. Greiner's *Deliverance* there is descent into the dark, unknown depths where demons are encountered. It is a journey into the underworld. But those who survive the savagery of the mountain people and the river are reborn. At the end of the journey they are prepared for the outward and inner demands of life.

According to Schechter, the shadow appears in the mythic trickster. The latter "compensates for feelings of impotence in the face of large, aggressive powers." In fairy tales and myths the trickster is the small boy or dwarf who defeats the giant, or the clever animal like Brer Rabbit who outwits the stronger and fiercer beasts. In films the trickster is Groucho Marx who demolishes the "society dame." On television he is Hogan who constantly befuddles Colonel Klink.[2]

Schechter thinks the disaster movie, such as *Earthquake*, evokes the Magna Mater who is both terrible and benevolent. She symbolizes the ambivalences of nature. The disaster movie appeared when feminism began to make itself felt. Perhaps it conveys the male viewer's unconscious awareness that his masculinity violates the life principles which the Magna Mater represents, and that if he mistreats her, he will draw down great retribution on himself and deserve it.

Schechter's most interesting suggestion is his interpretation of the counterculture of the 1960s as the surfacing of the *puer aeternus* or myth of the eternal child. Schechter sees the counterculture as the revival of the primordial image of Narcissus and Hyacinth. The *pueri* of classical mythology are androgynous innocents who defy the conventional wisdom and refuse to operate by the usual rules of profit and practicality.

The *puer* is neither sensible nor tough-minded. He was happy in his childhood fantasy land and finds no compensations for lost joys in the tough competitive adult world. Maturity offers a bad bargain. As Schechter sees it, the young people who became hippies and flower children during the 1960s were pampered in childhood then tossed into the maw of the Vietnam War when they reached military age. Thus, "Never trust anyone over thirty." The hippies and flower children were holy innocents who dropped out and copped out rather than join the establishment. They preferred oatmeal cookies and impoverished communal living to joining the work force, marrying, and moving to the suburbs to rear families. The hippie was the Peter Pan who never grew up and never wanted to.[3]

The *puer aeternus* is also evoked in the Disney films and theme parks of the late twentieth century. No Disney character typifies the *puer* more than Mickey Mouse, for instance. He also evokes the archetypal trickster.

Walt Disney's Magic Kingdom in Anaheim opened in 1956 and its Florida counterpart, Disney World, nearly two decades later. Adult visitors outnumber children four to one. Neither Disney World nor the new Epcot Center have the same effect as Disneyland. Disney himself is the reason. He died just after groundbreaking had begun on the Florida site. What appeals to children is what appeals to them in any amusement park, but what appeals to those adults who like Disneyland is the evocation of nostalgia. It is the one place in the world where those who were children before and just after World War II encounter a frozen fragment of the world of their childhood and early youth. It is a mood which gives one the feeling of going home. Part of it is because of Main Street with its toyland shops, popular music of the 1920s and 1930s, cherry cokes, marble-top soda fountain, and street railway tracks. During off season, when the park is not crowded, it is possible to recapture the leisurely simplicity of other times. Perhaps the recent past only seems simple because those of us who survive were children then, but this is indeed the point. Nothing in Disneyland is real, pressing, or urgent. The mandala design of the park contributes to the euphoric mood, as does the story book clock in the Small World. One rediscovers the inner child who is vividly remembered intellectually, but who is so very elusive in the depths of one's psyche. According to Disney, it all began with a mouse.

THE MASKS OF MICKEY MOUSE*

From time to time in his later years, Walt Disney tried to explain the enduring popularity of Mickey Mouse. The idea of an animated cartoon character which he created in 1928 always baffled him. Mickey continues to baffle critics today. Over the years since Mickey Mouse was released (just before the Wall Street crash), he has undergone a series of metamorphoses, and has actually grown up with the generation born during the early decades of the twentieth century. He was still popular when Disney died in 1966, and his fiftieth birthday was celebrated by national festivities including a black-tie party at the Library of Congress attended by the president of the United States.[4] The continued popularity of Mickey Mouse has been part whimsy, part nostalgia, but some critics find deeper significance in the little chap made of circles and clad in red short pants with white buttons. He has become an archetypal symbol, not only to Americans but to people everywhere, especially to the generation that was young during the 1930s. They are the Mickey Mouse generation.

The meteoric rise of Mickey Mouse and Disney astonished the film industry. In later years Disney sometimes mused over the vastness of his corporate empire and murmured, "We must never forget

* Published in *Journal of Popular Culture*, vol. 22, no. 4. Spring 1989.

that it was all built by a mouse." The phenomenal success of his character never ceased to amaze him and the critics. Not only was Mickey instantly popular among ordinary people young and old, but with intellectuals, artists, and heads of state.

By 1933 the Mickey Mouse craze was global. George V decreed that there must be a Mickey Mouse cartoon at all film performances attended at the palace by the royal family and their guests. The emperor of Japan wore a Mickey Mouse watch. Known by different names in many languages, Mickey was adored by the whole world. He was listed in *Who's Who* and *Encyclopedia Britannica* devoted an article to him. Further, the global fondness for Mickey Mouse has endured for more than five decades.[5] What is most fascinating is his complexity. Disney once tried to account for Mickey's appeal by his simplicity, saying that he is easy to understand. He is not. He is as complex as Disney was himself, and as profound in his symbolic and mythic implications as any mythic or fairy-tale character. He is what Harold Schechter calls a "new god."

The ultimate origin of Mickey Mouse may have been a pet field mouse named Mortimer whom Disney tamed when he was in Kansas City. Mice appear in an early *Alice's Wonderland* film. Disney claims to have conceived of the mouse during a train trip back to Los Angeles from New York in March, 1927. He had just lost his Oswald the Rabbit series and nearly all of his animators to the New York distributor Charles Mintz. "But was I downhearted?" he later wrote,

> Not a bit! For out of the trouble and confusion stood a mocking, merry little figure. Vague and indefinite at first. But it grew and grew and grew. And finally arrived—a mouse. A romping, rollicking, little mouse. . . . The idea completely engulfed me. The wheels turned to the tune of it. "Chug, chug, mouse! Chug, chug, mouse!" The whistle screeched it. "A m-moua-ouse," it wailed. By the time the train had reached the Middle West I had dressed my dream mouse in a pair of red velvet pants with two huge pearl buttons, had composed the first scenario and was all set.[6]

On his return to California, with all of his staff of animators but one signed up with Mintz and producing Oswald films, the Disney brothers and the one loyal animator secretly created the new character. He called the mouse Mortimer until his wife Lillian persuaded him to call him Mickey, which she thought was less pompous. (According to another version of the story, the name was suggested by a distributor.)[7]

Mickey Mouse was drawn by Ubbe Ert Iwerks, the son of a Missouri barber from Holland. Ubbe, which is Friese, sounds odd even to most Dutchmen. Iwerks shortened it to Ub. Walt and Ub, who were the same age, met in 1919. Both were trying to become animators. Of the two, Ub was by far the most talented at the drawing board. In fact, Disney was never able to draw his own creation.

Ub secretly drew the first two films, producing seven hundred frames a day. They were *Plane Crazy*, inspired by the Lindberg flight, and *The Gallopin' Gaucho*, in which Mickey was a swashbuckler like Douglas Fairbanks. Both animated cartoons were silent films. None of the distributors were interested in Mickey Mouse, and Disney decided to make an animated cartoon with sound. Although Lee DeForest had developed a practical sound system for film in 1923, none of the studios showed interest until Warner Brothers staved off bankruptcy in 1927 by producing *The Jazz Singer* with Al Jolson. After that all the studios produced talkies, but none of the animators, except Disney, dared try the new technique. Disney made another trip to New York and use of the Cinephone sound equipment from Pat Powers. On his return to Los Angeles, the Disneys hired a new staff of animators and, after much experimentation, developed a workable technique for making animated cartoons with sound. They made *Steamboat Willie*, in which Mickey and Minnie Mouse cavort aboard a boat carrying animals, piloted by Pegleg Pete, who was to become Mickey's archrival. Mickey rescues Minnie from Pegleg Pete's unwelcome advances and, in the course of the river journey, he plays a cow's teeth like a xylophone and her udders as bagpipes. Minnie twists a goat's tail and plays him like a hurdy-gurdy.

Steamboat Willie opened at the Colony Theater in New York on November 18, 1928. And thus Mickey Mouse was born. The movie appeared in theaters all over America during 1930. Powers, the distributor, contracted for more Mickey Mouse cartoons. The Disney studio hired more staff and remade and released *Plane Crazy* and *The Gallopin' Gaucho*. They also agreed to make six more cartoons and soon were producing Mickey Mouse reels at the rate of one every four weeks. Early in 1931 a syndicated Mickey Mouse comic strip, drawn by Iwerks, appeared. Hermann (Kay) Kamen, a New York merchandiser, licensed the manufacture of figurines, dolls, and other items, including a Mickey/Minnie handcar on a circular rail and Mickey Mouse watches. The first saved the Lionel Company from bankruptcy and the second saved the Ingersoll-Waterbury Watch Company. The tiny, obscure Disney studio became a corporate success, and Mickey Mouse was popular throughout the entire world.

Mickey's chief rival was Pat Sullivan's Felix the Cat, created by Pat

Sullivan and drawn by Otto Messmer. Felix was sometimes called the Charlie Chaplin of cartoon characters. "Like Chaplin, Felix is a loner in a hostile world, who combines resourcefulness and a touch of viciousness to survive."[8]

According to Max Langer, "What was most appealing about Felix was his personality. He had his distinctive pensive walk, head down and hands clasped behind. . . ." His versatile, prehensile tail could be a baseball bat, fishing hook, or telescope. The stories concocted by Raoul Barri were good. Leonard Maltin considers Felix to have been the equal of Mickey Mouse in every respect save sound. "Felix is as recognizable and rounded a character as any later cartoon character."[9] As the aging Iwerks recently told John Culhane, Mickey "was the standardized thing—Pear shaped body, ball on top, couple of thin legs. You gave it long ears and it was a rabbit. Short ears, it was a cat, ears hanging down, a dog. . . . With an elongated nose it became a mouse. . . ."[10] Iwerks's comment is overly modest. He improved the animating style of the day. The conventional style of drawing originated with animated cartooning itself, an art invented at the turn of the century by French and American pioneers such as J. S. Blackmore. Between 1910 and 1920, the art was developed by animators such as Winsor McCay with his "Gertie the Dinosaur." Little progress was made in drawing style during the 1920s until Ub Iwerks, who is sometimes called the forgotten man of animation, introduced a more fluid style as well as more refined drawing technique.[11]

The cartoon style of the 1920s was slapstick. While it has ancient and medieval antecedents, slapstick, as a comic film style, originated in France at the turn of the century and was enormously popular among the urban proletariat. According to Durgnat, French comics called *cascadeurs*,

> really did perform the plunge from the third story into a tub of washing; and at the exact moment that the floor of a room fell through, each man knew precisely where to leap—one on to the piano, another on to the aspidistra—silk hats still on their heads, lorgnettes dangling, beards a-quiver.[12]

The comic style which Disney exploited in the Mickey Mouse films of the early 1930s was derived from Mack Sennett's slapstick comedy. Sennett studied the French slapstick films and adapted the technique to produce the "Keystone Kops." According to Durgnat, "American comedy continued to derive its poetry from coupling simple and violent attitudes with a delirium of physical and mechanical knock-about." With Sennett there was a shift from the American music hall's older style of character comedy to that of mechanized man.

> Thus Sennett's films register not only the shock of speed but the spreading concept of man as an impersonal physical object existing only to work rapidly, rhythmically, repetitively. But Sennett parodies the conception, to concoct a universe where authority, routine, and the monotony of factory days are shattered as cars burst into bedrooms and beds race down the highway. Comedy, by exaggeration, veers toward revolt, an orgy of disorder, a Saturnalia of chaos.[13]

According to Durgnat, slapstick emerges from childlike impulsiveness, dream fantasy, and visual poetry. The "slapstick comedians are childlike, and . . . act out impulses which as adults we suppress." This was the style of comedians who delighted audiences during the 1920s. Chaplin, Arbuckle, Keaton, and Lloyd learned their craft from Sennett's "Keystone Kops" and went on to develop their own styles. The early animators such as Sullivan and Fleischmann exploited the same slapstick style and so did Disney.

During the 1930s, tastes changed. Durgnat notes that

> if anything, the comic tone took an upbeat turn. The earlier movies took poverty matter-of-factly. But when it became a national problem too, and the subject of optimistic pronouncements from complacent Republicans as from dynamic New Dealers, a more optimistic frame of reference was introduced. The cinema had, from its very beginnings, been steadily rising in the social scale, and the middle classes are far more decorous and squeamish about the seamy side of life than the lower classes; the Hays Code (1933) marks the middle class dominance. Further, the grimness of life made everyone all the more responsive to sentimental escapism.[14]

While slapstick continued to delight, there was public demand for new comic modes, and so Disney started *Silly Symphonies* in 1932. These short cartoons were masterpieces of charm, sentiment, and escape.

By 1934 Disney was complaining that Mickey had become a problem child. "He's such an institution that we're limited in what we can do with him. If we have Mickey kicking someone in the pants, we get a million letters from mothers scolding us for giving their kids the wrong idea."[15] The problem was solved by the introduction of a supporting cast which included Donald Duck, who made his debut in *The Wise Little Hen* in 1934. He soon upstaged Mickey as slapstick comic and the latter became a straight man. The barnyard bratty kid gave way to the likable small-town fellow in an oversized coat with brass buttons and braid who conducts the band in the town park on a Sunday afternoon. He is plagued by a bratty Donald Duck who keeps playing a flute while the band is trying to perform the *William Tell Overture*. If *Steamboat Willie* was the *rite de passage* marking Mickey's birth, *The Band Concert* was his initiation into maturity.

In later years, Disney said that the Mickey Mouse film was addressed to an audience "made up of parts of people; of that deathless, ageless, absolutely primitive remnant of something in every world-wracked human being which makes us play with children's toys and laugh without self-consciousness at silly things, and sing in the bathtub, and dream. . . ."[16]

The Mickey Mouse film was primarily addressed to the inner child in the adult rather than to actual children, few of whom had money of their own for theater tickets. While Mickey was ostensibly reborn for commercial reasons, the change had profound psychological implications. Disney often said, "There's a lot of Mickey in me!" There was. There was also a lot of Mickey in the Mickey Mouse audience. He and they were growing up.

As Jacob noted in 1939, Disney exhibited rare artistic idealism and integrity for a business man, especially during the 1930s. "Money is important indirectly," Disney said, "experimentation comes first. Quality is the thing we have striven most to put in our pictures." He added ". . . I don't favor much commercialization. Most producers think it is better to get while the getting is good. We have not operated that way."[17]

Disney was attuned to the soul of middle America; he shared its values himself, and was exceptionally sensitive to its changing moods. A theater-going public which liked Andy Hardy, the bashful Jimmy Stewart of *You Can't Take it With You*, and, above all, the Chaplin of *Modern Times* wanted a kindhearted and gentle, youthful but grown up Mickey Mouse. The new Mickey of the middle and late 1930s was sometimes the heroic dragon-slayer who rescues Minnie from the pirates, the desperadoes, and Pegleg Pete. More often he was the bourgeoisie do-gooder. He moved from the farm to the small town and from there to the suburbs. He became the neighborly middle American young fellow who lives next door, "Mr. Nice Guy."

New in-house instructions for drawing Mickey were prepared in 1934 by Ted Sears and Fred Moore. They wrote:

Mickey is not a clown . . . he is neither silly nor dumb. His comedy depends entirely upon the situation he is placed in. His age varies with the situation . . . sometimes his character is that of a young boy, and at times, as in the adventure type of picture, he appears quite grown up. . . . Mickey is most amusing when he is in a serious predicament trying to accomplish some purpose under difficulties or against time. . . .[18]

Moore adds

Mickey seems to be the average young boy of no particular age, living in a small town, clean living, fun loving, bashful around girls, polite and clever. . . . In some stories he has a touch of Fred Astaire, in others of Charlie Chaplin, and in some of Douglas Fairbanks, but in all of these there should be some of the young boy.[19]

In *Fantasia* (1940), Mickey is the apprentice in *The Sorcerer's Apprentice* based on Paul Dukas's musical piece and the story by Goethe. Mickey, when wearing the sorcerer's cap, dreams that he commands the sea, winds, clouds, and stars like a god.

No Mickey Mouse films were made during the war years. The few films made during the late 1940s and early 1950s portray Mickey as the likable suburbanite in pastoral settings, with the comic roles entirely taken over by Pluto and other supporting characters. His last movie was *The Simple Things* in 1954. The short film had become too expensive to produce and the 1930s-type presentation, with short subjects and cartoon followed by the feature, gave way to the double feature just before Hollywood succumbed to television. Again, Disney and his alter ego Mickey were quick to adapt to the new medium, and the Mickey Mouse Club appeared.

During the mid-1950s, as the genial host of Disneyland dressed in tails, Mickey underwent a third *rite de passage* in his life journey. He climbed to the top of the Disney empire as the corporate image. This was his most recent metamorphosis. The middle-aged Mickey mirrors the world of the corporate executive. He became an "organization man." He also became the king of the Magic Kingdom and his appearances took on the mystique of monarchy. He acquired *noblesse oblige* and patrician charm. He became avuncular; he was often seen nuzzling small children with nurturant affection on Main Street, U.S.A., in Disneyland. He became gentle and sentimental.

Disney was often taciturn in his later years. Mickey was not. When Disney died in 1966, *Paris Match* featured a cover in which a sad Mickey has a large tear in his eye.

The founding of a Magic Kingdom in Tokyo in 1983 attests to Mickey's continued popularity in Japan. Another Magic Kingdom was opened in France. By no means all of Mickey's loyal devotees are either very old or very young. Many are youthful and middle-aged. Many experience something akin to mystical experience in his presence.

During the 1980s, Disneyland was in trouble. Trade articles with titles like "Wishing Upon a Falling Star at Disney" lamented "What a great studio Disney used to be."[20] The crowds who attended Disneyland during the Los Angeles Summer Olympics in 1983 fell below corporation hopes and expectations. During the late 1980s a team from Paramount Studio revitalized Disneyland. Disney World continues to flourish, but Epcot Center is more popular. Yet Mickey continues to be a symbol. To test this point, Donald Bains showed the cartoon title card with Mickey's beaming face in a sunburst to an infant, who reached out for the cheerful image which made him feel happy. Bains invites anyone to try the same experiment.[21] During the late 1950s, Dr. Tom Dooley, who ran a hospital ship off the coast of Southeast Asia, found that he could not entice children to come for medical help until he obtained permission to paint Mickey Mouse on the hull of the ship. The children never had seen Mickey before, but they were drawn by the figure. Such experiences as these, and they have been numerous, intrigue commentators familiar with the archetypal theories of C. G. Jung.

Among those who have attempted to explain the popularity of Mickey Mouse in terms of analytic psychology are the aging Iwerks, who drew him, and John Hench, who was the vice-president of WED, the Disney corporation which manages Disneyland and Disney World. According to Iwerks, ". . . Mickey's face is a trinity of wafers"—and the circular symbol, as C. G. Jung has told us, "always points to the single most vital aspect of life—its ultimate wholeness." "Simple round forms portray the archetype of self which, as we know, in experience, play the chief role in uniting irreconcilable opposites and is therefore best suited to compensate the single-mindedness of the age."[22]

Hench, who came to Disney studio in 1939 as an artist, suggests that Disney art was able "to exploit very old survival patterns, a case in point being Mickey Mouse who is composed of circles."[23] Mickey

> has been accepted all over the world, and there is obviously no problem of people responding to this set of circles. I'm going to oversimplify this, but circles never cause anybody any trouble. We have bad experiences with sharp points, with angles, but circles are things we have fun with—babies, women's behinds, breasts. So Mickey was made this way, while a contemporary known as Felix the Cat didn't get anywhere. He has points all over him like a cactus. He has practically disappeared while we couldn't get rid of Mickey if we tried. . . .[24]

Circles are

> very reassuring—people have had millions of years experience with curved objects and they have never been hurt by them. It's the pointed things that give you trouble. Imagine putting a set of dynamic curves together in a design that has the power that this one does, so that he goes all around the world and no one thinks of him as an American import. They give him a name and then it's all a *deja vu* experience. They respond to the curves.[25]

According to Harold Schechter, who interprets popular culture in Jungian terms, Mickey is a trickster, the archaic and universally encountered god who, according to Jung, evokes the shadow, the seamy side of the personal unconscious, akin to the Freudian id. According to Jung, the shadow refers to impulses "which appear morally, aesthetically, or intellectually inadmissible, and are repressed on account of their incompatibility." When the shadow appears in dreams it represents that which is bestial.[26] "The dream confronts the individual with the very thing which he resents; it is presented as an integral part of his own personality and as one that may not be disregarded without danger."[27]

According to Edward Whitmont,

> The shadow can also stand for the less individualized part of the personality, the *collective* shadow which corresponds to the most primitive, archaic level of the human mind—the level which links us with our animal past—often symbolized by a beast or some sort of anthropomorphized animal.[28]

In myth the shadow is encountered as the trickster. The latter is an archaic and virtually universal mythic figure, such as Coyote among some American Indians and Loki among the ancient Norse. According to Jung, the trickster has persisted from archaic times to the present in the medieval jester and Punch and Judy. Since the antecedents of slapstick comics such as Sennett's "Keystone Kops" are of this tradition of farce, it follows that Krazy Kat, Felix the Cat, and Mickey Mouse are as well. Because of his various metamorphoses in the course of his development, Mickey Mouse is much more complex than the other animated figures, none of which progressed past the slapstick stage.

Disney posed as a philistine and often ridiculed intellectuals and their theories about his characters and creations. He always insisted that he was only an entertainer. Yet, though inarticulate in the expression of ideas, he frequently disclosed deep intuitive understanding and philosophical wisdom. He, too, recognized the archetypal nature of Mickey Mouse, though he did not put it in theoretical terms. Disney realized that he had unwittingly touched a very deep chord in the human psyche and that Mickey Mouse was far more than a comic-strip character.

UNCLE WALT'S MAGIC KINGDOM

As has been shown by the Marxist authors of *How to Read Donald Duck*, the Disney product is not innocent but on the contrary, is a cultural manifestation of American capitalism. It has been a subtle means for the indoctrination of people throughout the world in the ideology, myths, and illusions of the American Dream. This too, is a facet of the Disney phenomenon. Some critics attack Disney as a fascist. Yet few have given the world as much enjoyment as Walt Disney. There is a lot of good in the Magic Kingdom.

Disneyland is a kind of secular shrine, though this was never the intention. As with Shinto in Japan, or the ancient Roman civic religion, there is a sense in which Disneyland reminds one of the sacred precincts of archaic folk religions, a sense, too, in which Disney characters are like minor deities. In a way, Mickey Mouse and Donald Duck are avatars. The question is avatars of what? On the surface, they are obviously whimsical personifications of the American Dream. But, on deeper levels, they suggest something else. Perhaps it is where *Homo Ludens* and *Homo Religiosus* meet. Is there significance in Disneyland being a mandala? Perhaps.

I know of no better example of the mythic in modern dress than in Walt Disney's theme parks and films. Indeed, it is better exemplified there than in fantasy books such as Tolkien's or in films such as *The Dark Crystal* where myth and symbol are deliberately intended. The same is even true of science fiction films such as *Star Wars* in which, as we know, the scenario writers and directors had mythic themes consciously in mind. One does better to look for myths where they are not intended.

These places include genre literature such as detective fiction, Harlequin romances, gothic tales, and Westerns. They all tell the same old stories but in modern dress. The effect is something the same as in *West Side Story* which is Shakespeare's *Romeo and Juliet* set in Manhattan. In these scenarios too there is sometimes a glimmering at least of mythic intent. What is most interesting is the story in which mythic symbolism is not intended at all but appears anyway. There are many examples, but one in depth is better than brief mention of many. Let us consider Walt Disney and two of his many creations, Disneyland and Mickey Mouse. Disney's life itself exemplifies the American Dream. His success is founded on his very banality, by the fact that he was the very epitome of Middle America. Since American popular culture has become world popular culture his life and art therefore epitomizes world popular culture as well.

Disneyland is a mandala, as John Hench observed. Mickey Mouse is made up of circles. Both the theme park and the mouse are unconscious symbols. A mandala is a circular design made up of complex inner designs such as buddhas. Buddhists and Hindus draw them as meditative devices. They induce inner feelings of wholeness. Jung began painting mandalas as he emerged from his psychological crisis during the years 1913-1918. He discovered connections between these round designs and individuation, the realization of integration between the conscious and unconscious facets of psyche. I think that by sheer serendipity, Disney evoked deep archetypes, the *puer aeternus* and the "God Image," Jung's term for wholeness. Disneyland itself is a huge mandala.

Nearly a quarter of the American people as well as thousands of foreign visitors have made at least one pilgrimage to Walt Disney's Magic Kingdoms in California and Florida, Tokyo, and near Paris. Though most people think of the Disney theme parks as children's amusement parks, adult visitors outnumber children four to one. What is more, by no means all of the adult visitors are parents with children in tow.[29] Most adult visitors go for their own entertainment. This was as

Disney intended. He did not specifically design the theme parks for children but for people of all ages, from toddlers to old folks. People go to Disneyland to have fun and to escape. Some find a path back to childhood. Others experience euphoria, something akin to a mystical experience.

"Well, back to Reality Land tomorrow," a young fellow remarked with a sigh. He was ahead of me in line waiting to board the monorail bound for the Disneyland Hotel and exit. He was probably a suburbanite who commuted to work in Los Angeles twenty-three miles away. In all probability his wife had a job there as well. Both would be out of bed at 4:30 A.M. every weekday morning and in their cars before dawn, bucking the bumper-to-bumper traffic all the way in to their respective offices. They must do that to keep up the payments on their modest house in the exurbs, a house they can enjoy only on weekends because it is the same exhausting story five days a week: up very early and off to work and home late and then to bed. Five days a week there is not much in their lives besides work. Such is life today for the typical Californian. Yuppies are, of courser much better off than the low income blacks, Hispanics, and Asians who crowd the Los Angeles-bound bus every dawn, also to return home late to much less pleasant surroundings, and far more chores and demands from their latch-key kids who have been on their own all day. These, in turn, are better off by far than the homeless blacks who swarm the streets of downtown Los Angeles, the people who were abandoned in Reagan's turned around America. They sleep on the sidewalks, trundle their few belongings in carts, line up for meals at the "Sally Anne." There are also the impoverished families who carry signs offering to work for food. Such is the American Dream in the last decade of the century.

Reality Land, U.S.A., is made up of such attractions as the Rat Race, the Hum Drum, and the Cesspool. It is a workaholic ride for the swift, with clouds of smog to hide the sun and bathe the scene in shades of grey. Reality Land is also pervaded with the loud, cacophonous racket made by developers with their pneumatic drills which punctuate the never-ending traffic noise and the screeching of brakes. There is pain, suffering, and want in Reality Land, even in sunny California. It is violent. Most of its denizens live in fear.

When one steps off the monorail in Disneyland, the hard facts of life in America vanish. For the time one is in the park, reality is glossed over. Of course one knows that neither Marceline nor any other Midwest small town was ever like Main Street, U.S.A. Disney certainly knew.

When he put his "imagineers" to work, Disney told them to come up with a bright and shiny toy, not Main Street as it was, but a fantasy or illusion. Of course it is illusion. It is meant to be. No one lives in Disneyland. It is where one goes to escape. In Reality Land life is stern, even in the best of circumstances. But few people grow up completely and Disneyland is for the inner child in the adult. The monorail takes one back home for a little while.

Is the appeal only nostalgia? It is for some, especially the old. Those of us who grew up during the 1920s and 1930s were children in a world which was not very different from the world of our grandparents. In America, especially, the familiar Old World lingered on through two World Wars and Depression but finally evaporated during the 1960s. Since then, the ambience of life has been altered so profoundly that many scholars refer to our times as the postmodern.

Popular music is a case in point. The fragmented and raucous, raw, rhythmic new sounds from Africa, by way of the American South, have displaced the old European melodic and harmonic conventions. Disneyland enshrines the pre-rock popular culture even though it features rock bands and, in recent years, has become updated. Even so, the ambience remains. The Magic Kingdom is a model of a world which has been vanishing since the mid-1950s when the park was opened. In Disneyland time stands still, and there is an illusion of permanence.

Until the 1960s, Orange County was all orange groves sliced by narrow two-lane roads adorned by Burmah Shave signs. During the 1920s and 1930s, the high, square Plymouths and Oldsmobiles slowly cruised past fantastic refreshment stands in the shape of giant oranges and ice cream cones, all left over from the prosperous 1920s. Anaheim was a leisurely little town, in the midst of the orange groves. During the 1950s, Jack Benny's mythical railroad ran through Anaheim, Mazuzah, and Cucamonga. In those days, southern Californians enjoyed unpolluted air, leisurely days, and Sundays when families picnicked at Laguna or Oceanside. For longer adventures they set out on camping trips across the Mojave Desert and up into the High Sierras.

True, the 1930s were also the years of the Great Depression when a third of the nation was mired in poverty. But there were compensations. Prices were low and kids nickeled and dimed their way through the decade, most of them oblivious to the anxiety and stress of their elders.

Disneyland evokes that world. In Disneyland, one recaptures the feeling of being a kid again, if only for a few moments. The park was designed with such skill that the effect is hypnotic. In that, too, lies its perils. Mickey Mouse's glove conceals an iron fist. Disneyland is a voice of corporate America and is far from apolitical. It may not be partisan, but it is highly political. Too, though it is not sectarian, it has mythical if not religious implications.

The wary visitor to Disneyland is very aware that hidden persuaders abound, and that the intent to lull him or her into docile compliance with the neo-conservative values to which Disney subscribed. Corporate America is apparent at every turn, and is acknowledged to have subsidized virtually every event.

Even the most critically minded go on holidays, however, and one is not always disposed to be the adult of high principle and lily-pure virtue. Disney was an entertainer and had no other avowed purpose. One goes to Disneyland to have fun. To have fun is to play and to play is to regress. Disneyland is frivolous and escapist. It appeals to the narcissist in us, like all forms of self-indulgence.

To go to Disneyland is to recapture long-ago Saturday afternoons when kids were sent to the neighborhood movie house a block away to see Mickey Mouse cartoons and *Silly Symphonies*. Through these brightly colored animations, the mind of Walt Disney penetrated the collective unconscious of children throughout the world and created universal dreams. This worries Ariel Dorfman and Armand Mattelart, the Chilean Marxist authors of *How to Read Donald Duck*. Disney glosses the harsh realities of global capitalism, indoctrinates and seduces. Is Mickey Mouse's smile the smile of Big Brother in Orwell's *1984* after Winston Smith's conversion? Can one risk indoctrination as the attendant price of flight from reality? Will we leave behind in Disneyland any impressions we may have picked up there about the real World? I think we can. People with social conscience are sometimes too wary of the lighter side of life. Disney, after all, was first and foremost an entertainer.

Disney was the "idea man" of the Disney Studio, not an artist but a facilitator who coordinated and produced by firing the imaginations of the animators whom he hired. Disney's own imagination was conventional, but that was part of his secret. During the 1930s, he produced cartoon classics, such as *Silly Symphonies* and *Snow White and the Seven Dwarfs* which were much like the sentimental popular art of Late Victorian times. There is more than a little resemblance between the *Silly Symphonies* and Victorian storybook illustrations of elves and fairies in moonlit forest glades. They strike the same chord. At the same time, like these older fantasies, they also have sinister, subtle implications.

Disney creations are saccharin tranquilizers which lull the critical faculties and create the illusion that those who rule and exploit us are benefactors. They are opiates. However, we all need opiates now and then, and Disney's brand is very soothing. It is also a way to go home again.

Disney's *Snow White and the Seven Dwarfs* differs from the original Grimm folk tale by its sweetness and charm. It also teaches the capitalist ethos with the song "Whistle While You Work" and "Heigh Ho Heigh Ho It's Off to Work We Go." It conjures up optimistic dreams that "Some Day My Prince Will Come." The Disney version is very seductive, partly because the original cartoon drawings were exquisitely detailed works of art. This made them as effective for capitalism during the 1930s as Gothic cathedrals and their stained glass windows were in medieval Christianity. Both vindicate the ideologies of ruling elites. At Disney Studios, during the 1930s, cartoon art reached a summit it has never reached again.

After a long hiatus, the art of cartooning has returned thanks to the new animation techniques, some of which are because of computers. With advice from some of Disney's aging animators, the studio has created new masterpieces such as *The Little Mermaid*, a successful return to an art form we thought lost. In fact, the film is touted as a return to Disney. At this time of writing (1993), the studio has continued its successes with *Beauty and the Beast* and the top box-office grosser *Alladin*.

Above all, Disney evokes nostalgia for the recent past. During the 1930s, kids played with toys on the floor while parents hooted and laughed their way through bridge or monopoly. This was the Golden Age of radio, Little Orphan Annie and the Lone Ranger, banal even to old ears now. Oldsters remember taffy pulls, picnics at the park, playing hide-and-seek, making balsa airplane models and doll houses. As children, they played jacks and hopscotch. There were moments, too, when one caught the sweet scent of lilac while passing a bush in the back lane and when, at night, we looked up and saw the stars. They were visible, children were not yet so sated with sights and sounds as to miss the wild flowers on the verges as the high, square Buick rolled past on the Sunday family drive to Palm Springs.

Children of the first half of the twentieth century took in these sights and sounds without design or deliberation. They did not think about them, analyze them, or propound any theories about them, but simply enjoyed them without comment. To their elders they often seemed insensitive and emotionally shallow, because they scoffed at the views they tried to show. They still saw them. Much of what we later recall with pleasure is exactly what we scorned when we were young. To say it was a better world than now is both unfair and irrelevant. As children, those who grew up during the early twentieth century simply took experiences in and enjoyed them.

Without question, when people who are very young now are old enough to have their active working years behind them and leisured enough to reflect, they will become nostalgic for the world as it is now. Even the Black Death was probably recalled with nostalgia by someone in Chaucer's age. One is nostalgic for the times when the world seemed bright and new, when one discovered something new everyday, when one ran with abandon, feeling the wind in one's face, jumped, rolled, lay in the grass and gazed up at fleecy clouds seeing animal shapes and faces.

As Richard Schickel shows in *The Disney Version*, Disney created Disneyland as a memorial to himself. Frustrated by the transitoriness of films, he conceived of the theme park as a three dimensional, realization of his own memories, dreams, and aspirations. Because he was so atuned to the conventional Middle-American mind of his era, he also captivated the great mass of Americans of all ages.[30] As global popular culture became Americanized, moreover, that appeal became global as well.

Disney's Magic Kingdom in Anaheim is Nostalgia Land. Even Tomorrow Land is nostalgic; it is not the future as envisioned now, a bleak future to most prophets, but the bright, exciting future of space travel children dreamt of during the 1930s and earlier. It is not that progress has overtaken Tomorrow Land but rather that the futuristic dreams of the not-so-long ago now seem quaint and old fashioned in their hopefulness and anticipation.

Nothing in Disneyland is authentic. Nothing mirrors the past as it was. Nor is Disneyland an idealized version of the present or future either. The whole park is Fantasy Land. One climbs aboard the monorail and rides through the life-size model village as though one had shrunk to the lilliputian dimensions of one's childhood tootsie toys or the H.O. railroads of a slightly later era. Disneyland is a toy, a child's world big enough to walk around in. This why the traveller to Disneyland finds his or her way home, disproving Tom Wolfe's saying that "You can't go home again." In Disneyland you can because Disneyland is a way into the child's world which always hides in secret corners of the grown person's mind. As Disney remarked to Bob Thomas on the freeway to Anaheim while Disneyland was being built, "When does a person stop being a child?" He answered probably never.

Because it was designed by Disney himself, and because it opened when it did, Disneyland has deeper and more subtle dimensions. Some of these are not shared by the park in Orlando or those abroad. Disneyland has certain mythic implications, a thought which, at first glance, seems ridiculous. However, as one explores the deeper realms of the human psyche, one discovers that *Homo Religiosus* has a certain affinity with *Homo Ludens*. *Homo Religiosus* refers to the innate spirituality of human beings. *Homo Ludens* refers to the innate human capacity for fun and play.

The modern study of myths shows that they are neither falsehoods nor fictions but collective dreams, that dream is private myth and myth public dream. Such were the insights of the psychoanalytic and analytic schools of depth psychology and they have had impact on the theories of myth, especially as discussed by Joseph Campbell and Mircea Eliade, both of whom were deeply influenced by C. G. Jung. All show that myth is a language of the soul. The cyclops, dragons, gorgons and gods of the archaic world have their post-modern counterparts in the surrealist fantasy figures and realms of the twentieth century. Disney's Mickey Mouse is one of these and Disneyland another.

Disneyland is where we can go home again, if only for a few hours. It may be a highly subtle and complicated propaganda device, but, while one is wandering about the kingdom, one chooses to suspend judgment and simply enjoy. There is much that is bowdlerized, much that is false, but even the most critical admit that the show is well produced. It is done well. Disneyland, like the movies, is entertainment. That is its purpose and it does that well. There is no obligation for it to do anything else. What makes one wary is the fact that, despite disclaimers, there are hidden persuaders. American corporate propaganda is far more skilled and subtle than Nazi or Communist propaganda ever was, and is also far more effective. The corporate sector lies with exquisite charm, carefully exploits depth psychology to the full, and makes the maximum use of symbols. Capitalist propaganda aims at the unconscious and is subtle. The techniques which have been found so useful in the advertising industry and applied to politics are highly effective. They have transformed the world.

Disneyland is a corporate showpiece par excellence, and one needs to be aware of the hidden persuaders in Disneyland. Some, like Mr. Lincoln are as obvious as the plaque above the exit which proclaims "Free Enterprise is the Fifth Freedom." Others are deeply disguised in whimsy and nostalgia. One is easily taken in because one wants to be. The techniques that have worked so well in commercial advertising are effectively applied and they work all too well. Disneyland is thus a cathedral of capitalism. Mickey Mouse and Donald Duck are its saints and its events and attractions attract the way sculpted images and stained glass windows did. The message is that hard working employees who serve their masters well are rewarded.

Disneyland is where *Homo Ludens* and *Homo Religiosus* meet. The Sumerians and Greeks laughed at their gods, so do native people in the Americas. We call these comical gods tricksters, and they abound in all cultures. The deities of folk religions are not always awesome, nor do they always exemplify the highest virtues and values in a culture. Sometimes they are ironical figures whom we look down on. There is much humor in archaic popular religions and the same is true of the unrecognized popular religion. There is also pathos as well.

An American secular religion coexists with Christianity, a religion which no one identifies as such. Yet it is identical to folk religions in other cultures such as the new religions of Melanesia and elsewhere in the Pacific, the so-called cargo cults in which the god is Joe Frum who came from across the sea with Hershey bars and who may come back some day with more. He is G. I. Joe who left behind wrecked airplane parts and bits and pieces of gear from which the natives have made temples. Disneyland is a shrine of the same kind of religion, one that is not acknowledged to be a religion at all, certainly not by its founders who only wanted to make money entertaining. But then, Joe Frum did not come as a god but as a draftee in World War II, and his Hershey bars were not manna from heaven but by courtesy of the United States Army. He has his counterparts in Shinto shrines such as Nikko or in the Roman Forum. (The latter, it must be admitted, bears a closer resemblance to another facet of the American secular religion, the Lincoln Memorial.)

The theologians of the Disney Cult are the imagineers; the priests are the costumed guides, the healthy, young people who exemplify Middle America in its most attractive guise. By Middle America we mean the middle income, middle-brow, conventional American culture most of us live in. It is not a derogatory term. The Disney version weaves illusions. Having once been mugged just outside the Disneyland fence, I am all too aware of the stark contrast between the theme park with its sanitized illusions and Reality Land at the exit of the monorail ride. But those who go willingly pay the admission price for the moments of euphoria which can sometimes be akin to religious experience. Disneyland is more convincing in this respect than nearby churches such as Crystal City precisely because it makes no moralistic or critical demands. It simply is. It is there for *Homo Ludens* to enjoy, but it is tinged all the same with what people of other cultures would instantly recognize as the numinous. We have not come very far from our Ice Age ancestors except in our technology. Mickey Mouse and Donald Duck are among our cave paintings and figurines. Very likely the emotions aroused by the palaeolithic Venus of Laussel and Minnie Mouse were much the same.

8

MYTHS ABOUT MYTHS

As FAR AS IS KNOWN, the Greek Pre-Socratic philosophers were the first to take a critical view of myth. This does not mean that they were free of mythic thinking themselves, but it does mean that they had theories about myths. They had myths about myths. Xenophanes, Protagoras, and other skeptics regarded myths as traditional stories. Plato had a poor opinion of them because of the bawdiness and caprice of divine behavior in Homer and Hesiod. He regarded myths as fantasies and illusions, a view still held by most people. Aristotle defined *mythos* as "plot," what the story is about. Someone does something. By his day, the fourth century B.C.E., the myths had become literary works based on folk tales. This attitude, as we have seen, prevailed throughout the Hellenistic and Roman Eras, and was adopted by the Christians.

One of the earliest interpreters of *múθos* was Euhemerus ; (fl. 316 B.C.E.), a writer of fanciful tales, who argued that myths are history in disguise. All the gods were once men whose real feats have been embellished and distorted. Euhemerism was widely accepted throughout the Roman Empire. The Latin terms were *fabula* and *historia*, both of which meant "story."

While Neo-Platonic philosophers used the names of the Greek and Latin deities as metaphors, belief in their metaphysical reality had long since vanished. The old stories were now told for literary delight. Publius Ovidius Naso (Ovid) wrote his *Metamorphoses* during the first century C.E. as a purely literary work. It was read in the same spirit.

The early Christians regarded the Greek and Roman gods as illusions inspired by the powers of darkness and thus waged war against their cults. Thus, Diana of the Ephesians, for example, was a prime target for John's missionary campaign. The chief rivals to Catholic Christianity were the mystery religions such as the Cult of Isis and Serapis, Mithraism, and Gnosticism. During later classical times, Manichaenism rose. All of the foregoing were rich in sacred histories which were denounced as *fabula* by Christians such as Lactantius and Augustine: they were "lies," "deceptions," and "illusions" inspired by Satan and his fallen angels. Christians regard their own theology, angelology, and demonology as "revealed truth" based on sacred scripture.

During late classical and medieval times, Christian missionaries such as St. Boniface and Adam of Bremen encountered the Celtic, Teutonic, Baltic, and Slavic religions in northern Europe. The Norse and German stories about gods and heroes were called *saga* in Old High Norse, meaning "something said." The Christians classed these as demonic illusions as well, but also noted that the words *saga, fabula,* and *historia* essentially meant the same thing, "traditional stories, usually about gods and heroes." They tolerated some of these, such as *Beowulf*, just as they tolerated Ovid's *Metamorphoses*. Both, however, were regarded as literary works and without any religious connotations whatsoever.

During the Italian Renaissance, the knowledge of Greek was recovered from the Islamic world, and interest in the Greek classics revived and also interest in the classical myths was revived. During this time, Masilio Ficino of the Platonic Academy of Florence embarked on a search for primordial revealed texts. He was excited by his discovery of *The Corpus Hermeticum* which he thought was an ancient Egyptian text older than the Bible. In that way, he regarded myth as sacred history and therefore something to be regarded with respect.

Philosophes of the eighteenth-century Enlightenment, such as the erudite and versatile Johann Gottfried Von Herder and Jean Le Rond d'Alembert, were fascinated with world mythology. According to Cassirer, the scholarly study of myth began with the eighteenth-century Italian philosopher and jurist Vico, a solitary soul out of harmony with the spirit of the times. The Neapolitan scholar turned to law because it was the only study which flourished in Naples at the time. Inspired by the history of Roman law of Giovan Vincenzo Gravina, Vico traced the origin of law in the human mind as well as historical change. By so doing he created his *Scienza nuova* or psychology of history. In his *Universal Law (Diritto universale)*, he espoused the deist view that God rules through natural laws not miracles, and that the source of the laws of historical change are in the human mind. Law emanates from conscience. The sentiment for justice is initially confused, uncertain, and instinctive; it is an unconscious, universal sentiment. The law to which it gives birth is enmeshed in religious forms, including myths. The legislators recorded in the history of primitive peoples are symbols and myths which mark historical stages. These early, confused conceptions of law gradually give way to rational, abstract formulae which are themselves replaced in time by rational legal principles.

According to Vico, both the history and religion of primitive people are mythical. Both evolve from the savage state to civilization passing through three phases: the divine, heroic, and human. Each phase has a corresponding form of government: aristocracy, tyranny, and democracy, respectively. Democratic excesses cause the rise of empire which becomes corrupt and declines into barbarism. This is the *law of cycles*. According to Vico, the eternal ideal history of humanity is cyclical. All nations and cultures have their life stages, birth, growth, maturity, decline, death, followed by rebirth in new forms.

Another eighteenth-century contributor to mythic thought was Johann Gottfried Von Herder (1744-1803), born in East Prussia the year Vico died. In 1762, at the age of eighteen, he went to Königsberg to study medicine. Instead he abandoned his studies, became a disciple of Immanuel Kant, and developed much interest in cosmological and anthropological problems, as well as literature. Later, he broke with classicism and became one of the founders of the *Sturm und Drang* (Storm and Stress) movement, which was the forerunner to German romanticism. This brought him into association with Goethe. Van Herder was a voluminous but fragmentary writer and, although his writings were long neglected, interest in them has revived.

Friedrich Maximillian Müller (1823-1900), better known as Max Müller, was an Orientalist and philologist who was born in Dessau. He studied Sanskrit at Berlin and his language studies led to an interest in world religions. He translated and edited the *Rg veda* which was published by Oxford University Press in 1848. He settled in Oxford and was appointed professor of modern languages in 1850 and to the chair in Sanskrit ten years later. His studies in mythology led him to develop a science of comparative religions. He published *An Introduction to the Science of Religion* (1873) and became editor of *The Sacred Books of the East* (1875). He wrote extensively about Indian philosophy, stimulated the search for Oriental manuscripts and, in the course of his religious studies, developed a theory of myth.

Müller's *Essay in Comparative Mythology* (1856) was the earliest significant discussion of comparative religion. It could be said that he was the founder of *Religionswissenschaft*, or religious studies. At any rate, he coined the term. Müller approached the study of religion from his knowledge of Sanskrit, being primarily a philologist. Interested in archaic forms of religion, he suggested that contemporary primitives might preserve some very ancient mythologies, rituals, and beliefs which could be taken as survivors from prehistoric times. From them, the originals could be discerned.

Müller thought that etymology was the key to decoding the beliefs of early peoples. In his view, "Even if we go beyond the age of literature, we explore the deepest levels of human thought, we can discover in the crude ore which was made to supply the earliest coins or counters of the human mind, the presence of religious ingredients." He analyzed Sanskrit terminology on the assumption that the Vedas were the earliest religious scriptures. He was particularly fascinated by the relationship between *deva* meaning "god" and *div* meaning "to shine." The latter hinted at solar worship and, with such etymological grounds as these, Müller proposed that early man worshiped divinity mediated in concrete natural forces such as the sun. It was not that the sun itself was worshiped but rather that the sun was an important concrete expression of the inexpressible, infinite, and intuitively perceived ultimate reality.

Müller's interest was not in the origins of religion, because he was convinced that there was no way to reach them. Instead, he was intrigued by the Sanskrit names for deities, the fact that Varuna means "sky," Indra means "thunder," and the Maruts, "wind."

However, Müller discredited his own thesis by taking it to absurd lengths. He became obsessed with the solar myth theme and found it cropping up everywhere. Thus, the myth of Apollo and Daphne is about the sun driving away the dawn. To him, religion is a "disease of language," a comment which did little good to his scholarly reputation. His reputation was further damaged by his assertion that the *Iliad* is a solar myth, all of which inspired Andrew Lang to say that Müller himself was a solar myth.

The Golden Bough

It is no exaggeration to say that *The Golden Bough* is the font of all modern studies of mythology, even though both the voluminous, multivolume discussion itself and its author have fallen into disrepute among anthropologists. Frazer was a classical scholar who thought he was an anthropologist because he read so much anthropology. His achievement was a massive and erudite study which initially inspired Malinowski to leave physics for anthropology and Lévi-Strauss to make the same intellectual journey from philosophy. Freud read *The Golden Bough* and was moved to embark on his own study of mythology which led to *Totem and Taboo*; Toynbee tried to do for history what Frazer had done for mythology. It has been said that the twentieth century has learned its mythology chiefly from Frazer. While this is an exaggeration, it cannot be denied that Frazer's impact has been enormous. Frazer had his limitations. He did not understand symbolism, nor did he grasp the subtleties of myth. However, he did have some interesting insights. He also wove a quest myth himself which tells us a great deal about the twentieth-century European mind.

James George Frazer was born in Glasgow in 1854. He learned his Greek and Latin at Larchfield Academy, and, instead of entering his father's business, went to Glasgow University to study more Greek and Latin. In 1873 he entered Trinity College, Oxford, studied law (which was his father's idea), and was admitted to the Middle Bar; however, he never practiced. At Cambridge he continued on with his classics studies and became a Fellow.[1]

Frazer was one of those fortunate few of the Victorian era who was affluent enough to be relieved of all of the practical exigencies of life in an uncrowded, leisurely world where he could enjoy books, good companions, and be bothered with few intrusions. He lived to be eighty-seven. He died in 1941.

Frazer was busy with his edition of Pausanias when his attention was called to E. B. Tylor's *Primitive Culture* (1871). It was the turning point of his life. He plunged into a study of what was then called "primitive religion," having discovered the vastness, complexity, and antiquity of human culture and become fascinated with origins. However, the only "primitive" he ever met was when the Wild Man of Borneo chased him at a carnival when he was a small child. What he knew was what he read in the thirty thousand books of his library, and what he learned from questionnaires which he sent out to missionaries, travelers, and colonial officials throughout the world. Anthropologists from Malinowski on have faulted him for his "If I was a horse" approach. The phrase comes from a joke about a Yorkshire farmer who was looking for a horse. The farmer ate a clump of grass and then mused, "Well, if I was a horse I'd go that way." Frazer, E. B. Tylor, R. R. Marrett, and Andrew Lang all tried to understand primitive cultures by imagining what they would think if they were prehistoric savages. Their data was hearsay, and they made no attempt to verify it. None of the pioneer ethnologists were professional anthropologists. That discipline did not blossom until the 1920s. Instead, these men were classics scholars who attempted to understand world mythology from the perspective of their Greek and Latin studies.

Shortly after he began his studies of mythology, Frazer met William Robertson-Smith who, because he was a free thinker, had been expelled from Free College, Aberdeen, where he had been university librarian. Frazer helped him secure an appointment as professor of Arabic at Cambridge. He also helped him with *Religion of the Semites* (1889). This project roused Frazer's interest in world mythology and spurred him to write the first edition of *The Golden Bough*, which was published in two volumes in 1890; the second edition of three volumes appeared in 1900. Frazer continued his studies and produced the massive twelve-volume edition between 1911 and 1915.[2] A thirteenth volume was added in 1936.

The Golden Bough is a vast, encyclopedic study of magic, totemism, and myth. According to Lionel Trilling, "no book has had so decisive an effect on modern literature as Frazer's."[3] It is itself a work of literature, an epic, and, as such, is itself displaced from myth. The plot of *The Golden Bough* is presented in the story with which the first volume begins:

> Who does not know Turner's picture of the Golden Bough? The scene, suffused with the golden glow of the imagination in which the divine mind of Turner steeped and transfigured even the fairest natural landscape, is a dream-like vision of the little woodland lake of Nemi—"Diana's Mirror," as it was called by the ancients . . . Diana herself might still by the lonely shore still haunt the woodlands wild. In a sacred grove on a cliff above the lake a figure might be seen to prowl. In his hand he carried a drawn sword, and he kept peering warily about him as if every instant he expected to be set upon by an enemy. He was a priest and he was also a murderer. He was on guard lest his own murderer catch him unawares. Such was the rule of the sanctuary. A candidate for the priesthood could only succeed to office by slaying the priest, and, having slain him, he retained office till he was himself slain by a stranger. . . .[4]

The theme of *The Golden Bough* is the god who dies and rises from the dead, a motif which Frazer thought was universal and basic to all myths, therefore the origin of religion. In "Adonis, Attis, Osiris," volume five, Frazer analyzes the dying and resurrected gods of Near Eastern mythology. He discusses those of Greece such as Dionysus in the sixth volume, and then concludes with his study of "Balder the Beautiful" and the dying and reviving god of the Norse. In all of these myths there is a beloved individual who is in the full bloom of life when he is attacked and killed by a wild animal (Adonis), betrayed by a traitor (Osiris), slain by a physically trivial but magically lethal wound (Balder), or set upon and dismembered (Orpheus). The god dies and descends into the underworld. There is grief. However, a hero or heroine deity risks his or her own life by a perilous journey into the underworld where he or she persuades the infernal powers to let the departed one return to the land of the living. By so doing, he or she conquers death. By participating in the god's death and resurrection, his mortal votaries also have eternal life.[5]

At the end of *The Golden Bough*, Frazer comes to the obvious conclusion. Was not Christ born to a virgin, like Attis? Was he not slain through the treachery of an enemy, hung on a tree like the Phrygian god? Did his mother not weep for him and his disciples show sorrow? There is an echo of the dismembered Dionysus in the parting of his garments among his executioners. He was buried, descended into hell, and on the third day he rose triumphant, like Attis, Adonis, Osiris, Dionysus, and Balder.

Frazer suggested that Christian theology was based on a Hellenistic myth. Even though Jesus was an historical figure, the story of his life, death, and resurrection is very much like that of Osiris, Attis, or Balder. In turn, these gods were fertility deities whose myths were based on the death and resurrection of vegetation. In this way, most of the religions of the Near East and Europe were mythopoeic interpretations of natural forces. Frazer thought that the age of religion had been preceded by a prehistoric age of magic in which it was believed that natural forces could be manipulated and controlled. Frazer coined the term "sympathetic magic," by which he meant the influence or control of a distant object or force by the ritual manipulation of a model. Thus, a magician can control the weather by rolling stones to simulate thunder and splashing water to simulate rain. One can maim or kill a distant enemy by sticking pins into a doll which represents the victim.

Frazer reasoned that religion arose when prehistoric peoples discovered that magic did not work and that the natural powers were beyond their control. After that discovery, priests appeared who tried to propitiate the powers, to flatter them with praise and make sacrifices to them in the belief that they could persuade them to be benevolent. Religion persisted until the rise of science in modern times. Since then, humanity has been discovering that what were once thought to have been supernatural forces are actually natural forces. Once they are understood, they can be coped with using reason and the scientific method. Frazer predicted that religion would eventually wane and give way to the scientific world view.

Frazer's vast erudition gave him great stature during the opening decades of the twentieth century. Those who read him were deeply impressed by both his arguments and his knowledge. He had a great impact on religious thinking as well, and he confirmed unbelievers of the day in their skepticism. While he was not exactly an atheist, he undermined traditional religious authority by showing its all-too-human origins. In particular, he showed the unity of humanity and that all religions shared the same basic presuppositions. By so doing, he anticipated later students of myth such as Freud, Jung, Eliade, and Campbell who shared his universalism of outlook.

The Golden Bough has one big idea. The death and resurrection of the gods is a mythical interpretation of the natural death and revival processes of vegetation. Like all great ideas, Frazer's has its limitations. The death and resurrection motif chiefly occurs in Western mythologies, in those of the cultures from Iran to Ireland and from Egypt to Iceland. It is less significant in India, the Far East, the Pacific Islands and the Americas, or in Africa south of the Sahara.

Frazer identified the masculine "myth of the hero and the dragon," all of the theme of death and resurrection in which the victory of the risen god is victory over death and the Devil. Frazer showed how the death, departure, and resurrection of the god was celebrated in rituals which became sacred dramas in which the suffering, eclipse, and revival of the god is presented mimetically either by images or actors. In the rites of the Cult of Adonis, according to Frazer, mourning followed the ritual death of the god. The rite was a dramatic reenactment of the myth. Adonis was symbolically buried or cast into the sea. Frazer describes his resurrection as follows:

> When night had fallen, the sorrows of the worshippers were turned to joy. For suddenly the light shone in the darkness: the tomb was opened: the god had risen from the dead; and as the priest touched the lips of the weeping mourners with balm, he softly whispered in their ears the tidings of salvation.[6]

Frazer traced the origins of this rite to the cycles of nature. Freud and Jung thought that something deeper than the rational interpretation of death and rebirth in animals and vegetation was involved. Freud and Jung became interested in myth about the time that the first volumes of Frazer's twelve-volume edition of *The Golden Bough* began to appear (1911-1915). Both became interested in the hero myth because of Frazer's work. Inspired by Frazer, Freud traced the origin of all myth and religion to the Oedipus complex in *Totem and Taboo* (1913). During World War I, Jung traced it to the archetypes of the collective unconscious. He was also much influenced by Frazer.

As Frazer remarks in his preface to the first volume,

> The present volumes, forming the first part of the whole, contain a preliminary ingoing into the principles of Magic and the evolution of the sacred Kingship in general. They will be followed shortly by a volume which discusses the principles of taboo in their special application to sacred or priestly kings. The remainder of the work will be mainly devoted to the myth and ritual of the Dying God.[7]

Diana's King of the Wood is the microcosmic priest-king. Kings must have divinity and magical powers. According to Frazer,

> Kings were revered, in many cases not merely as priests, that is as intermediaries between man and god, but as themselves gods, able to bestow upon their subjects and worshippers those blessings which are commonly supposed to be beyond the reach of mortals and are sought, if at all, only by prayers and sacrifices offered to superhuman and invisible beings.[8]

Since the gods were magicians so were the kings. Both magicians and kings are divine creatures. The magical man-god is a man who wields wide powers of the same type that others do on a small scale. The religious man-god is the receptacle of the divine spirit.

> His whole being, body and soul, a touch of his hand or a turn of his head may send a thrill vibrating through the whole universal framework of things: and conversely, his divine organism is acutely sensitive to such slight changes of environment as would leave ordinary mortals wholly unaffected.[9]

Frazer was one of the great synthesizers of the first half of the century. Like Oswald Spengler, Arnold Toynbee, Freud, and Jung he presented grand designs and schemas based on a big idea. Since Frazer's death in 1941, our knowledge of archaic cultures has expanded considerably. Far more is known about prehistory than in his day and we are far better informed in the history of religions. However, Frazer in his ideas concerning the dying god has not been substantially affected. To the contrary, Frazer has been confirmed. Despite the enormous variety and diversity of religious ideas and myths, the dying god is still a very compelling concept.

Thanks to the investigations of James Mellaart, Samuel Kramer, Marija Gimbutas, and many other recent archeologists, we know a great deal about ancient Sumer, Palestine, Syria, and Anatolia—far more than was known in Frazer's time. Archeological and anthropological methodology has been perfected and is rigorously scientific. There is an enormous store of data.

Some of these particulars are important. During the opening years of the century, many ethnologists were fascinated with totemism. Beginning with Robertson-Smith and his *Religion of Semites*, many scholars, including Frazer, attributed the origins of religion to totemism. Emile Durkheim argued the case with particular vigor in his *The Elementary Forms of Religious Life* (1912). Totemism, of course, was the basis for Freud's *Totem and Taboo*. Jung bought the theory as well. Indeed, Frazer was the major source of totemistic data, and his studies on the subject were accepted as authoritative.

Demolished by Malinowski, Frazer's theories of totemism have become ethnological mythology. Far from being universal, totemism has been found to be a comparatively uncommon phenomenon among primitive peoples. The theory that religion began with totemism is no longer viable even as speculation.

Other features of Frazer's thought have not fared well either. There is no evidence that a magical age preceded the rise of religion. Also, contemporary anthropologists do not draw the sharp distinction between magic and religion that Frazer did. Instead, the two phenomena are now seen as intimately related, and the term "magico-religious" is sometimes used. Yet, Frazer's theory of sympathetic magic is still useful, and, though limited, his ideas of totemism still apply where that phenomenon flourishes.

Frazer's theory of the dying god has been sustained by research in neolithic and bronze Age cultures in western Eurasia, though less so elsewhere. The dying god theme occurs in ancient Hawaiian religion. According to Marshall Sahlins, Captain Cook was the dying god Lono to the Hawaiians who killed him and then revered him as the risen lord *(Hako)* after his death. However, the motif is chiefly characteristic of Indo-Europeans and Semites.

By way of summary and tribute, Frazer's impact on literature and literary criticism has been particularly significant. T. S. Eliot drew heavily on *The Golden Bough* when he wrote *The Waste Land*, as did James Joyce when he wrote *Ulysses*. Eugene O'Neill was profoundly influenced, especially in plays such as *Mourning Becomes Electra*. The literary school of archetypal criticism owes much to Frazer. Frye, for example, was profoundly influenced by him. Frazer was to the literature of the early twentieth century what Ovid was to the literature and art of the Renaissance.

Freud and Jung probably learned more about myth from *The Golden Bough* than from any other single source. As mentioned, Frazer also had enormous impact on both Malinowski and Lévi-Strauss. He is therefore the single most significant modern scholar in the field of mythology. All schools of modern mythic study began with him. Thus, Malinowski, Lévi-Strauss, Freud, and Jung all became interested in myth because they read *The Golden Bough*. In later years, Northrop Frye and Joseph Campbell were profoundly influenced by Frazer, whom they read when they were young. Indeed, it is no exaggeration to say that everyone interested in myth from the turn of the century to World War II was initially inspired or strongly influenced by reading *The Golden Bough*.

Frazer was the first modern scholar to recognize mythic displacement to literature. As a classics scholar, Frazer began with the literary myths of the ancient Greeks and noted the underlying themes. Many classics scholars, such as Jane Harrison, did the same during the last decade of the nineteenth century and the first two of the twentieth. Frazer, however, pursued the matter further and worked his way back to universal motifs on the basis of his collection of ethnological literature. He also traced the connections between living world religions and their archaic antecedents. Others were working in the same field, Leo Frobenius, for example, but Frobenius was virtually unknown outside the German-speaking world. To this day only a fraction of his work is available save in German. Frazer, on the other hand, was as well known to continental European scholars as to those in the English-speaking world.

Thus, far from being alone in the field, Frazer was one among many. His stature was based on his voluminous evidence, most of which was accepted as given until the 1920s, and the demolishing of literary ethnology by Malinowski and Radcliffe-Brown. To scholars interested in myth of the early twentieth century, he was the font. Harrison, Frobenius, Rose, and other students of myth concurred with him on most points, so that the whole made a very formidable edifice. Ethnological thinking still has not recovered from its collapse during the 1920s, and Frazer has had no successors, unless it is Joseph Campbell. Since the 1920s, virtually all authorities have avoided general theories and instead concentrate on particular studies.

Freud, Jung, Eliade, Campbell, and Toynbee were nurtured in Frobenius, Nietzsche, and Frazer. All were long lived and productive to the end. As a result, the ideas and assumptions of the early twentieth-century ethnologists persisted until now, albeit outside academic archaeology and anthropology. Few if any scholars of stature have carried on. Instead, most scholars are specialists. Those few who preserve the generalist tradition are disciples of Jung, Eliade, and Campbell.

The scholar who pursues the wider tradition of scholarship beyond the psychodynamic or archetypal might be called the *generalist*. These people have synthetic rather than analytic inclinations; they are essentially people who are in the tradition of the eighteenth-century philosophes. Indeed, one could call them philosophes, as they would have been called had they lived two hundred years ago.

The broad, general characteristics of the contemporary philosophes are the same as those of the philosophes of the Enlightenment. Whereas the specialists tend to be professionals, scholars and scientists, philosophes are amateurs. They love what they do. They have very broad interests. The philosophes are interested in ideas for their own sake and are not particularly interested in their practical application. This implies detachment from priorities which give most intellectuals today a sense of practical urgency.

Frazer typified the philosophe ideal, as did both Freud and Jung. Like Jung, Frazer was insulated by wealth, which he employed as an aristocrat would. That is, he was less interested in power than in the pursuits of leisure. This was also true of Jung. Both were free to pursue their interests and they did. The intellectual interests were ends in themselves and not means to an end.

In pursuing their studies, however, they made enormous contributions in thought and scholarship. This more than justified their aloofness from the practical demands of the world around them. Despite two World Wars and the Great Depression, neither Frazer nor Jung deserted the ivory tower. Instead, they showed how the tower contributes to humanity even in the most urgent of times. Practical people denounce the ivory tower because of its aloofness. Its denizens gaze out on the world without participating in it. This very loftiness, however, enables them to see the countryside whole. It is always useful if at least some people do that and tell us what they see. Otherwise, we lose our way. Those in the ivory tower see where we have come from and where we are going. They are like spotters for artillery, especially in the days of the observation balloons. Those immersed in the struggle with all its urgencies and demands have their important roles, but so do the observers.

Frazer was a spotter, an observer. Both he and Jung glimpsed the topography of the human quest and furnished insights which are still valid. By so doing, they carried on the great tradition of the philosophes which, in turn, had its origins among the Ionians. They did their work precisely because they did not have a sense of urgency to act in the world, precisely because they lived in the ivory tower. One wonders if the ivory tower has any inhabitants at all anymore, especially when one considers what the modern university has become. They too serve who do not have a strong sense of duty.

Speaking specifically of myth, Frazer, Freud, and Jung are the three giants of the twentieth century, even though Frazer offered few theories and Jung offered only comments in passing in the course of discussing dreams, archetypes, symbols, and other topics which preoccupied him more. In the case of all three, the impact on mythic thinking has been chiefly in terms of implications rather than in precise extended discussion. They offered suggestions which others have since followed. All three plucked the golden bough.

Until the work of Claude Lévi-Strauss during the 1950s, the most prominent name among myth-studying anthropologists was Bronislaw Malinowski. Unlike Cassirer, Malinowski enjoyed high regard outside academic circles. Unlike Eliade and the historians of religion, he based his theories on actual field-work experience. In his case, it was work with the Trobriand Islanders, a maritime people located near the Bismarck Archipelago off New Guinea. According to Strenski, Malinowski argued the ideological and moral superiority of field work as "exemplifying the romantic view of the transcendent value of 'life'." Most scholars class Malinowski with A. R. Radcliffe-Brown as a "functionalist" anthropologist, akin to the "behaviorists" in psychology.

In *Four Theories of Myth in Twentieth-Century History* (1988), Strenski links Malinowski with Fritz Ringer's *German Mandarins* of the early years of the twentieth century. Ringer stressed the importance of understanding *(Verstehen)* and lived experience *(Erlebniss)*. Malinowski had an aversion to utilitarian and pragmatic values, according to Strenski. I have the very opposite impression of him from my reading of *Argonauts of the Pacific* and *Myth Science and Reli-*

gion. Strenski classes him among the Germans, intellectually speaking, because of his indebtedness to Wilhelm Wundt at Leipzig and Wilhelm Dilthey. I am also certain. According to Strenski, Malinowski showed that the Trobriand Islanders were not instrumental or utilitarian. My impression is that Malinowski was both, and that his chief interest was in the roles which myths played in societies. However, as Strenski shows, Malinowski's diaries show affinities with the German Volkish background as "the source of his feelings for landscape and for his idealist association of myth and soil." Malinowski saw the Trobriand Islanders mythically "'rooted' in their own natural surroundings." The "heart of Malinowski's theory of myth is that myths are the important stories a society tells," which is what the Trobriand word *lili* means.[10]

Lévi-Strauss has a logical approach to myth which is stereotypically French. His structuralist anthropology stems from the linguistic school of myth analysis but with a very different approach than Max Müller, Cassirer, and other German linguistic thinkers.

Lévi-Strauss holds that every civilization tends to overestimate the objective orientation of its thought. People in native cultures do the same. So called primitive people thirst as much for knowledge as do so-called civilized people. What we call "primitive" thought is the same demand for order as so-called civilized people experience. The differences between magical and scientific thinking are not that the former are irrational and the latter rational; both are rational. But magic is deterministic while science is not altogether so but allows for random factors. Mythical thought is as precise as scientific thought.

To Lévi-Strauss, myths communicate wisdom, knowledge, and tradition. He refers to the French word *bricoleur*, or "handyman," the nearest English equivalent. Unlike the craftsman, the *bricoleur* improvises. He is an ingenious tinkerer who invents solutions to practical problems. *Bricolage* is akin to improvisation.

> Like "bricolage" on the technical plane, mythical reflection can reach brilliant unforeseen results on the intellectual plane. Conversely, attention has often been drawn to the myth-poetical nature of "bricolage" on the plane of so called "raw" or "naive" art [as] in the case immortalized by Dickens in *Great Expectations* but no doubt inspired by observation of Mr. Wemmick's "castle" with its miniature draw bridge, its cannon firing at nine o'clock, its bed of salad and cucumbers thanks to which its occupants could withstand a siege if necessary. . . .[11]

Science is a system of verification by testing. Myth and ritual are based on improvisation. Science looks for new messages; myth is the received or revealed message. It is there already. Myth is therefore conservative, whereas science is innovative and the scientist is an explorer looking for new answers. Mythical thought, like science, generalizes and, in that way, can be scientific even though entangled in imagery. It too works by paradigms, models, analogies, and comparisons. Mythical thought is intellectual *bricolage*. Its characteristic feature is that it builds structural sets by using the remains and debris of the past. Its limitation is that it is imprisoned in the past, but, at the same time, it gives meaning to reality.

> One can go further and think of the rigorous precision of magical thought and ritual practice as an extension of the unconscious apprehension of the *truth of determinism*; the mode in which scientific phenomena exist. In this view, the operations of determinism are divined and made use of in an all-embracing fashion before being known and properly applied, and magical rites and beliefs appear as so many expressions of an act of faith in a science yet to be born.[12]

Mythical thought is not rudimentary but is a well-articulated system. It is an alternative to scientific thought, which is another well-articulated system.

> Myths and rites are far from being, as has so often been held, the products of man's myth-making faculty . . . their principle value is indeed to pursue until the present time the remains of methods of observation and reflection which were precisely adapted to discoveries of a certain type: those which nature authorized from the starting point of a speculative organization and exploitation of the sensible world in sensible terms.[13]

Myth is the science of the concrete which is necessarily by its nature, restricted to results other than those obtained by the exact sciences. But myth "is no less scientific and its results no less genuine. They were secured ten thousand years earlier and still remained the basis of our own civilization."[14]

Mircea Eliade began writing *Myths, Dreams, and Mysteries* when he was Rumanian cultural attache in Lisbon during World War II. He continued it and *Comparative Religions* while he was in London and Paris after the war. The books led to an invitation to lecture at the University of Chicago which, in turn, led to his academic appointment. He died in 1987.

In the foreword to *Myths Dreams Mysteries*, Eliade wrote:

> ... in writing [this book] I limited myself to discussion of the differences of stricture between myths and dreams, and then to comparisons of the respective points of view of the historians of religion and of the depth-psychologists. . . . The central theme of the present work is, in fact, the meeting and confrontation of the two types of mentality which might be called for simplicity's sake, the traditional and modern, the first being characteristic of man in archaic and Oriental societies, the second of man in modern societies of the western type.[15]

Concerning myth, Eliade wrote:

> Myth defines itself by its own mode of being. It can only be grasped as myth, in so far as it *reveals* something as having been *fully manifested*, and this manifestation is at the same time *creative* and *exemplary*, since it is the foundation of a structure of reality as well as a kind of human behaviour. A myth always narrates something as having *really happened*, as an event which took place, in the plain sense of the term whether it deals with the creation of the world, or the most insignificant animal or vegetable species, or of an institution. The very fact of *saying* what happens reveals *how* the thing in question was realized. . . . For the act of coming to be is, at the same time, the emergence of a reality and the disclosure of its fundamental structure; it is also revealing the emergence of that totality of the real which is the cosmos, and its ontological laws. It shows in what sense the world is. Cosmogony is always ontophany, the plenary manifestation of being. And since all myths participate in some sort in the cosmological type of myth—for every account of what came to pass in the holy era of the beginning *(in illo tempore)* is but another variant of the archetypal history, how the world came to be—it follows that all mythology is ontophany. Myths reveal the structure of reality, and the multiple modalities of being in the world, that is why they are the exemplary models of human behavior. They disclose the *true* stories, concern themselves with the *realities*. But onophany always implies theophany or hierophany. It was the gods or semi-divine beings who created the

world and instituted the innumerable modes of being in the world from that which is uniquely human to the mode of being of the insect. In revealing the history of what came to pass *in illo tempore,* one is at the same time revealing an irruption of sacred into the world. When a god or civilizing hero ordained a mode of behavior—for instance—a particular way of taking good—he is not only assured the reality of that behavior (for until then the practice in question was non-existent, was not in use and it was "unreal"), but by the very fact of this behavior was . . . a divine creation. By feeding himself in the same manner as God or civilizing Hero, man repeats their gestures and, in some sort, participates in their essence.[16]

According to Peter Gay in *The Enlightenment: The Rise of Modern Paganism* (1967), mythical thinking is true thinking. It is a collective term describing a wide variety of mining operations. "It can be observed in its purity among primitive peoples, while it was overlaid among advanced ancient civilizations by touches of rationality, beauty of expansion and, complexity of institutions." This speaks to the contrast between original myths which are usually tedious and artless and works of literature based on myths. What is more, the mythopoeic mind could not achieve *Sachlichkeit*—objectivity—both because it was incapable of dealing with experiences coolly, quantitatively, and because it could not experience objects as objects."[17]

However, when one turns from the theory of science to history of science one is in a very different realm, one which is closer to mythopoeic thinking than scientists and their apologists acknowledge. The scientific mind has not been able to achieve *Sachlichkeit* either. Scientists do not usually deal with experiences coolly, quantitatively, and experience objects as objects. That is the ideal, but, like all ideals, it is seldom realized. Scientists, too, have sudden insights, as do practitioners of *zazen*, or gradual dawning insights, like yogis engaged in disciplined meditation. There is much emotional commitment as well, both in the actual discoveries and in their interpretation. There is nothing wrong with this. It is only to say that scientists are also human.

No scientist lives in a vacuum. All are subject to prejudice, jealousy, and possessiveness. These and other personal traits inevitably color and shape the hypotheses of every scientist. The modern scientist works with better tools than his or her archaic mythopoeic counterpart, but both are subject to the vagaries of their personalities. No scientist is ever completely detached and impersonal. None can be completely objective. In fact, there is no such thing as objectivity unless it is a myth in the sense of illusion or fiction.

Theories are often presented as established truth, as if proven, and take on the character of religious dogma. Thus, the mathematical theories of René Descartes led to the fixed conclusion on his part that human beings are machines mysteriously endowed with a mind and that animals are machines which do not have minds and therefore the cries of an injured animal mean no more than the creaking of the machine. Descartes also concluded that the universe is a machine as well, that it ticks through eternity like a clock. Neither Bacon, Descartes, Newton, nor Darwin tried to disprove their own theories in order to subject them to the most rigorous of tests. Instead, they defended them as the adherents of religious or political creeds do their most cherished convictions.

The scientific method is really not very different from what has been followed since the days of the Sumerians and very probably much earlier. There are initial discoveries which are like sudden mystical experiences. These are followed by mopping up operations which go on until anomalies occur. Something does not quite work, then something else. Critics discover holes in the theory and, at this point, it either collapses or is modified. If the latter, then it has made its appropriate contribution to progress.

This method is not very different from the mythopoeic. Myths are not static or fixed but are constantly revised by bards, minstrels, scribes, and scholars. The insights which are expressed in metaphorical language reveal reality on the basis of the best evidence at hand. With the myth, as well as with the scientific theory, the anomalies appear and the myth either collapses or is revised.

Certain discoveries shatter old myths and scientific theories. One was the discovery by Aristarchus that the earth is a globe, another that the earth is the third planet in the solar system, yet another that the solar system is a small speck in a vast galaxy of which there are several hundred million galaxies with more constantly being identified. The three tiered shamanic cosmos, the Sumerian tin can floating in the sea, and the Hebrew world in the midst of the Deep with waters above and below had to give way to the Ptolemaic cosmos of crystalline spheres, revolving sun, moon, and planets. This was fully as much a break with the familiar as when the Copernican theory challenged the Ptolemaic, the Newtonian the Copernican, and the Big Bang the Newtonian.

Thus, science and myth coexist whether we want them to or not and both are constantly subject to revision. science is the way of disciplined empirical investigation and testing, something all children begin to do almost from the moment that they are both. Myth is made up of our inner insights and intuitive visions if the myth is cosmological, sociological, or psychological and not an adventure story, as in *The Iliad* or a comical tale as in the Cree trickster stories. Thus, the ancient Egyptians might think of the sky as a cow or as the goddess Nut bending over the world, or of a god as a man, a falcon, or a falcon-headed man, and a king as the sun, star, bull, crocodile, lion, falcon, or jackal. In the Memphite Theology Ptah creates his body, other gods, and all living things by naming them. In the beginning was the Word; the Word has power because it is not merely a sign but partakes of the essence of the thing it names.

Gay writes:

> I am not suggesting that myth floated disembodied above reality, uncontaminated by life and untouched by change. Quite the contrary. The myths were grandiose projections of the ancients' experience—the blessing of irrigation, the calamity of drought. The Babylonians treated their cosmos as a vast cosmic state resembling their own and their cosmologies reproduced what they saw daily. Indeed, for all these changes, the myths always retained their aversion to analysis and their anthropomorphism; they continued to explain the unknown by the known and to postulate the universe with beings resembling the believers themselves. . . . The mythopoeic mind saw the world through the iridescent veil of immediate experiences, things as living powers. Deeply and usually enmeshed in realities; it had no logic for reality.[18]

Today most people are still in a mental mishmash of archaic mythopoeic and modern scientific views. The world religions are all of archaic origin, and although most have been modified by the impact of modernism, most do not. Thus, fundamentalist Islamic Saudi Arabia is strictly based on the *Koran* and rejects the Western scientific world view but not Western technology, especially military technology.

It always has been so. At every time in history, and everywhere in the world, traditionalists and innovators have coexisted. The so-called scientific revolution of the seventeenth century did not bring about the birth of science, nor were science and philosophy born in Greece during the sixth century B.C.E. Instead, there has been a gradual cumulation of knowledge from the Ice Age on which in our times has culminated in the modern information explosion. But, parallel to that is the persistence of traditional mythopoeic thinking: religion, occultism, mysticism, and various forms of word and number magic. Scientists, too, are affected. Thus, Freud was superstitious about numbers; Einstein was a theist, and Oppenheim was drawn to Hindu mysticism.

While it is possibly true that the ancients did not think historically prior to the Greeks and Romans, they did think chronologically. That kind of thinking paralleled timeless mythopoeic thinking. In some ways, the Babylonian priests who first recorded the movements of the planets were scientists even though their purposes were to foretell the future. Their mathematical reckonings were quantified and cumulative. They engaged in systematic observation. But they were also astrologers. Astrology, too, persists, side by side with astronomy.

At the same time, to give Bacon, Descartes, and Locke their due, the pioneer philosophers broke with tradition and experimented. This made a difference. There had been experimenters before, even during the High Middle Ages, but the pressures of tradition and conformity were very strong. It took an economic revolution to create a community of people who could sufficiently free themselves from the struggle for survival to explore non-utilitarian pursuits. There had been such times before, times of prosperity and plenty, but it still took many centuries for civilization to advance to the stage when there could be a Descartes, a Newton, or a Locke.

The Enlightenment was brought about by amateurs, people who did what they did because they loved it. These were the philosophes. Most were not trained philosophers but individuals who had curiosity and who enjoyed tinkering at a time when one could master most of human knowledge without the benefit of universities. Their chief concern was to find the limits of reason, and, by the end of the century they had. However, philosophy is the only seaworthy craft afloat.

There were ways in which they broke with the past. David Hume asserted that a miracle cannot be because it violates the laws of nature and such violations are impossible. It is very possible that such thoughts had been voiced before, by someone somewhere, just as it is possible what someone before Thales asked, "Of what substance are all things made?" The difference is that Hume published his essay *On Nature* and it was widely read at a time when many people in Western Europe were ready to read such an essay and debate such propositions as the impossibility of miracles. That had not been true during the thirteenth century. Consequently, the lonely rebel who perhaps voiced such thoughts had no means to publish his or her ideas before the invention of the printing press and too little was known about nature to make his or her denials plausible. We need not assume that such heretical statements were necessarily silenced. It is probable that they were ignored. The same fate undoubtedly befell whatever Egyptian or Mesopotamian asked "Of what substance are all things made?" He or she was like a lone dancer without a partner and "it takes two to tango."

APPENDIX

SOME DICTIONARY AND ENCYCLOPEDIC definitions of myth are as follows:

OXFORD ENGLISH DICTIONARY

MYTH, MYTHUS 1. A purely fictional narrative usually involving supernatural persons, actions, or events, and embodying some popular idea concerning natural or historical phenomena.—properly distinguished from *allegory* and from *legend* which implies a nucleus of fact but often used vaguely to include any narrative having natural or historical phenomena.

WEBSTER'S THIRD NEW INTERNATIONAL DICTIONARY

Myth from the Greek *mythos*, perhaps akin to Gothic *mandan*, "to remind," Old Irish *smuainim* "I think," Old Slav *mysil* "thought," Lithuanian *mausti* "to desire ardently."
   1. A story that is usu. of unknown origin and at least partially traditional, that ostensibly relates historical usu. of such character as to serve to explain some practice, belief, institution, or natural phenomenon, and that is esp. associated with religious rites and beliefs. 2a. a story invented as a veiled explanation of a truth. . . . b. the theme or plot of a mythical tale occurring in forms differing only in detail . . . often the word is used to designate a story, usu. fanciful and imaginative, that explains a natural phenomenon or social practice, institution, or belief. . . . It is also used to designate a story, belief, a notion commonly held to be true but utterly without factual basis. . . .

Larousse

Recit des temps fabuleux et heroiques. Antiq. Recit imaginaire qui, sous la figure de l'allegorie, traduit une grand géneralité historique, physique ou philosophique; un myth saláire. l'histoire de Promethée est un mythe. On a defini le mythe de diverses façons. Il est malaise de la distinguer avec precision de la legende. Toutefois, il comprie souvent une signification symbolique [cosmogonique, tres souvent] et met en scene des dieux.

Brockhaus

Mythos: die dem ürsprunglich-naiven Empfinden als zeitlose Gegenwart erscheinende Aussage über die Zussanhange der Welt mit seiner eigenen Existenz, im engeren Sinne eine rational micht beisbare Assage über Gottliches, der doch ein Wahrheitanspruch eigen ist.

ENCYCLOPEDIA AMERICANA

Myths may include elements of oral literature, such as fairy tales and legends, but myths are distinct from them in two ways: First a myth is understood in its own society as a true story. (It is only when it is seen from outside its society that it has come to acquire the popular meaning of a story that is untrue.) A myth relates the most comprehensive and ultimate narrative about its subject, whether it be the origin of the world, the origin of death, the meaning of a gesture, or the structure of a temple. Second, it achieves comprehensiveness and intimacy, because it refers its society back to primordial reality, which is not merely prior in time but is a qualitatively different time, place, and mode of being. This primordial time is the reservoir and repository of the models on which all the significant knowledge, expressions, and activities of the present society are based. Although a myth may appear illogical and nonrational from the point of view of these later forms of intellectual and social order, it portrays its origins. In this sense, the myth exists as an expression of first principles, that is, as an archaic form.

THE NEW ENCYCLOPEDIA BRITANNICA MACROPAEDIA

Myth is a collective term used for one kind of symbolic communication and specifically indicates one basic form of religious symbolism, as distinguished from symbolic behavior (cult, ritual) and symbolic places or objects (such as temples and icons). Myths (in the plural) are specific accounts concerning gods or superhuman beings and extraordinary events or circumstances in a time that is altogether different from that of ordinary human experience. As with all religious symbolization, there is no attempt to prove that these unusual, transcendent, or divine events are "possible," or otherwise to justify them. For this reason, every myth presents itself as authoritative and always as an account of facts, no matter how completely different they may be from the ordinary world. The original Greek term for myth (mythos) denotes "word" in the sense of a decisive final pronouncement. It differs from *logos* the word whose validity or truth can be argued and demonstrated. Because myths present extraordinary events without trying to justify them, people have sometimes assumed that myths are simply unprovable and false stories and thus have made the word myth synonymous for fable. In the story of religion, however, the difference between myth and fable must be borne in mind.

ENCYCLOPEDIA OF RELIGION

Kees Bolle

The English word *myth* comes from the Greek *múthos* ("word" or "speech") which owes its significance precisely to its contrast with *logos*; the latter can also be translated as "word," but only in the sense of a word that elicits discussion, an "argument." *Múthos* in its meaning of "myth" is the word for a story concerning gods and human beings. A myth is an expression of the sacred in.words it reports realities and events from the origin of the world that remain valid for the basis and purpose of all there is. Consequently, a myth functions as a model for human activity, society, wisdom, and knowledge.

NOTES

CHAPTER 1

1. Mircea Eliade, *Myth and Reality*, trans. Willard R. Trask (New York: Harper Colophon Books, 1963), pp. 6f.

2. Joseph Campbell, *Creative Mythology, The Masks of God* (New York: Penguin Books. 1985), p. 90.

3. C. G. Jung, "Archetypes of the Collective Unconscious," *The Collected Works of C. G. Jung*, Bollinger Series XX, Volume 9.1 (Princeton: Princeton University Press, 1969, par. 7, p. 5f.

4. Northrop Frye, *Anatomy of Criticism, Four Essays* (Princeton: Princeton University Press, 1957), p. 33.

5. G. S. Kirk, *The Nature of Greek Myths* (London: Penguin Books, 1982), p. 14, cf.; also Richard Chase, "Notes On the Idea of Myth," in *Myth and Literature*, John B. Vickery, ed. (Lincoln, Nebraska: University of Nebraska Press, 1969), pp. 3-13; and David Bidney, "Myth, Symbolism, and Truth," *Ibid.*, pp. 68ff.

6. Peter Berger, *The Sacred Canopy: Elements of a Sociological Theory of Religion* (Garden City, New York: Anchor Books, 1969), p. 40.

7. Claude Lévi-Strauss, *The Savage Mind* (Chicago: University of Chicago Press, 1966), pp. 1-16.

8. Erich Fromm, D. T. Suzuki, and Richard De Martino, Zen Buddhism and Psychoanalysis (New York: Harper and Row, 1960), pp. 10-24.

9. Jung, *Memories, Dreams, Reflections*, recorded and edited by Aniela Jaffé, trans. Richard and Clara Winston, rev. ed. (New York: Vintage Books/Random House, 1965), p. 3.

10. Cf., Wilfred Cantwell Smith, *The Meaning and End of Religion: A Revolutionary Approach to the Great Religious Traditions* (1962, reprint, San Francisco: Harper and Row, 1978).

11. Ivan Strenski, *Four Theories of Myth in Twentieth Century History* (Iowa City: University of Iowa Press, 1987), p. 1f.

12. *American Heritage Dictionary* (Boston: Houghton Mifflin, 1976).

13. Ernst Cassirer, *The Philosophy of Symbolic Forms* Vol. 2 of *Mythical Thought* (New Haven: Yale University Press, 1955), pp. 2f.

14. E. M. Forster, *Aspects of the Novel* (London: Penguin Books, 1962), pp. 34f.

15. Ibid., 94.

CHAPTER 2

1. Harry Nelson and Robert Jurmain, *Introduction to Physical Anthropology* (St. Paul: West Publishing Co., 1991), ch. 14.

2. Allan C. Wilson and Rebecca L. Cann, "The Recent African Genesis of Humans, *Scientific American*, April 1992, p. 68.

3. Ibid.

4. Alan G. Thorn and Milford H. Wolpoff, "The Multiregional Evolution of Humans," *Scientific American*, April 1992, p. 77.

5. Ibid., 78.

6. John McCrone, *The Ape That Spoke* (New York: William Morrow and Co., 1991), pp. 160-66.

7. Raymond Dart, personal communication.

8. E. O. James, *Prehistoric Religion* (London: Thames and Hudson, 1957), p. 9.

9. Alexander Marshack, *The Roots of Civilization* (New York: McGraw-Hill, 1972), p. 114.

10. Ibid.

11. Ibid., 112.

12. Ibid., 119.

13. Ibid., 114.

14. Brian M. Fagan, *Journey From Eden* (London: Thames and Hudson, 1990), p. 141.

15. Cf. Louis Dupré, "Neolithic Religion," *Encyclopedia of Religion* (Chicago: University of Chicago Press, 1988).

16.Marja Gimbutas, *Goddesses and Gods of Old Europe 6500-3500* B.C.E. (Berkeley: University of California Press, 1982), p. 18.

17. Ibid., 88.

18. Ibid., 91.

19. Ibid.

20. Ibid., 93.

21. Ibid.

22. Ibid.

23. Ibid., 112.

24. Ibid., 113.

25. Ibid., 145.

26. Ibid., 146.

27. Ibid., 150.

28. Ibid.

CHAPTER 3

1. Samuel Noah Kramer, *The Sumerians* (Chicago: University of Chicago Press, 1967), p. 112.

2. Ibid.

3. Ibid., 113.

4. Ibid.

5. Ibid., 115.

6. Ibid., 161f.

7. A. Leo Oppenheim, *Ancient Mesopotamia: Portrait of a Dead Civilization*, rev. ed., completed by Erica Reiner (Chicago: University of Chicago Press, 1977), p. 171.

8. Ibid., 173.

9. Kramer, *The Sumerians*, p. 169.

10. Ibid., 171.

11. Ibid., 197.

12. G. S. Kirk, *Greek Myths* (London: Penguin Books, 1982), pp. 96f.

13. Cf. M. I. Finley, *The World of Odyesseus* (London: Penguin Books, 1954), pp. 142-58; M. P. Nilsson, *The Mycenaean Origin of Greek Mythology* (New York: Norton, 1963); W. K. C. Guthrie, *The Greeks and Their Gods* (Boston: Beacon Press, 1955).

14. Oliver Taplin, "Homer" in *The Oxford History of the Classical World*, John Boardman, Jasper Griffin, Oswy Murray, eds. (Oxford: Oxford University Press, 1986), pp. 72-75.

CHAPTER 4

1. Theophilus James Meek, *Hebrew Origins* (New York: Harper Torchbooks, 1960), p. 123; Werner Keller, *The Bible as History* (New York: William Morrow, 1981), pp. 59-69.

2. Keller, *The Bible as History*, pp. 157-68; Cf. W. O. E. Oesterley and Theodore H. Robinson, *An Introduction to the Old Testament* (New York: Meridian Books, 1958), *Passim*; Northrop Frye, *The Gread Code* (Toronto: Academic Press, 1982).

3. Robert Graves and Raphael Patai, *Hebrew Myths* (New York: McGraw-Hill, 1966).

4. Jesse L. Weston, *The Quest of the Holy Grail* (New York: Barnes and Noble, 1964), pp. 486-94.

5. Roger Sherman Loomis, *The Grail: From Celtic Myth to Christian Symbol* (New York: Columbia University Press, 1964), pp. 8-18.

6. Ibid., 176.

7. Lord Raglan, "The Hero of Tradition" in *The Story of Folklore*, Alan Dundes ed. (Englewood Cliffs, New Jersey: Prentice-Hall, 1965), pp. 142-57.

8. Joseph Campbell, *The Hero With a Thousand Faces* (Princeton: Princeton University Press, 1987), p. 31.

9. Ibid., 51.

10. Ibid., 77f.

11. Ibid., 91f.

12. Ibid., 118.

13. Ibid., 147.

14. Ibid., 167.

CHAPTER 5

1. René Descartes, *A Discourse on Method*, Part 1, trans. by John Veitsch, in Robert H. Nash, *Ideas of History* (New York: E.P. Dutton, 1969), p. 27.

2. Ibid., 27.

3. Patrick Gardner, *Theories of History* (New York: The Free Press/MacMillan, 1959), pp. 9-11.

4. Helmut Fleischer, *Marxism and History*, trans. by Erich Mosbacher (New York: Harper and Row, 1969), pp. 13ff.

5. Ibid.

6. Ibid.

7. Ibid.

8. Ibid., 14ff.

9. John F. Fennelly, *Twilight of the Evening Lands—A Half Century Later* (New York: Brookdale Press, 1972), pp. 14-17.

10. Oswald Spengler, *The Decline of the West*, Volume 1 (New York: Alfred A. Knopf, 1926), p. 21.

11. Ibid., pp. 183ff.

12. Ibid.

13. Ibid., Volume 2, p. 224.

14. Arnold Toynbee, *A Study of History*, a new edition revised and abridged by the author and Jane Caplan (New York: Weathervane Books, 1979), p. 11.

15. Ibid., 161-66.

16. Ibid.

17. Toynbee, *Study of History*, p. 319.

18. Ibid., 334.

19. Ibid., 285.

20. Ibid., 350.

21. Karl Jaspers, *The Origins and Goals of History* (New Haven: Yale University Press, 1953), ch. 1.

22. Ibid., 73f.

23. Ibid., 2.

CHAPTER 6

1. Sheldon Cheney, *A World History of Art* (New York: Viking Press, 1944), p. 3.

2. Ibid., 14.

3. Ibid.

4. Sigmund Freud, "Creative Writers and Daydreaming," *The Standard Edition of the Complete Psychological Works of Sigmund Freud*, Volume 4 (London: Hogarth Press, 1960), pp. 143-55.

5. Ibid.

6. Ibid.

7. Ibid., 146.

8. Ibid.

9. Ibid.

10. Lilian Feder, *Ancient Myth in Modern Poetry* (Princeton: Princeton University Press, 1977), pp. 19ff.

11. Ibid.

12. James Lundquist, *J. D. Salinger* (New York: Frederick Ungar, 1979), pp. 37-69, 120-36; J. D. Salinger, *Franny and Zooey* (Boston: Little, Brown & Company, 1961), p. 36-39.

13. Robert Hopkiss, *Jack Kerouac: Prophet of the New Romanticism* (Laurence: Regents Press of Kansas, 1976), p. 38.

14. Ibid.

15. M. H. Abrams, *A Glossary of Literary Terms*, 3d ed. (New York: Holt, Rinehart, and Winston, 1971), p. 11.

16. Maud Bodkin, *Archetypal Patterns in Poetry* (London: Oxford University Press, 1934), pp. 4f.

17. Ibid., p. 42.

18. Ibid.

19. Northrop Frye, *Spiritus Mundi: Essays on Literature, Myth and Society* (Bloomington, Indiana: Indiana University Press, 1976), pp. 4f.

20. Ibid., 5.

21. Ibid., 14.

22. Ibid., 17.

23. Frye, *Anatomy of Criticism* (Princeton: Princeton University Press, 1957), p. vii.

24. Ibid., 33f.

25. C. F. Derek Hudson, *Lewis Carroll* (London: Constable, 1959), pp. 121ff.

26. Florence Becker Lennon, *The Life of Lewis Carroll* (New York: Dover, 1972), pp. 137f.

27. Henri Ellenberger, *The Discovery of the Unconscious* (New York: Basic Books, 1970), pp. 105ff.

28. Ibid., 276.

29. Mircea Eliade, *Shamanism: Archaic Techniques of Ecstasy* (Chicago: The University of Chicago Press, 1970), p. 101.

30. Mircea Eliade, *Zalmoxis: The Vanishing God* (Chicago: The University of Chicago Press, 1972), pp. 100f.

31. P. O. Morton, Robert Lenardon, *Classical Mythology* (London: Longmans, 1977), p. 24.

32. C. G. Jung, Psychology and Alchemy in *Complete Works*, vol. 12 (Princeton: Princeton University Press, 1968), p. 53.

33. Philip Wicksteed, "Hell" in *Discussions of the Divine Comedy*, Irma Brandeis, ed. (Boston, L.D.C., Heath, 1961), p. 121, cf. also Frances Ferguson, "The Metaphor of the Journey," *Discussions of the Divine Comedy*, p. 62.

34. Giorgio de Santilla, Hertha von Dechend, *Hamlet's Mill* (Boston: David Godine, 1977), pp. 103ff.

35. A. M. E. Goldschmidt, "Alice in Wonderland Psychoanalyzed," in *Aspects of Alice*, Robert Philips ed. (London: Victor Golancz, 1972).

36. Judith Bloomington, "Alice as Anima: The Image of Woman in Carroll's Classic," *Aspects of Alice . . .*, pp. 380ff.

37. *The Annotated Alice: Alice's Adventures in Wonderland and Through the Looking Glass*, Lewis Carroll, with an introduction and notes by Martin Gardner (New York: Bramhall House, 1948), p. 37.

CHAPTER 7

1. Joseph Campbell, *Masks of God: Creative Mythology* (London: Penguin Books, 1977), pp. 90, 93.

2. Harold Schechter, *Psyche and Symbol in Popular Art* (Bowling Green, Ohio: Bowling Green University Popular Press, 1980), pp. 40ff.

3. Ibid., 144ff.

4. Ibid.

5. Ibid.

4. John Culhane, "A Mouse for All Seaons," *Saturday Review*, November 11, 1978, p. 50.

5. Richard Schickel, *The Disney Version* (New York: Avon Books, 1968), p. 125.

6. Culhane, "A Mouse For All Seasons," *Saturday Review*, p. 51.

7. Ibid.

8. Lewis Jacobs, *The Rise of the American Film* (New York: Teachers College Press, 1968), pp. 97, 100.

9. Leonard, Maltin, *Of Mice and Magic: A History of American Animal Cartoons* (New York: American Library, 1980), pp. 2, 4, 23.

10. Ibid.

11. Ibid.

12. Raymond Durgnat, *The Crazy Mirror: Hollywood Comedy and the American Image* (New York: Dell Publishing Company, 1969), p. 67.

13. Ibid.

14. Ibid.

15. Bob Thomas, *Walt Disney, An American Original* (New York: Dell Publishing Company, 1969), pp. 97.

16. Ibid., 100.

17. Jacobs, *The Rise of the American Film*, p. 51.

18. Ibid.

19. Bart Mills, "Disney Looks for a Happy Ending to its Grim Fairy Tales," *American Film*, July-August, 1982, p. 52.

20. David Bains and Bruce Harris, *Mickey Mouse: Fifty Happy Years* (New York: Harmony Books, 1977), p. 1.

21. David Bains and Bruce Harris, *Mickey Mouse: Fifty Happy Years* (New York: Harmony Books, 1975), p. 35.

22. "Two Disney Artists," *The Harvard Journal of PIctorial Fiction*, Spring, 1975, p. 35.

23. Ibid.

24. Ibid.

25. Ibid.

26. Schechter, *Psyche and Symbol in Popular Art*, p. 40.

27. Ibid.

28. Edward C. Whitmont, *The Symbolic Quest: Basic Concepts of Analytical Psychology* (New York: Harper and Row, 1973), pp. 161f.

29. Richard Schickel, *The Disney Version* (London: 1966).

30. Ibid.

31. Ibid.

CHAPTER 8

1. R. Angus Downie, *Frazer and the Golden Bough* (London: VIctor Gollancz, 1970), pp. 12-18.

2. Ibid., 33f.

3. Ibid.

4. James George Frazer, *The Golden Bough*, one volume edition (New York: MacMillan, 1963), p. 1.

5. John B. Vickery, *The Literary Impact of the Golden Bough* (Princeton, New Jersey: Princeton University Press, 1973), p. 54.

6. Frazer, *The Golden Bough*, p. 273.

7. Ibid., viii.

8. Ibid., 342.

9. Ibid., 242f.

10. Ivan Strenski, *Four Theories of Myth in Twentieth-Century History* (Iowa City: Iowa City Press, 1987), pp. 47-51.

11. Claude Levi-Strauss, *The Savage Mind* (Chicago: University of Chicago Press, 1962), p. 17.

12. Ibid., 11.

13. Ibid., 16.

14. Ibid.

15. Mircea Eliade, *Myths, Dreams, and Mysteries* (New York: Harper & Row, 1960), p. 7.

16. Ibid.

27. Peter Gay, *The Enlightenment: The Rise of Modern Paganism* (New York: Von Nostrand, 1967), p. 91.

28. Ibid., 92.

BIBLIOGRAPHY

Bodkin, Maud. 1934. *Archetypal Patterns of Poetry*. Oxford: Oxford University Press.

Campbell, Joseph. 1988. *The Inner Reaches of Outer Space*. San Francisco: Harper Press.

Cassirer, Ernst. 1952. *Language and Myth*. London: Dover Publications.

Cheney, Sheldon. 1944. *A World History of Art*. New York: Viking Press.

Eliade, Mircea. 1960. *Myths, Dreams, and Mysteries*. New York: Harper Torchbook.

Eliade, Mircea. 1963. *Myth and Reality*. New York: Harper & Row.

Fennelly, John. 1972. *Twilight of the Evening Lands—A Half Century Later*. New York: Brookdale Press.

Fagan, Brian. 1977. *Journey From Eden*. London: Thames & Hudson.

Forster, E. M. 1962. *Aspects of the Novel*. London: Penguin Books.

Feder, Lilian. 1977. *Ancient Myth in Modern Poetry*. Princeton: Princeton University Press.

Frye, Northrop. 1957. *Anatomy of Criticism*. Princeton University Press.

Frye, Northrop. 1971. *Spiritus Mundi: Essays on Literature and Myth and Society*. Bloomington: University of Indiana Press.

Gay, Peter. 1967. *The Enlightenment*. New York: Van Nostrand.

Gimbutas, Marija. 1982. *Goddesses and Gods of Old Europe*. Berkeley: University of California Press.

Hopkins, R. 1971. *Jack Kerouac: Prophet of the New Romanticism*. New York: Holt, Rinehart & Winston.

Kramer, Samuel Noah. 1967. *The Sumerians.* Chicago: The University Chicago Press.

Loomis, Roger S. 1964. *The Grail From Celtic Myth to Christian Symbol.* New York: Columbia University Press.

Marshack, Alexander. 1972. *The Roots of Civilization.* New York: McGraw Hill.

McCrone, John. 1991. *The Ape that Spoke.* New York: Hulton Monroe & Co.

Oppenheim, A. L. 1977. *Ancient Mesopotamia.* Chicago: University of Chicago Press.

Schickel, Richard. 1968. *The Disney Version.* New York: Avon Books.

Spengler, Oswald. 1926. *The Decline of the West,* 2 vol. New York: Alfred Knopf.

Srenski, Ivan. 1987. *Four Theories of Myth in Twentieth Century History.* Iowa City: Iowa City Press.

Voegelin, Eric. 1962. *Order and History: The World of the Polis,* vol. 2. Baton Rouge: Louisiana State University Press.

INDEX

Abbassid, 61
Abzu, 42, 115
Alice in Wonderland, 109, 113-114, 116
An, 41
Alice Stories, 113-114
Analytic psychology, 6
Antigone, 50
Apollinian, 87
Australopithecus Africanus, 19, 21, 23
Australopithcines, 20, 21, 22, 23
Axial Age, 92

Bible, 60, 61, 62, 64, 65, 104, 106-107
Bird and Snake Goddess, 37
Bodkins, Maud, 104, 105
Bull and moon symbols, 36

Campbell, Joseph, 67-9; *Hero With a Thousand Faces*, 67-9
Canaanites, 56, 57
"Candelabra" School, 20, 21
Capra, Fritjov, 5
Carroll, Lewis, 109, 113, 114, 115
Casablanca, 120-21, 122, 123
Cassirer, Ernst, 2, 10, 159
Çatal Hüyük, 32-3
Choukoutian, 23, 24
Christian, 60-64, 66, 70, 103, 106
Columbus, 74-5, 77, 78
Cornford, F. M., 47
Cosmology, 40, 75, 106
Creative writers, 99-102

Dante, 73, 111-112
Dart, Raymond, 23
Descent of Ishtar, 45
Descensus ad inferos, 109-110
Dingir, 41
Disney, Walt, 128-133, 134, 135, 140-145
Disneyland, 136-141, 142-145
Divine Comedy, The, 109
Dodgson, Charles, 115-116
Dorothy (in Oz), 121-122, 124
Dubsar, 39
Dupré, André, 32
Dying God, 156

Eden-New Jerusalem Myth, 95
Edubba, 39
E (Elohist) writer, 56-57
Eliade, Mircea, 1, 110, 162-3
Enki, 42, 44, 46
Enkidu in the nether world, 46
Enlightenment, the, 64, 166
Enlil, 42, 44
Enuma elish, 54
Epic of Gilgamesh, 45
Eternal Return, Myth of, 51-2, 53-4, 66-7
Euhemerus, 147
"Eve," 21

Fagan, Brian, 27
Fairy tales, 11
Faustian Man, 87-88

DATE DUE